Pro NuGet

T0094043

Maarten Balliauw
Xavier Decoster

Apress®

Pro NuGet

ISBN-13 (pbk): 978-1-4302-4191

ISBN-13 (electronic): 978-1-4302-4192-8

President and Publisher: Paul Manning
Lead Editor: Ewan Buckingham
Technical Reviewer: Fabio Claudio Ferracchiati
Editorial Board: Steve Anglin, Mark Beckner, Ewan Buckingham, Gary Cornell, Louise Corrigan, Morgan Ertel, Jonathan Gennick, Jonathan Hassell, Robert Hutchinson, Michelle Lowman, James Markham, Matthew Moodie, Jeff Olson, Jeffrey Pepper, Douglas Pundick, Ben Renow-Clarke, Dominic Shakeshaft, Gwenan Spearing, Matt Wade, Tom Welsh
Coordinating Editor: Brent Dubi
Copy Editor: Heather Lang
Compositor: Bytheway Publishing Services
Indexer: SPI Global
Artist: SPI Global
Cover Designer: Anna Ishchenko

Distributed to the book trade worldwide by Springer Science+Business Media New York, 233 Spring Street, 6th Floor, New York, NY 10013. Phone 1-800-SPRINGER, fax (201) 348-4505, e-mail orders-ny@springer-sbm.com, or visit www.springeronline.com.

For information on translations, please e-mail rights@apress.com, or visit www.apress.com.

Apress and friends of ED books may be purchased in bulk for academic, corporate, or promotional use. eBook versions and licenses are also available for most titles. For more information, reference our Special Bulk Sales–eBook Licensing web page at www.apress.com/bulk-sales.

Any source code or other supplementary materials referenced by the author in this text is available to readers at www.apress.com. For detailed information about how to locate your book's source code, go to http://www.apress.com/source-code/.

Contents at a Glance

Contents

Foreword

Try as they might, Microsoft can never meet the code needs of every developer. The world is simply too rich and diversified, full of many niches of functionality. It wouldn't make sense for Microsoft to try and supply libraries to meet all these needs.

Instead, Microsoft focuses on more foundational libraries while its community of developers have taken it upon themselves to write thousands upon thousands of useful libraries and utilities.

Microsoft recognized this and started the NuGet project to make it easier for developers to discover and distribute one another's libraries. A healthy ecosystem of developers who share code and build libraries is good for Microsoft and good for developers.

But then, an interesting thing happened. Microsoft donated the project and its employees time to the Outercurve Foundation, a foundation meant to foster open source collaboration with corporations. NuGet is an Apache v2 licensed open source project that accepts contributions from outside of Microsoft.

In doing so, Microsoft truly made NuGet a project that belongs to the community. At the same time, Microsoft plans to ship it within its products. It's already shipped as part of ASP.NET MVC 3, and will ship as part of the next version of Visual Studio. NuGet represents a new way for Microsoft work with the community while they deliver a great product.

NuGet was designed to be very easy to get started with. Making use of a NuGet package is pretty much as simple as adding an assembly reference. But there's also a lot of depth to NuGet. NuGet supports more than one workflow, such as checking in packages to source control, or restoring them during compilation. Packages can contain PowerShell scripts that add new commands to the NuGet PowerShell Console. For example, the MvcScaffolding package contains commands for scaffolding a site based on a model.

This is why there is room for a book on NuGet. It's simple to get started, but there are so many ways to make use of its full power. From very early on, Maarten and Xavier have been involved with NuGet contributing ideas and building products based on NuGet such as `http://MyGet.org`, a site for hosting custom (and optionally private) NuGet repositories.

What I hope you get from this book is a sense of all the ways that NuGet can help streamline your day to day development and even make it more fun to write code. And for those of you who want to take it further, why not come over and contribute?

Phil Haack
Project Lead, NuGet

NuGet is the best thing to happen to Open Source and Microsoft since, well, since the beginning. I enjoy working for Microsoft and I've been doing Open Source for well over a decade, but getting open source libraries into my projects has always been a hassle. Where is the site? Which file to download Where do I put it? Which DLL do I get and what framework version? Too many clicks.

We in the .NET community have been jealous of Ruby GEMs and Java Maven and all the other package management solutions for developers. It took a while, but Microsoft finally released an open source project that takes commits from non-Microsoft developers and enhances the .NET developer ecosystem. NuGet was a little late in coming, but it's here and I don't know how I wrote software without it.

You can measure the success of a project like NuGet not by downloads, (although at the time of this writing there were over 3.5 MILLION package downloads and nearly 20,000 packages in the NuGet repository) and not be how many people are using it (although the NuGet package manager is coming up on a million downloads itself) but rather how fundamentally it changes your daily workflow. Everyone who uses NuGet suddenly can't live without it.

Why a book on NuGet? Because NuGet is a building block on top of which many other things can be build. Not just NuGet packages and .NET libraries, but innovative services, starter kits, web frameworks, scaffolders, installers and all sorts of crazy stuff that NuGet team never imagined.

We've already seen commercial software vendors like JetBrains build NuGet support directly into their TeamCity product as well as tools and component companies like DevExpress create private NuGet feeds to support the Enterprise. NuGet is open source, but it's more than just open source. It's about making building software with new, original and pioneering libraries in YOUR application as easy as File | Add Reference.

I'm happy to be a part of this community and to, in some small part, contributed to NuGet and its success. I hope that now by reading this book that YOU will become a part of that success story!

Scott Hanselman
Principal Community Architect – ASP.NET/IIS/NuGet Microsoft

About the Authors

▥ **Maarten Balliauw** is a technical consultant in web technologies at RealDolmen, one of Belgium's biggest ICT companies. His interests are ASP.NET (MVC), PHP and Windows Azure. He's a Microsoft Most Valuable Professional (MVP) for Windows Azure and has published many articles in both PHP and .NET literature such as MSDN magazine and PHP architect. Maarten is a frequent speaker at various national and international events such as MIX (Las Vegas), TechDays, DPC. His blog can be found at http://blog.maartenballiauw.be.

Blog: http://blog.maartenballiauw.be
E-mail: maarten@maartenballiauw.be
Twitter: http://twitter.com/maartenballiauw

▥ **Xavier Decoster** is a certified Technology Specialist ASP.NET/Silverlight and Scrum Master. He works as a Technical Consultant for RealDolmen Belgium. He's passionate about .NET software development in all its facets, including but not limited to tooling such as Visual Studio, Team Foundation Server, NuGet etc.

He is a co-founder of MyGet.org, which is a NuGet-as-a-Service platform on Windows Azure, where he builds further on top of his experience as a web developer and his broad ALM interests. From the point of view that every software developer deserves to work with proper tools in an environment that supports efficiency and productivity, he does a best effort to contribute to the community, as a speaker (Agile.NET, VISUG, UgiAL.NET), as an author, as a blogger, and through various open source projects.

Blog: http://www.xavierdecoster.com
E-mail: pro.nuget@xavierdecoster.com
Twitter: http://twitter.com/xavierdecoster

About the Technical Reviewer

Fabio Claudio Ferracchiati is a senior consultant and a senior analyst/developer using Microsoft technologies. He works for Brain Force (`www.brainforce.com`) in its Italian branch (www.brainforce.it). Fabio is a Microsoft Certified Solution Developer for .NET, a Microsoft Certified Application Developer for .NET, a Microsoft Certified Professional, and a prolific author and technical reviewer. Over the past ten years, he has written articles for Italian and international magazines, and coauthored more than ten books on a variety of computer topics.

Acknowledgments

We're not sure about the date. It must have been somewhere in August 2011 since we've had the crazy idea of writing a book. Having worked together on `www.myget.org`, we've learned we cooperate quite effectively. And being a member of the NuGet ecosystem, just like SymbolSource.org, Octopus, Chocolatey and many, many others, we felt there could be said enough about NuGet. Why not take the plunge to write a book? Maarten had written one before on ASP.NET MVC (v1) and swore he would never write a book again, ever. Xavier had never written one but liked the idea of trying it, at least once. NuGet has been around since the beginning of 2011 and we've both explored, experimented and integrated this simple yet effective concept in our life as a developer.

Writing a book is never the work of the authors alone. We've had great support by the folks at Apress on forcing us with deadlines to keep the writing process going. They've given us "carte blanche" after we had submitted some proposed chapter ideas. We had the idea that this should be both a getting started book as well as explore the power of the idea behind NuGet. Thank you, Brent and Ewan for having that much trust in us as we've never met in real life. Fabio, we also wish to thank you for reading our book thoroughly and making sure we were clear enough on the technical side. It was good to have you as a technical reviewer.

NuGet is built by a community. Some develop, some give feedback on how they use it. We've had the chance to work with some great guys like Phil Haack (GitHub), David Fowler (Microsoft), Rob Reynolds (Chocolatey), Paul Stovell (Octopus) and Hadi Hariri (JetBrains). They've given us valuable input for the book you are currently holding in your hands. They offered us their mindset and ideas around using NuGet, we've brain-picked them and introduced these concepts in our book to provide insights that go way beyond using NuGet just as a tool to pull packages from a feed and consume them.

Thanks to our wives as well. They've done a great job in giving us the time and space to explore the NuGet ecosystem without demanding anything in return.

Finally, thank you, dear Reader, to buy this book. It recognizes our hard work but more importantly, it makes us feel the community around NuGet is growing and more people are going to introduce NuGet in their development practices.

Maarten & Xavier

The Bigger Picture

NuGet is a free, open source, package management tool for the .NET platform. It is developed by Microsoft and has been contributed to the ASP.NET Gallery on Outercurve Foundation, formerly known as the Codeplex Foundation. It also ships as part of the ASP.NET MVC 3 tooling. NuGet enables .NET developers to easily find packages, including any dependencies, and manage them within Visual Studio projects.

A NuGet package can consist of assemblies, configuration files, source code and more. Software package management is not a new concept, although the tools have been notably missing for years by .NET developers. Some open source tools were available but like with many things life a chicken-egg problem existed between having tooling and having a package publishing ecosystem.

In this chapter, you'll learn why the .NET platform needed a package management tool, how NuGet compares to other package management tools, and finally, how you could benefit from using NuGet in your projects.

Leveraging the Community

One thing any .NET developer should be aware of, is that the .NET ecosystem is much bigger and not limited to the .NET Framework itself. There are literally thousands of open source libraries and components available for your perusal.

Those who are aware of this vast ecosystem often ask themselves the same questions:

- How do I know if there already is a suitable solution available?

- Where can I find it?

- How do I install it?

- How do I configure it properly?

- How do I know there is a newer version available?

Usually, this meant searching the web for the best solution, try to find your way through different blog posts, discussion forums, project sites and hopefully some documentation as well, and eventually pulling some source code or compiled libraries for reference in your projects. The adventure is just beginning! How do you know what to reference? Do I reference all libraries or only some of them? How do I use these libraries?

By the time you were satisfied with your work and got the thing working, you'd usually lost valuable time. Of course, the next time you needed this dependency, you already knew what to do: been there, done that! That is, if the library had not evolved into some new major version full of new features and breaking changes, merged assemblies and obsolete libraries etc. If you found out about a new, improved version of the dependency during development, justifying an update of this dependency, then this exact same pain could be waiting already!

Wouldn't it make more sense to leave the hassle of going through all these potential installation and configuration changes up to the people who created it in the first place? Who knows better than the creators of the library about what has changed, or which steps are to be taken to upgrade from an older version to the new one?

If any of the above makes sense to you, NuGet will sound like music to your ears. This book will help you in leveraging NuGet and make sure these situations belong to history.

Get Latest Version

When working on software projects and joining a development team, it's always pleasant to be able to do a "Get Latest Version" on the source control system being used, press *F5* in Visual Studio and run the application to get accustomed to it.

Unfortunately, this dream scenario of being able to *get latest and run* is not always reality: many times developers reference assemblies from the GAC (Global Assembly Cache) that are not present in a default .NET installation. This means every developer needs to be doing some tooling and library installations on their systems in order to get the application to run.

Note Each computer running the common language runtime (CLR) has a machine-wide code cache called the *global assembly cache* (GAC). The GAC stores assemblies specifically designated to be shared by several applications on the computer. More info on `http://msdn.microsoft.com/en-us/library/yf1d93sz(v=vs.71).aspx`

If you are lucky, smart developers add their external libraries to source control as well so this *get latest* scenario just works. However, there's still the pain of keeping everything up-to-date.

Did all of the above sound awfully familiar? NuGet is the perfect match to overcome such pains in your development process and this book will help you with optimizing for the *get latest* scenario.

Escaping From Dependency Hell

To understand the goals of and the reasons behind a package management tool for the .NET platform, it's worth considering how developers have been managing software dependencies so far. If you ever struggled updating a referenced assembly to a new version, or searched for documentation on a third-party library to perform a specific task, to find out such documentation did not exist, you have encountered dependency management issues. If you ever had a build failing or a runtime exception because of a reference collision, you have entered dependency hell.

Dependency hell is a term for the frustration of software users who have installed software packages which have dependencies on specific versions of other software packages.

—Wikipedia, http://en.wikipedia.org/wiki/Dependency_hell

Note If you have not heard about dependency hell, the term "DLL Hell" is a similar concept to that which existed in earlier versions of Microsoft Windows where software developers were always struggling to find and work with the correct DLL in their software.

An Introduction to Dependency Management

Following industry best practices, a good software architect, technical lead or developer designs his application with reusability and modularity in mind. There are tons of good books and resources out there that will explain you the reasoning behind, but that would quickly lead us beyond the scope of this book. Creating or consuming reusable components and libraries is generally considered a good thing. In fact, all developers building on top of the .NET Framework already do this implicitly, without paying too much attention to it, as the .NET Framework is the core framework on top of which we all build our solutions.

Over the years, an increasing number of people in the .NET community initiated open source projects or started contributing to such open source initiatives. Some of them gained a huge amount of popularity due to the quality and maturity they had reached, others due to the unique functionality they provided. Many software projects began referencing these third-party libraries and as such became dependent on them.

Both origins of such software dependencies have one thing in common: *you don't control them.* This is exactly the root cause of the frustration that many developers have experienced when fighting dependency issues: you can't control the third-party reference you rely on.

Table 1. Example dependency matrix for a modular application

Application	Module	Dependencies
Application A	Module X	Library U, Library V
	Module Y	Library S, Library T
	Module Z	

Imagine you're part of a development team working on a single module, module X, for an application, as illustrated in Table 1. Your team's module is depending on two libraries, while one of the other modules has its own dependencies. So far so good, all teams are working on isolated modules

xix

without interdependencies. It seems however, as shown in figure I-1, that library U, on which module X depends, has a dependency itself to library T from another module. This could be a potential source of headache when one of the two teams requires another version of T, or upgrades T to an incompatible version for library U. You've just encountered a version collision on one of your dependencies.

This very simple example illustrates you don't need to have a huge dependency graph for an application to encounter dependency issues. Real life enterprise solutions that can consist out of hundreds of modules increase the change of entering dependency hell exponentially. You can safely conclude that the larger an application's list of dependencies, and its dependencies' interdependencies, the more of a pain point this becomes. Because most business applications are more complex than the simple example above, most development teams don't even realize they will hit these issues, until they feel pain and frustration is their part.

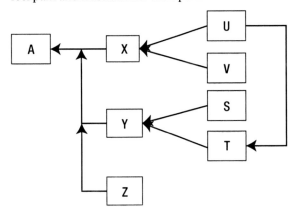

Figure 1. Example dependency graph for a modular application

Many development teams have struggled with dependency issues due to incorrect versioning applied to such third-party libraries or components. A typical example would be a library version 1.0 that just released an update using a minor version increment, version 1.1, but nonetheless contains breaking changes. Those companies that hit these issues, preferred reinventing the wheel and have control over this dependency. They started creating their own frameworks trying to solve similar problems. Although this indeed mitigated the risk of dependency issues, it has proven to be a costly workaround due to significantly increased development time, and actually created the illusion of reusability: everyone was applying reusability principles within their own isolated environment. Some smart people realized this, but the reality is that even those people often ended up in an environment where company policies and the economic reality forced them to work this way.

Another approach is to lock down all dependencies at the start of a project: although you'll never have this kind of dependency issues, your project will never benefit from any new functionality or improvements a newer version of those dependencies can bring. A variation to this, is to unlock the dependencies right after a release, when work starts on the next version. At this point in time, you pick newer versions of your dependencies, and lock them again until after release. The first approach is harsh and your project doesn't benefit from it in the long term, while the latter has been proven quite successful. If you want to be *agile* and pick any version of a dependency when you feel fit, you'll be continuously fixing your project instead of driving it towards stable milestones.

You probably have a gut feeling by now that none of these approaches are really satisfying and have a reactive touch to it. You're always running behind the fact you'll be dealing with all of this yourself, every single time, over and over again. To understand how NuGet solves these issues, it's important to learn how people came up with answers to these problems over the years, and how they evolved.

A Brief History of Dependency Management

In the early days of the Internet, developers used some sort of repository-based approach, such as the Apache Jakarta Project in Java, where the community surrounded the development platform with lots of open source projects. This helped forging a new approach to dependency management. Around the use of source control, they discouraged checking in binaries and other output of your project. The Apache Ant framework, an XML-based Java build library, helped facilitating this best practice. This tool was a first in its kind because it also allowed to retrieve files using HTTP. Typically, an internal site was put in place to be responsible for hosting shared libraries within an organization. At build-time, the Ant build files were used to download the libraries locally when not already present. This approach had a shortcoming however: there was no standard way of setting up these repositories. Also, caching was not uniformly dealt with.

The lessons learned from these experienced were meant to be solved by Java's second generation build framework, Maven. Maven was an attempt to standardize the dependency management process and introduced recommendations around repository management and versioning conventions.

As opposed to what the Unix development community was used to, .NET developers found it a convenient practice to put all referenced dependencies into source control, next to their project. Convenient, because it was very easy for getting projects set up. In similarity to what the Java community experienced, this approach also lacked a standardized strategy for managing different versions of dependencies.

The release of Microsoft MSBuild was a turning point for the .NET community. This free XML-based build platform is bundled with the .NET Framework and is used by Visual Studio as the underlying build engine. Although a port of Ant was available for .NET at the time, MSBuild quickly became the tool of choice. However, MSBuild did not come with any tasks that supported downloading dependencies.

Note You can read more on MSBuild on MSDN: http://msdn.microsoft.com/en-us/library /0k6kkbsd.aspx.

Towards mid-2010, the .NET community seemed to move towards the right direction with the introduction of OpenWrap, immediately followed by a Microsoft announcement that they joined forces with a .NET package management project called Nubular (Nu). Based on RubyGems, a well-known package management system in the Ruby-world, it has been rewritten to get rid of the Ruby dependency. The Nu command line package management system was now to be called NuPack. Shortly hereafter and one more rebranding, NuGet was born.

Tip Did you know that Visual Studio project files are actually MSBuild project files? Open the files in Notepad (or any other text editor) to see how it is built out of MSBuild tasks, targets, properties and items.

What's Wrong With What I've Always Been Doing?

Before the existence of a package management tool such as NuGet, dependency management in .NET has been a big problem. There was no uniform way to tackle them, there was no practical guidance that provided a "one-solution-fits-all" approach to all development environments.

The various approaches to tackle these problems often relied on the development tools being used. For instance, teams using Team Foundation Server's source control system could use shared Team Projects to manage their internal dependencies. On a smaller scale, you could also have Visual Studio projects shared between multiple solutions. Although in some cases this worked, the main issue with this solution is the fact that the code in those shared projects could be easily changed in any of those solutions. Such change in the code often resulted in one solution building correctly, while the other solutions were broken all at once. If some kind of version or change management was applied to those solutions, you'd often experience problems with this as well because every single time a solution builds the shared project, the other solutions would get a new version as well.

Others preferred putting all compiled dependencies in a local folder relative to the Visual Studio solution, often called References, Referenced Assemblies, Libs, or something else, clearly an indication that there was no uniform convention. A positive note in this approach is that a proper release has to be picked for every single dependency, including internal ones, which made some sort of change management possible. Until today, this is the most common approach taken by .NET development teams, independent of which software configuration management tool they use. Nevertheless, for those using Team Foundation Server, upgrading a dependency is often a pain in the behind because of the insufficient tracking of binary differences in source control. When a developer changed a dll in the folder and wanted it to be checked in, he would often be presented with a dialog that "Team Foundation Server did not detect any changes. Undoing check-out.". As a developer wanting to upgrade an assembly under source control, you had to remember that you need to explicitly check-out the file first, before replacing it and checking it in. This is often used as an argument against Team Foundation Server's source control system, but, although it is indeed a weakness, the argument is actually an indication that the approach itself is maybe not as perfect as one would think it is.

In general, if you think about it, does it make a lot of sense to:

- Store compiled code in a source control system?

- Duplicate those compiled dependencies relative to a solution all over your source control system?

- Store third-party libraries and components, which may be restricted by license and are the intellectual property of others, into *your* source control system?

We'll go in depth into the answers to these questions in Part III of this book, where we will guide you through various scenarios and practices to stay as far away as possible from dependency hell.

An Introduction to Package Management

The idea of a package management system for software libraries and components is actually derived from the concept of operating system package managers that install system-wide software packages or libraries, much like Apt-Get and similar package management tools do in the non-Microsoft space. Linux based operating systems and other Unix-like systems typically consist of hundreds of distinct software packages, making it a package management system a real necessity. On Microsoft Windows, where the .NET runtime relies on dynamic library linking, the runtime also looks in the Global Assembly Cache, or GAC in short, for shared libraries to remove the issue of DLL hell. As the central repository for shared DLL's, the GAC is often the place into which applications will find or install common assemblies.

In the area of software development, a package manager is responsible for the automation of the installation, update, configuration and removal process of software packages in a consistent manner within the scope of solution. Typically, this tool is also responsible of interpreting package metadata such as version information or package dependencies to prevent conflicts or missing prerequisites.

Note When talking about 'package manager' or 'package management' throughout this book, we'll refer to application-level package management unless otherwise noted.

You might be wondering why we discuss package management instead of dependency management. That is because there is a difference between a package and a dependency. A package typically consists out of software libraries that, when installed in a target project, form a dependency the target project relies on. But there's more! A package can also contain source code, configuration files, content such as images, scripts and other files. Discussing dependencies would limit us to only a part of what a package can contain or what a package manager can contribute to the development process. Package contents and how to create them will be discussed in detail in Chapter 5: Creating Packages.

It is also very tempting to confuse a package manager with an installer, often caused by common or very similar terminology and functionality. An installer is usually specific to a given product. In other words: a given product often comes with its own installer. This results in the installer often being tightly coupled to the product being installed, due to product specific options or installation steps, making it harder or even impossible to reuse the installer. There are also multiple vendors of installers resulting in different installer formats being used. This is very different for a package manager, which is the one and only installer of packages. Packages need to be of a specific format understood by the package manager. This difference makes a package manager very distinct from an installer.

Because a package manager is aware of package versioning and its dependencies, it is smart enough to detect any potential conflicts. It can add the appropriate binding redirects if needed or warn you upon installation time that a versioning conflict occurred.

Note You can redirect an assembly binding reference to another version of an assembly by using entries in the application or machine configuration files. More info on `http://msdn.microsoft.com/en-us/library /2fc472t2.aspx`.

This makes installing packages and dependency conflict management more convenient, especially if it can detect and solve issues with binding redirects, or abort package installation by telling you where the problem occurs. Because the format of packages is restricted by a manifest specification (more on that in Chapter 5: Creating Packages) and the package manager is the same for all packages, there is a uniform approach independent of the development environment you are working on.

There are only two things you depend on: the package manager, and the package publisher. The package manager is a single point of failure of which you can be certain it has been well tested and functions as it should. Don't expect major issues from that side. The package publisher however is an unknown third-party that is subject to human error. This is however not any different from relying on a third-party component without a package manager: you assume the component or the package contents are well tested and function as expected. Have you seen developers writing unit tests or other kinds of tests on a third-party component before using it? Would it be easy to find budget to do this? Do you feel this is a natural precaution? The structure of the package contents however is well-defined according to a manifest that the package manager understands. The only human error the package publisher can make in order to provide you with a dependency issue, is an incorrect versioning pattern. Versioning is also topic of interest in Chapter 5: Creating Packages.

Key Benefits of NuGet

NuGet brings you all the benefits of any package manager: it takes care of dependency chains and versioning conflicts at installation time, and it facilitates finding, installing, updating and uninstalling packages on application level. Besides these common must-have functionalities, NuGet has much more to offer.

NuGet is more than just a package manager. When changing perspectives, which we will assist you with in Chapter 11: NuGet Outside Visual Studio, you'll notice that you can leverage NuGet as a protocol for other means, due to its extensibility, its tooling, its integration and the fact that it is open source.

NuGet Is Open Source

Although NuGet has been developed by Microsoft, it has been made open source and contributed to the ASP.NET Gallery on Outercurve Foundation. Because it is open source, the .NET community has picked it up quite fast and forged an ecosystem around it by providing tools, guidance and support. Some even came up with innovative solutions for other scenarios based on NuGet, such as scaffolding, hosted private NuGet feeds in the cloud, system-wide package management and an application plugin system. Of course you can also just get the sources and tweak it further to your needs.

Tooling And Integration

NuGet provides us with a lot of tooling allowing us to use NuGet in any .NET environment. Whether you use Visual Studio or another IDE, whether you use Team Foundation Server or another source control system, whether you use the public NuGet Gallery or a custom NuGet feed hosted in the cloud or within company firewalls, you'll be able to integrate NuGet into your development environment with a minimum of effort. As NuGet becomes a major citizen into our .NET development stack, we feel certain that this integration will become even smoother in the future, as some third-party development tool vendors already demonstrated recently.

The command line tool allows you to interact with NuGet from a simple console window. This tool can also be leveraged by continuous integration systems or deployment environments to fetch or publish NuGet packages using some simple commands.

The Powershell enabled Package Manager Console allows you to interact with NuGet from within Visual Studio. Providing you with useful cmdlets ("commandlets") for standard NuGet operations, you'll be able to manage the NuGet packages your projects rely on without leaving the IDE. The ability to register your own cmdlets into this shell provides you with even greater flexibility.

The NuGet Package Manager is a graphical user interface allowing you to visualize and edit package contents and metadata. It also allows you to create and publish your packages directly into a feed of choice. The NuGet Package Manager also has a plugin system, allowing you to extend this application even further to your needs.

The NuGet Package Manager Visual Studio extension integrates flawlessly with the Visual Studio IDE, which makes installing a package as easy as adding a reference to a project. The Visual Studio extension also comes with configurable settings for caching and package sources.

All these tools will be used in combination, so you'll be able to mix them as you want, as well as stick to a tool and work with it through the book. In the next chapter, we'll show you how to set up your computer with these tools to get started.

Chapter 2 of this book will help you find and install these tools.

Extensibility

Because NuGet is an open source project, it is also very easy to extend it or its usage. There are some nice examples out there that leverage NuGet and extended its purpose or functionality.

- **Chocolatey** – A system-wide package manager leveraging NuGet, enabling the quick installation of several useful software packages.

- **MvcScaffolding** – Installing this NuGet package extends the Visual Studio IDE with new functionality, referred to as *scaffolding*. Provided you have a template, either using the standard ones or a custom one, you can easily generate any type of project item (such as CRUD views and controllers for a given model).

- **MyGet** – A cloud solution providing you with what we call NuGet-as-a-Service (NaaS). Avoids the hassle of developing your own NuGet Server and quickly get started levering NuGet in your software development environment.

Competition

The wide spread usage of NuGet also has another effect: it creates extra competition for Microsoft products. Microsoft is not the only package provider on the NuGet Gallery and its packages are listed amongst other third-party components and frameworks. For instance, the choice of using Entity Framework, NHibernate, Dapper.NET or a similar product, is now a matter of picking a package and install it. If people query the NuGet feed for the word 'database', they'll find a whole lot more than just Entity Framework.

This means that it will be equally as easy to find and use a non-Microsoft solution for reference in your project, and based on good reviews of those solutions, you might choose the non-Microsoft package. We think this evolution is good and should result in an improved quality of those solutions. The more people who use it, the better the feedback.

Who Should Use NuGet

If you feel so familiar with the problems sketched in this chapter that it scares you, then you have definitely been waiting for NuGet put your mind at ease. If you don't like to go through the manual process of installing third-party frameworks yourself, or experience issues trying to keep up with new releases of those dependencies, then NuGet is your next best friend. Even if you do know your dependencies very well and are very familiar with its installation, configuration and different versions, you could benefit from using NuGet by gaining precious time you could spend on more valuable tasks.

In short, the use of a package manager for .NET development is a best practice every developer should consider, and with the proper guidance of this book, you'll wonder one day how you managed to live without it.

Summary

In this chapter, we have described how dependency issues have struck many .NET development teams and how people tried to come up with a proper solution or workaround. We've also discussed the pain points involved, and how a package management tool can help you solve them.

In the next chapter, we'll get you started with everything you need to be up and running with NuGet with a minimum amount of effort. By chapter 7, you'll be ready for more realistic enterprise scenarios, including hosting your own NuGet server, integrate with source control and continuous integration scenarios and automated deployment. Finally, we'll also change our perspectives and take a look at different ways of leveraging NuGet, such as in a plugin system.

CHAPTER 1

Getting Started

To get started with NuGet, some software components will be required on your system. While NuGet, in essence, is just a small, command-line executable, a lot of value comes from its integration with Visual Studio or the Visual Studio Express editions. Taking advantage of this integration offers you a seamless development workflow and enables you to work with NuGet right from within your Visual Studio installation; you'll even have a nice user interface to work with.

We'll elaborate on working with NuGet from within Visual Studio in Chapter 2. Before that, this chapter will help you prepare your workstation and get all the prerequisites to work with NuGet in your development process, including installing Visual Studio, additional components, and NuGet itself.

Preparing Your Workstation

A small set of tools is essential to develop with NuGet. Whether you are a VB.NET or C# developer, whether you develop in Windows Forms, Web Forms, Silverlight, ASP.NET MVC (Model-View-Controller) or for a Windows Phone, you will need Visual Studio 2010 or one of the Visual Studio 2010 Express editions.

NuGet is supported in the following development environments:

- Visual Studio 2010 Express

- Visual Web Developer 2010

- Windows Phone Developer Tools 7.1

- Visual Studio 2010 Professional

- Visual Studio 2010 Premium

- Visual Studio 2010 Ultimate

- SharpDevelop

If you do not have access to the Professional, Premium, or Ultimate editions, you can find some free Visual Studio Express versions at www.microsoft.com/express.

In this book, most examples will use Visual Studio 2010 Ultimate. Keep in mind that the Visual Studio integration is identical across all versions listed in this section, and all versions are equally suited to our purposes. This book will not cover SharpDevelop, but its NuGet integration is similar to that of Visual Studio 2010.

■ **Note** If SharpDevelop is your favorite integrated development environment (IDE), don't throw away this book. SharpDevelop and Visual Studio 2010 share similar ideology and features. If you wish to install NuGet with SharpDevelop, have a look at `http://community.sharpdevelop.net/blogs/mattward/archive` `/2011/01/23/NuGetSupportInSharpDevelop.aspx`.

Installing Visual Studio 2010

After obtaining one of the Visual Studio versions listed in the previous section, install Visual Studio as you would install any other Windows application, and make sure that all service packs and updates are installed. The features to select during the Visual Studio 2010 installation are shown in Figure 1-1. Do note that, if you prefer languages like VB.NET or F# over C#, you can install those languages as well.

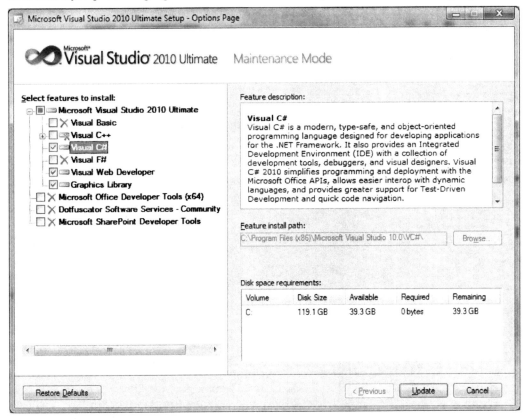

Figure 1-1. Selecting the features of Visual Studio 2010 to install

Installing the Essential Software

Some examples in this book require you to install specific software. For example, some require the ASP.NET MVC 3 framework. Visual Studio 2010 ships with the ASP.NET MVC 3 framework installed, but you may want to upgrade to the latest version.

Other applications used throughout this book are Microsoft WebMatrix and the Orchard Content Management System (CMS). The easiest way to install these components and configure your development environment is through Microsoft's Web Platform Installer, or Web PI as everyone calls it.

The Web PI allows you to select a set of application components and frameworks, install them all at once, and take care of dependencies. For example, if you install the ASP.NET MVC framework, the Web PI will also install .NET 4 on your machine. If you wish to have the default configuration for your local development web server installed, the Web PI will both install and configure this for you.

Installing the Web Platform Installer

The Web PI can be downloaded at http://microsoft.com/web. Click Downloads menu at the top of this page, and then click the Web Platform Installer link shown in Figure 1-2 to acquire the Web PI tool.

Figure 1-2. The Download link to the Web Platform Installer

Once you arrive on the download page, click the large Download It Now button, shown in Figure 1-3, to download it to your computer. Note that Internet Explorer will ask you to run or save the installation file. Click the Run button (also shown in Figure 1-3) to run the Web Platform Installer. Other browsers often have similar option hidden under the Open button, for example.

Figure 1-3. The download page for the Web PI

Installing Components and Configuring Your Environment Using the Web PI

Once the Web PI is running, you can select a variety of tools, applications, and frameworks to install on your machine from the Web PI main screen, which will look like Figure 1-4. Web PI also enables you to configure some of the components that are already on your machine.

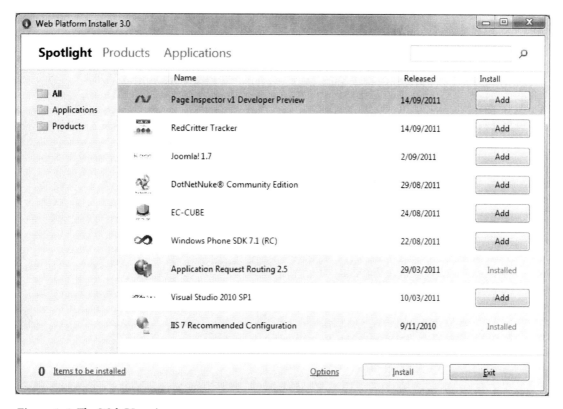

Figure 1-4. *The Web PI main screen*

You'll use the search box on the top-right corner of this screen to find the essential components used in this book. When the Web PI finds a component, simply click the Add button on the right side to add it to the list of software to install.

Find and add the following components:

- Windows PowerShell 2.0

- ASP.NET MVC 3 or higher

- IIS 7 Recommended Configuration

- Microsoft .NET Framework 4

- Microsoft WebMatrix

After you've added these components, click the Install button near the bottom of the Web Platform Installation window. This action will display a confirmation dialog listing the components you've selected plus their required dependencies, as shown in Figure 1-5. Click the I Accept button to install all these components.

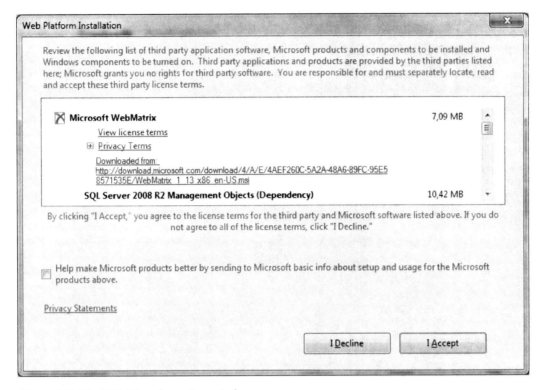

Figure 1-5. The Web PI confirmation window

Installing NuGet

Since you are reading a book titled *Pro NuGet*, you can imagine one of the required components to work your way through this book is NuGet itself.

NuGet is a collection of several tools, including the NuGet executable, a small .exe file that you can use from the Windows command line, and the NuGet Visual Studio extension. Throughout this book, we'll mostly be using the Visual Studio extension (both the graphical user interface and the PowerShell console). However, some sections will be using the command-line version of NuGet. This section covers finding and installing these two components.

Throughout this book, we will also use the NuGet Package Explorer tool. NuGet Package Explorer is not an official Microsoft product; it's an open source project hosted on CodePlex. NuGet Package Explorer (NPE) is required in your developer tool belt once you start working with NuGet: it allows you to open, edit, inspect, and validate NuGet packages from an easy-to-use graphical user interface.

Installing the NuGet Visual Studio Extension

To get started, navigate to www.nuget.org, the official web site hosting the NuGet tool and a variety of useful NuGet packages to use in your software. Find and click the Install NuGet button. After that, you'll be taken to the Visual Studio gallery where the actual download of the latest version of NuGet is located.

The Visual Studio gallery displays a purple Download link, as shown in Figure 1-6. Click this link to install the NuGet Package Manager into your Visual Studio environment.

Figure 1-6. The Visual Studio gallery, where the NuGet Visual Studio extension can be downloaded

Installing the NuGet extension into Visual Studio is very straightforward. The Visual Studio Extension Installer (VSIX) will prompt you to install NuGet into one or more versions of Visual Studio available on your system (Maarten happens to have three of those on his machine, as you can see in Figure 1-7). Click the Install button to register NuGet in Visual Studio.

Figure 1-7. The NuGet installer lists the versions of Visual Studio into which it can be installed.

■ **Note** NuGet can be installed directly from Visual Studio. In the Tools ➤ Extension Manager menu, you can search for Visual Studio extensions. Search for NuGet, and click the Install button to install NuGet into Visual Studio.

The Visual Studio Extension Manager is also the place where you can install updates to the NuGet Visual Studio extension. NuGet typically is updated every two months. The Updates panel on the Visual Studio Extension Manager will allow you to easily update NuGet to its latest version.

Downloading the NuGet Command-Line Tool

The NuGet command-line tool is used in this book as well. You can download its latest version at http://nuget.codeplex.com (on this page, you can also download the NuGet source code and even contribute if you want to add a feature to NuGet).

Select the Downloads menu, as shown in Figure 1-8, and the resulting page will present you with three download options: NuGet Visual Studio extension, NuGet.exe Command Line, and NuGet Package

Explorer v2.0. The second download is the NuGet command line tool. Click its link, accept the license terms, and save NuGet.exe to a location on your hard drive that you can easily find later.

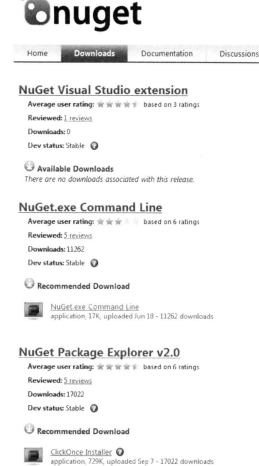

Figure 1-8. The NuGet downloads page on CodePlex

Installing NuGet Package Explorer

Although NPE is not required to work with NuGet, as we mentioned before, it is handy because it allows you to open, edit, inspect, and validate NuGet packages from an easy-to-use graphical user interface.

NPE is a ClickOnce application that can be installed from inside your browser. To add it to your machine, simply navigate to http://nuget.codeplex.com, and find the Downloads page. As Figure 1-8 shows, the third download features NuGet Package Explorer. You can install and run NPE by clicking the ClickOnce Installer link.

> ▪ **Note** ClickOnce is a Microsoft technology that allows you to download and run an application from the Internet. Although that concept is not new or special, ClickOnce adds one additional feature: applications installed through ClickOnce are automatically updated as needed. This means that your NuGet Package Explorer software will always be kept up-to-date automatically.

After installing NPE, you will be greeted by its welcome screen, as shown in Figure 1-9. You can close NPE for now, because we won't need it again in this chapter. In other chapters, we'll make extensive use of it though.

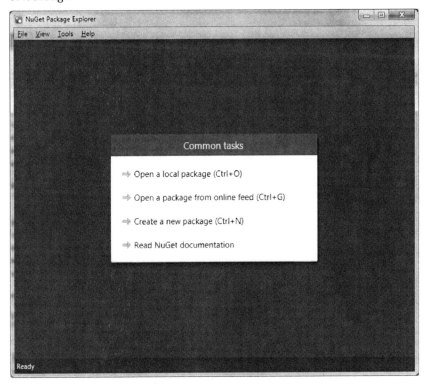

Figure 1-9. The NuGet Package Explorer welcome screen

Getting Further Information

If you require additional information on installing NuGet, the NuGet command line tool, or NuGet Package Explorer, navigate to http://docs.nuget.org, where the people maintaining the NuGet open source project keep an up-to-date documentation wiki.

If you experience technical problems with NuGet, the NuGet Visual Studio Extension, or the NuGet command line executable, the discussion forum and issue tracker at http://nuget.codeplex.com should provide you with support on these topics. This URL can also be used to ask for additional features in the NuGet stack.

Last but not least, NuGet (and NuGet Package Explorer) are open source projects. This means that you can have a look inside to see how a specific feature is implemented, track down bugs, or even add your own contribution to one of these projects. Don't feel shy: if you have a great idea either file a feature request or build it by yourself and share it with the world. Who knows? Our next version of the *Pro NuGet* book may feature something you contributed to NuGet.

Summary

In this chapter, we covered setting up your workstation and all required tools for developing applications using NuGet. You've also seen how you can install NuGet, the NuGet Visual Studio Extension, the command line tools, and NuGet Package Explorer. Finally, you learned that both `www.nuget.org` and `http://nuget.codeplex.com` offer valuable additional information on working with NuGet.

In the next chapter, we'll show you how to consume your first NuGet package.

CHAPTER 2

Consuming and Managing Packages in a Solution

The Introduction of this book introduced you to the bigger picture: the general concept of package management and why it is so extremely powerful. We also introduced NuGet as a solution-wide package management tool and explained its key benefits. Chapter 1 showed you how to get your development environment ready to fully leverage NuGet on your machine. This chapter will build on that knowledge and show you how you can consume your first NuGet package in Visual Studio.

In our first simple scenario, a package will be added to an ASP.NET MVC project. Afterward, we'll explore additional options for installing, updating, and uninstalling NuGet packages in your projects. You will also learn how to adjust NuGet to your needs by configuring custom package sources. There's a nice graphical user interface to do all that, in addition to PowerShell commands and a command-line tool. We'll show you how to use all of those, so you can decide for yourself which method best suits you.

Finally, we'll demonstrate how you can analyze packages installed into a project and how those packages relate to your project and to each other.

Consuming Your First NuGet Package

In this section, we'll show you how you can consume your first NuGet package. Using the tools that are integrated into Visual Studio by installing the NuGet Visual Studio Extension, as explained in Chapter 2, we'll search for a NuGet package from the public NuGet repository.

■ **Note** To most NuGet users, the term "NuGet repository" describes the source of NuGet packages, but to others, this is a "NuGet feed." In essence, both names are correct: since we're talking about a source of NuGet packages, it is a repository. Since those repositories are exposed to the world as an ATOM (XML) feed, the term "feed" is also appropriate.

NuGet packages can be consumed in any type of Visual Studio project, so go ahead and create a new Visual Studio project, for example, an ASP.NET MVC project or a WPF project. You can also open an existing project and add a NuGet package there.

For this section, we're using a new ASP.NET MVC project, since there's something special about that type of project in relation to NuGet (we'll come to that in a second). Figure 2-1 shows the settings used to create a new ASP.NET MVC project named ConsumingNuGet to demonstrate this NuGet version of "Hello, World". After creating a new ASP.NET MVC project in Visual Studio, you're finished with this section.

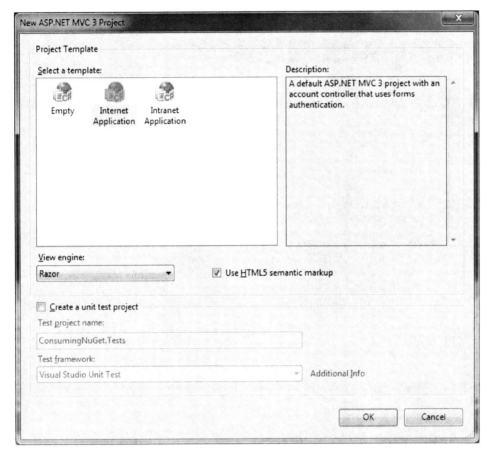

Figure 2-1. Settings used in Visual Studio 2010 to create a new ASP.NET MVC project

Integrating Visual Studio and NuGet

Once you have a Visual Studio 2010 project opened and have installed the NuGet Visual Studio Extension as described in Chapter 2, some new menu options will be available in Visual Studio 2010. For example, the Tools menu contains a new entry called Library Package Manager, which features a number of submenus (see Figure 2-2).

Next to this new menu under Tools, a new context menu is available on a solution and project level. Find the Manage NuGet Package context menu by right-clicking either the solution or one of the projects in a solution. If you're not a command-line person and prefer working using the UI, you'll find yourself using these menus quite regularly.

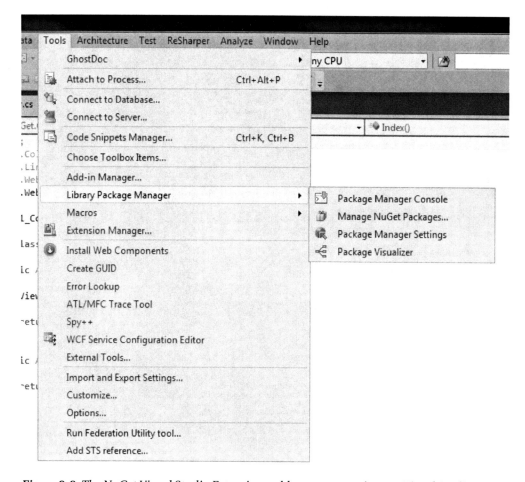

Figure 2-2. The NuGet Visual Studio Extensions adds a new menu item to Visual Studio 2010.

■ **Note** In Figure 2-2, you may notice the Package Visualizer submenu if you have installed Visual Studio 2010 Ultimate edition. Although this submenu is not available in all Visual Studio versions, it is a valuable tool when working with NuGet packages, so it will be covered later in this chapter.

Finding the Package You Need

The NuGet Visual Studio Extension adds some search functionalities to find a NuGet package. Right-click your project in Visual Studio, and click Manage NuGet Packages. This will open a search form with basic filtering options, as shown in Figure 2-3.

The window presented consists of three panes: one to switch among installed packages, package updates, and a list of packages that you have recently used; another to search packages; and a third to display details of selected packages. Make sure to open the Online pane. From there, you can work with the search functionalities available in the Search Online field.

Figure 2-3. *The NuGet Package Management dialog which enables searching for NuGet packages*

Searching for packages is a difficult job when you don't know what to search for. The best way to start exploring NuGet is by entering the technology you are working with in the search box in the top-right corner of this window. For example, type **mvc** as a search query when you are working with ASP.NET MVC. If you are looking for something related to Windows Phone 7, enter **wp7**.

The list of NuGet packages will be filtered based on your query but may still yield a large number of NuGet packages. Refine your search by adding a second keyword. For example, if you want to work with HTML5, change the search query to **mvc html5** to get a smaller list of packages to explore. Of course, this method is not ideal, because it is based on filtering title, description, and tags added to NuGet packages. If the package author forgot to add tags to the published packages, they will probably not be visible when you search for specific keywords. Nevertheless, this way of filtering is the only method of getting a short list of NuGet packages that may provide the functionality you need.

At the time of this writing, over 2,500 NuGet packages are available on Microsoft's public NuGet repository. Some of these packages have multiple versions available, resulting in a total of over 7,000 unique packages in the official NuGet repository! By the time you are reading this book, these numbers have probably gone stale, and even more packages are available. Even once you've searched for your technology, how do you find the specific package you need?

Once you filter the list of available NuGet packages based on the technology you are using and an additional keyword that refines that search, the list of packages at your disposal will be easier to process. Since the official NuGet repository contains various packages of a variable quality, it is important to take some other clues into account in choosing packages. It's very similar to all app stores out there where not every app you install has the same quality baseline.

Luckily, every NuGet package comes with a number of details to inform your choice. If you look back at Figure 2-3, the right-hand pane shows a variety of details about a package:

- The package creator, which may influence whether you deem the NuGet package to be trustworthy.

- The package ID, which will probably not influence your decision but is great to remember if you really like the package and want to reuse it in future projects.

- The package version and last update date, which may give you an idea of how mature and how well-maintained the NuGet package is.

- The number of downloads and rating are good indications on a package. Don't judge a package by its number of downloads alone: less-popular but great-quality packages sometimes have no ratings and a handful of downloads.

- The Project Information hyperlink brings you to the NuGet package's project information page where you can learn a lot about a package.

- The package description, dependencies, and release notes can also give a strong indication about whether the NuGet package will fit your needs.

Be wise in your decisions, and always try out new packages in a sample application (not on your actual project) if you are not familiar with them!

Installing a NuGet Package

Let's add a package to our still-blank ASP.NET MVC project. Right-click your project in Visual Studio, and click Manage NuGet Packages. Find the package named ELMAH, an error-logging framework for ASP.NET. As shown in Figure 2-4, it is pretty obvious what to do next: click the Install button and watch what happens.

Figure 2-4. Finding and installing the ELMAH package in a project

The NuGet Visual Studio Extension added a new Reference to your project. Also, if you look at the Web.config file in the ASP.NET MVC project, some additional configuration settings have been added as well, as shown in Listing 2-1.

Listing 2-1. The Modified Web.config File After Installing the ELMAH NuGet Package

```xml
<?xml version="1.0" encoding="utf-8"?>
<configuration>
  <configSections>
    <sectionGroup name="elmah">
      <section name="security" requirePermission="false"
            type="Elmah.SecuritySectionHandler, Elmah" />
      <section name="errorLog" requirePermission="false"
            type="Elmah.ErrorLogSectionHandler, Elmah" />
      <section name="errorMail" requirePermission="false"
            type="Elmah.ErrorMailSectionHandler, Elmah" />
      <section name="errorFilter" requirePermission="false"
            type="Elmah.ErrorFilterSectionHandler, Elmah" />
    </sectionGroup>
  </configSections>
  <!-- ... -->
```

```
<system.web>
  <!-- ... -->
  <httpModules>
    <add name="ErrorLog" type="Elmah.ErrorLogModule, Elmah" />
    <add name="ErrorMail" type="Elmah.ErrorMailModule, Elmah" />
    <add name="ErrorFilter" type="Elmah.ErrorFilterModule, Elmah" />
  </httpModules>
  <httpHandlers>
    <add verb="POST,GET,HEAD" path="elmah.axd" type="Elmah.ErrorLogPageFactory, Elmah" />
  </httpHandlers>
</system.web>
<system.webServer>
  <!-- ... -->
  <modules runAllManagedModulesForAllRequests="true">
    <add name="ErrorLog"
         type="Elmah.ErrorLogModule, Elmah" preCondition="managedHandler" />
    <add name="ErrorMail"
         type="Elmah.ErrorMailModule, Elmah" preCondition="managedHandler" />
    <add name="ErrorFilter"
         type="Elmah.ErrorFilterModule, Elmah" preCondition="managedHandler" />
  </modules>
  <handlers>
    <add name="Elmah" path="elmah.axd" verb="POST,GET,HEAD"
         type="Elmah.ErrorLogPageFactory, Elmah" preCondition="integratedMode" />
  </handlers>
</system.webServer>
<!-- ... -->
</configuration>
```

Browse the Solution Explorer tree, and you'll see that ELMAH has been added to the list of references. If you right-click the ELMAH reference, and select Properties, the properties pane in Visual Studio will show you where the package has been downloaded and referenced: C:\....\ConsumingNuGet\packages\elmah.corelibrary.1.2\lib\Elmah.dll. Looking at the evidence gathered, the following happened automatically just by clicking Install in the Package Manager dialog:

- The latest version of ELMAH was downloaded from the Internet.

- The required assemblies and other files have been added to a folder under the solution root.

- The ELMAH assembly has been automatically referenced in the current project.

- The Web.config file was automatically modified and updated with all required settings for Elmah.

Impressive, no? Imagine having to search the Internet for the latest version of ELMAH, find the correct download, extract it to your system, read through the documentation to understand what's required to install it into your project, change Web.config, and so on.

It gets even better. When a package has a dependency on another package, NuGet will download and install the additional required package together with the one you were installing in one go. Some packages add extra functionality to Visual Studio; others add extra source code files to your project. A few even extend PowerShell and allow you to generate lots of code in your project (check the MvcScaffolding package if you want to play around).

Where Did It Come From?

NuGet packages always originate from a package source, that is, a NuGet repository or NuGet feed. Since Microsoft backs the development efforts of NuGet with time and materials, these materials include hosting an official, default, and public NuGet repository, which you can explore at www.nuget.org.

As you will see later in this book, you can also create your own NuGet packages and publish them to this official repository. What if you want to distribute your private, corporate, in-house developed base framework to just your development team, and not the entire world of .NET developers? We will cover how you can host your own, private NuGet repository later in this book as well.

By default, the NuGet repository at http://go.microsoft.com/fwlink/?LinkID=206669 (no need to remember that by heart) will be registered as the "NuGet official package source" in the NuGet Visual Studio Extension. Open the Visual Studio Tools ➤ Library Package Manager ➤ Package Manager Settings menu, and click the Package Sources item to register additional repositories or to replace the default, public repository with a repository that contains only those packages that you want to use in your projects. Figure 2-5 shows you the dialog in which you can register additional package sources.

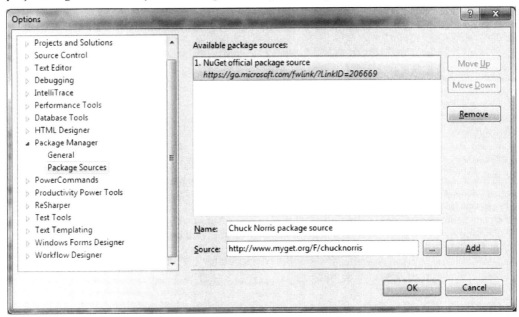

Figure 2-5. Register an additional package source.

There is more to tell about where a NuGet package originates. If you click the General item in this dialog, you'll see an entry named Package Cache. The NuGet Visual Studio Extension will always create a copy of installed packages on your local hard drive, so packages don't have to be downloaded every time they are installed. Therefore, NuGet checks its repositories when installing a package in the following sequence:

1. *Package cache*: When a package does not exist in the package cache, the actual package sources will be checked.

2. *Package sources*: Next, NuGet checks the list of defined package sources, in order of appearance. This means a package source higher up the list of package sources will be consulted prior to a repository lower on that list.

░ **Tip** The package cache can be a source of frustration. For example, the cached version of a specific package will be used if a NuGet package author forgets to update the version number of a package. If you encounter problems or see the wrong version of a package installed in your projects, the source of failure is probably either that a stale version of a package is located in the package cache or that the package is being downloaded from the wrong package source. The package cache can currently not be disabled.

Updating a Package to the Latest Version

What do you do when a dependency you are using in your project publishes a new version? Do you immediately update to the new version? Do you wait? Do you wait because you want to make sure it's stable first, or do you wait because upgrading a dependency again means downloading software, reading manuals, updating configuration, and so on?

If you find yourself waiting to save yourself the work of updating, NuGet offers a clean upgrade path for any NuGet package installed to your project that respects semantic versioning (read more on semantic versioning in Chapter 1 of this book).

Just like when installing a new NuGet package into your project, right-click your project in Visual Studio, and click Manage NuGet Packages. In the dialog that opens, select the Updates tab. As shown in Figure 2-6, this tab shows the list of all updates available for NuGet packages installed into your project.

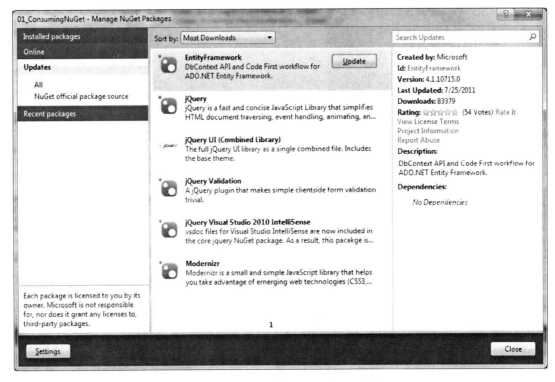

Figure 2-6. Updating a package using the Manage NuGet Packages dialog

Since we've installed the Elmah package earlier in this section and NuGet typically installs the latest version of a NuGet package into your project, the Updates tab will not be showing ELMAH. Nevertheless, you will see some updates available for this fresh, blank project. ASP.NET MVC projects are created with some NuGet package references automatically added, such as EntityFramework, jQuery, jQuery UI, jQuery Validation, and Modernizr. Updates can easily be installed by selecting the reference and clicking the Install button.

■ **Note** For this section of this book, we've chosen to work with an ASP.NET MVC project because it reflects the future vision of Microsoft on building software in Visual Studio and adding extra functionality to your projects.

The ASP.NET MVC framework features a predefined set of NuGet package dependencies enabling you to automatically update external dependencies like jQuery with just a few clicks. Microsoft envisions NuGet being used even more in future Visual Studio versions for adding additional menu items and tooling to Visual Studio through NuGet. For example, plans for ASP.NET MVC 4 are to have all tooling installed into Visual Studio only when someone installs the ASP.NET MVC 4 NuGet package.

Whenever a package update requires additional configuration settings, additional .NET framework dependencies, or dependencies on other NuGet packages, these will also be installed in one go, just like when you are installing a fresh NuGet package into your project.

Be aware that when you change files that have been installed through NuGet, such as configuration files or other artifacts added to your project, these changes will never be overwritten. This has been done to protect your work from being replaced by a clean, blank state of the NuGet package. This also means that if an update requires changes in these files, you will have to make those changes yourself.

Uninstalling a Package

When you're refactoring a project, chances are that some dependencies on external libraries may be removed along the way. We've already seen that NuGet offers a clean way of installing and updating NuGet packages; the good news is that uninstalling NuGet packages is equally frictionless.

Open the Manage NuGet Packages dialog, and click the "Installed packages" tab. This will list all packages installed in your project, including their dependencies. To uninstall a package, simply click the Uninstall button next to the package. If you try to uninstall a package that is still required by another NuGet package, the NuGet Visual Studio Extension will provide you with an error message like the one shown in Figure 2-7.

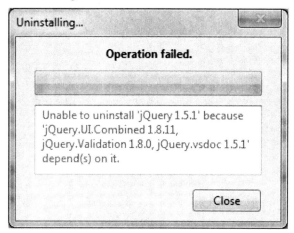

Figure 2-7. Uninstalling a NuGet package that is still required by other Nuget packages generates an error message.

Uninstalling a package goes through the inverse process of installing a NuGet package into your project. For example, when uninstalling Elmah from the project, the following process will be executed:

1. The Web.config file will be automatically modified, and all required settings for ELMAH will be removed. Note that if you have modified these settings, the modified version of the settings will be left sitting in your Web.config and may have to be removed manually.

2. The ELMAH reference will be removed from your project.

3. The required assemblies and other files that have been extracted from the original package into the solution root will be removed from the file system if no other projects in your solution are dependent on them.

As you can see from this process, uninstalling a package will almost never leave behind any artifacts from the previously installed package.

Using the Package Manager Console

You have now learned the basic operations of working with NuGet using the graphical user interface provided by the NuGet Visual Studio Extension. While working with a graphical user interface is easy, many developers using NuGet prefer working with the Package Manager Console that is also installed as part of the NuGet Visual Studio Extension.

The Package Manager Console is a new, interactive window you can dock in your Visual Studio IDE that allows you to interact with NuGet through commands or, in a broader sense, to automate Visual Studio. This window is special because its PowerShell enabled, and as such, you can run NuGet commands as well as PowerShell commands. In proper PowerShell terms, we speak about cmdlets (pronounced "commandlets"). The fact that the Package Manager Console enables you to use PowerShell commands inside Visual Studio is probably the main reason why many developers prefer working with the Package Manager Console instead of the NuGet Visual Studio Extension: it enables you to work with NuGet and script Visual Studio in a familiar yet powerful manner.

Before we cover a more specific scenario and work with an explicit version of a package, we would like to give you some quick tips on how to make optimal use of the Package Manager Console.

Don't worry if you are not familiar with PowerShell or its syntax. Most operations you will do while working with NuGet packages can be done in one command. You don't have to learn the various commands by heart either, as they are easily discoverable using the built-in auto-completion feature.

As you can see in Figure 2-8, pressing the *Tab* key in the Package Manager Console at any time opens an IntelliSense-like window showing the commands available. Once you are using a command, pressing the TAB key will display a list of options available for that command, as you can see in Figure 2-9.

Once you are more familiar with the Package Manager Console, you'll see that the naming pattern used for these commands is so intuitive that you'll be able to perform all these actions spontaneously.

⬛ **Tip** The Package Manager Console also provides you with auto-completion when using the Tab key.

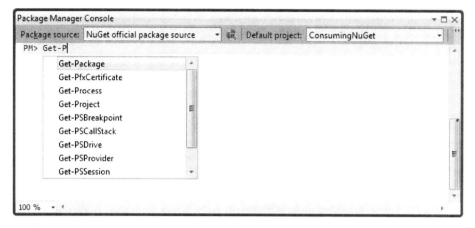

Figure 2-8. *List the available cmdlets in the Package Manager Console using the Tab key for auto-completion.*

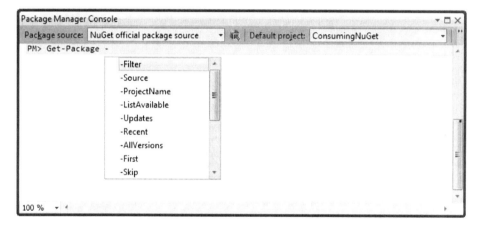

Figure 2-9. *List the available command switches for a given cmdlet using the Tab key for auto-completion.*

■ **Tip** You can always find out more information about the available commands and how to use them by executing the Get-Help cmdlet. To find out more about a specific command, you can type **Get-Help** followed by the name of the cmdlet, e.g., Get-Help Get-Package.

Finding a Specific Version of a Package

There are several ways to find a package without using the Manage Packages Dialog: you can query http://www.nuget.org for a package; you can use the command line, and you can use the Package

Manager Console. Lazy as we are, we don't want to leave our Visual Studio IDE, so we won't use the command line or the NuGet Gallery. We'll cover those later in this book.

To find a package using the Package Manager Console, you'll need to list the packages available matching your query. This is the purpose of the Get-Package cmdlet. By default, this cmdlet will show you the packages installed in your project. To query the package source, which is by default the NuGet Gallery, you'll have to add the -ListAvailable switch, as illustrated in Figure 2-10. Add a -Filter switch to the command to filter the results and search for a specific package.

By default, only the latest version of a package will be returned. If you want to list all versions of this package available on the package source, you can add the -AllVersions switch, as shown in Figure 2-11.

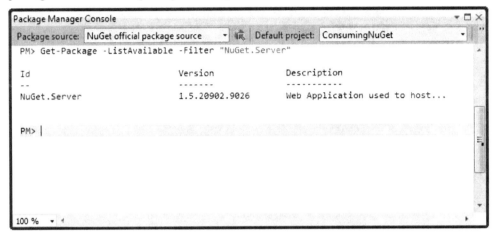

Figure 2-10. Getting a list of packages available on the NuGet Gallery matching a given name

```
Package Manager Console                                                    ▼ □ ×
Package source:  NuGet official package source   ▼ 🔍  Default project: ConsumingNuGet     ▼
PM> Get-Package -ListAvailable -Filter "NuGet.Server" -AllVersions

Id                      Version              Description
--                      -------              -----------
NuGet.Server            1.2.20331.10         Web Application used to host...
NuGet.Server            1.2.20331.11         Web Application used to host...
NuGet.Server            1.2.20331.12         Web Application used to host...
NuGet.Server            1.2.2210.35          Adds a nuget endpoint to an ...
NuGet.Server            1.3.20426.373        Web Application used to host...
NuGet.Server            1.4.20609.9012       Web Application used to host...
NuGet.Server            1.4.20623.9012       Web Application used to host...
NuGet.Server            1.5.20818.9011       Web Application used to host...
NuGet.Server            1.5.20902.9023       Web Application used to host...
NuGet.Server            1.5.20902.9026       Web Application used to host...


PM> |

100 %   ▼ ◄
```

Figure 2-11. Getting a list of all available versions of a package matching a given name

Installing a Specific Version of a Package

Once you have found the package you need, you'll have to install it. Again, you can install a package in several ways, but if you want to install a specific version of a package (i.e., not necessarily the latest version), you'll have to stick with the Package Manager Console or the command line. We have dedicated a specific section to the command line after this one, so you still won't have to leave the Visual Studio IDE for this operation.

To install a package into a project, you need to use the Install-Package cmdlet. To install a specific version of a package, you can simply add the -Version switch to the command as illustrated in Figure 2-12. Straightforward isn't it? The only thing left to do is to pick a project in the Default Project drop-down list to make sure the Package Manager Console targets the correct one.

You'll notice that the Package Manager Console will output the progress of the installation procedure. As Figure 2-12 illustrates, any required dependencies that need to be installed or updated will be taken care of. This is a first indication of how useful NuGet can be for managing your dependencies: no more time wasted reading through release notes for installation steps and prerequisites. NuGet will figure it out for you!

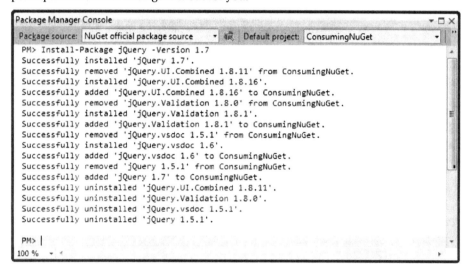

Figure 2-12. Installing a specific version of a package using the Package Manager Console

Configuring Package Sources

We've explained you how you could use the Default Project drop-down list to target a specific project using the Package Manager Console. However, we've ignored the other drop-down list, Package Source. By default, the NuGet official package source is listed and selected. But what if you want to use another package source, such as an internal NuGet server, a local repository, MyGet, or a combination of any of those? To do so, you'll have to configure the package sources in the Package Manager Settings dialog. You can find it under Tools ➤ Library Package Manager ➤ Package Manager Settings.

Figure 2-13 shows you two already-configured package sources, one online and one local. The NuGet official package source is by default there (though you can remove it if you would like to). To add another package source, simply provide a name and a path to the package source, and click the Add button. If you want to configure a local folder or network share to be used as package source, you can paste in the path to the directory or use the Browse button. To order the package sources in a specific way, you can select a package source from the list and play with the Move Up and Move Down buttons to position the item in the list. When searching for a package, NuGet will respect the order of the package sources as defined here, meaning the first one in the list will be queried first, then the second one, and so on.

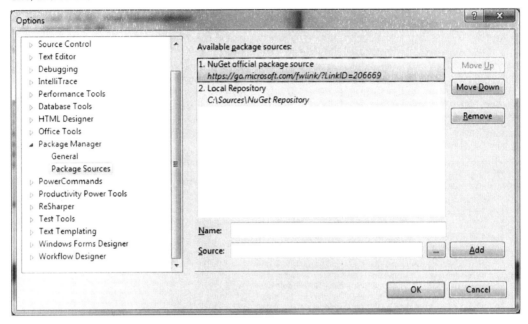

Figure 2-13. Managing NuGet package sources

It might sometimes seem a bit counterintuitive to have a default project selected when running a cmdlet in the Package Manager Console. We have summarized the use of a default project in Table 2-1. Don't worry if you don't know some of the commands yet; they will be explained shortly.

Table 2-1. Using the Default Project in the Package Manager Console

Cmdlet	Uses the Default Project?
Get-Package	No
Install-Package	Yes
Update-Package	No
Uninstall-Package	Yes

Updating a Package to a Newer Version

At some point in time, you'll want to update one of your packages to a newer version. The Manage Packages Dialog will, by default, show you the latest available version of any updates that are available. The same can be accomplished using the Package Manager Console, as shown in Figure 2-14.

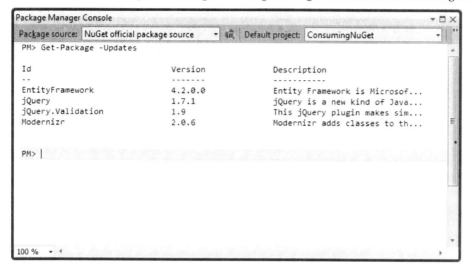

Figure 2-14. Listing the available updates for a project using the Package Manager Console

If you want to update to one of these package versions, you simply run Update-Package followed by the ID of the package you want to update. If you want to update to a specific version of a package, you can do so by adding the -Version switch to the Update-Package cmdlet in the Package Manager Console, as illustrated in Figure 2-15.

The default behavior is to update any dependencies that require an update as well, but you can override this behavior by adding the -IgnoreDependencies switch. Notice that we did not provide any target project for this command. This command targets all projects within the solution, unless you explicitly target a project using the -ProjectName switch. The default project drop-down list at the top of the dialog does not have any impact on the Update-Package cmdlet. Being aware of these defaults and caveats will allow you to make optimal use of the Package Manager Console.

■ **Tip** Did you know you can update all packages all at once for an entire solution with one simple command? That's exactly what the Update-Package statement will do by default if you don't add anything else to it!

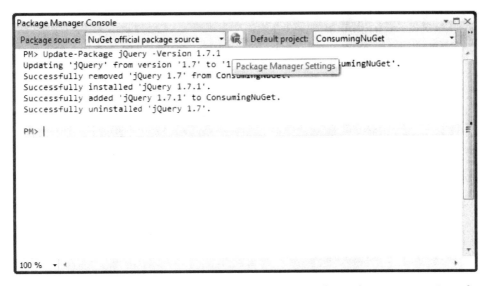

Figure 2-15. Updating a package to a specific version using the Package Manager Console

Of course, some human intervention may be required to complete the update process of a NuGet package. Think about updating the references to the new jQuery script files in your HTML or a changed API. These are things that the producer of a package cannot anticipate, so no automation will be available for you to perform these custom steps.

An option is available, though, that will allow you to perform *safe* updates. To do so, you use the -Safe switch in combination with the Update-Package cmdlet. Please note that using this switch means fully relying on the correct versioning of the package producer, as that is the only way NuGet, or any other package management system for that matter, is able to detect potential issues. In Chapter 3, we will elaborate a bit more on versioning, but know, for now, that major and minor version changes are considered unsafe. For example, if version 1.0.0 of a package is installed, and versions 1.0.1, 1.0.2 and 1.1 are available in the feed, version 1.0.2 will be considered the latest safe version available and will be the version that gets installed.

Uninstalling a Package

In the event you need or want to uninstall a package from a project, you can use the Uninstall-Package cmdlet. This command's default behavior is to rely on the default project selected in the drop-down list at the top of the Package Manager Console window. To uninstall a package from the default project, simply pass the package ID to the Uninstall-Package command, as shown in Figure 2-16. Notice that we did not specify any target project name.

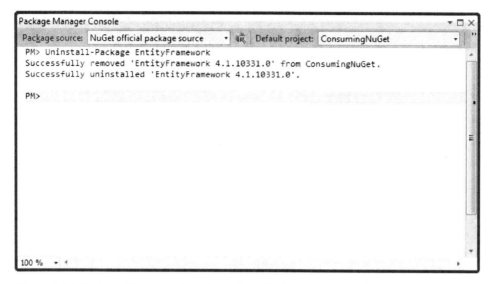

Figure 2-16. Uninstalling a package from the default project using the Package Manager Console

Uninstalling a package can impact the other packages you reference in your project. NuGet will assist you by detecting these dependencies and inform you about any conflicts that might occur. For instance, if another package depends on the package you want to remove, the command will fail. This is a safety precaution and default behavior for this command. However, you can *force* the removal of a package using the -Force switch, which will instruct NuGet to remove the package, even while another package depends on it.

Another useful switch to this command is the -RemoveDependencies option, which will make sure that not only the specified package will be uninstalled but also all *unused* dependencies of that package. Any dependency depended on by another package will be skipped.

Using the NuGet Command Line

So far, you didn't need to leave the Visual Studio IDE for any operation you wanted to perform using NuGet. Actually, you'll rarely have to do that at all! The NuGet Visual Studio Extension provides a great integrated experience, one which many developers will quickly be able to adopt. "Then why is there a need for a command line?" you ask. The reason is straightforward: NuGet is a package management tool for the .NET platform. It is open source and freely distributed, and anyone should be able to benefit from its usage.

In some scenarios, you will fall back onto the NuGet command line however. One of them is continuous integration. We'll dive deeper into this topic in Chapter 7. Typically, a build environment contains the bare minimum to be able to build your software. NuGet could be one of those tools that will enable your build servers to consume and produce NuGet packages as part of automated builds. To be able to do so, you'll need a simple tool that allows you to interact with NuGet repositories and packages, preferably a command line. That's exactly what the NuGet command line is for.

All of the operations supported by the NuGet cmdlets in the Package Manager Console are also available in the NuGet command line. If you are more familiar with the command style syntax of a DOS prompt, you might feel more comfortable using the command line tool than the Package Manager

Console, although the differences could be essentially reduced to a matter of syntax. Nevertheless, we will show you how you can get started quickly using the command line for various NuGet operations.

To work with the NuGet command line, you should open a command prompt in Windows. You can do this in many different ways:

- Press the Windows key + R, type **cmd**, and press Enter. Navigate to the folder where you stored nuget.exe, and interact with it. If you *manually* downloaded nuget.exe from the Internet, do not forget to unblock it by right-clicking the file, and selecting Properties ➤ Security ➤ Unblock.

- On Windows 7, you can browse to nuget.exe using Windows Explorer. Shift-right-click the folder containing nuget.exe, and select "Open command window here".

■ **Tip** The NuGet command line tool comes with a built-in help function: type **nuget help** to get a list of available commands, as illustrated in Figure 2-17. If you want help about a specific command, for example, the install command, you simply execute nuget help install. Another way to do so is by executing nuget install -help.

You might notice one very interesting description near on of the commands listed in there. Take a closer look at the update command: its description tells that you can use it to update the NuGet command line itself—how neat!

■ **Tip** To update the NuGet command line to the latest version available, execute nuget update -self from the command line.

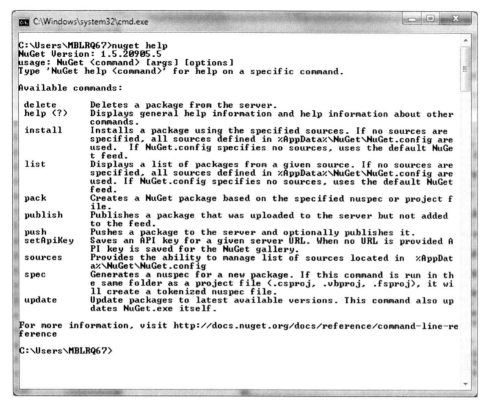

Figure 2-17. Getting help from the NuGet command line tool

Installing a Package

To install a package using the NuGet command line, you'll have to run the `install` command, which can be used in two different ways. You can specify a package source or multiple package sources to be used, or you can specify no package source, in which case the NuGet command line will fall back on using the `nuget.config` file in your local application data folder. If the configuration doesn't specify any package sources, it will fall back to a hard-coded NuGet feed URL.

■ **Note** The NuGet command line is unaware of any context in contrary to the NuGet Visual Studio extensions. As such, you'll have to specify a *target* for the commands used in the NuGet command line. Some commands will use the current directory where the `NuGet.exe` tool is located: in that case, you usually can specify an output directory for the command.

Installing the Latest Version

By default, the install command will always pick the latest version of a given package. Similar to the Install-Package cmdlet in the Package Manager Console, the install command has some switches that allow you to be more specific in your request.

To install the latest version of a specific package in the current directory, execute the command shown in Listing 2-2.

Listing 2-2. Installing the Latest Version of a Package Using the NuGet Command Line

```
nuget install {packageId}
```

Simply replace {packageId} with the ID of the package you want to install, for instance nuget install WebActivator. Notice that the command line will download the package and extract it in the current directory, unless another location is specified by the -OutputDirectory option. Because the NuGet command line has no context for the solution or projects you might want to target, it will limit the install operation to the extraction of the package in a specific place. Typically, you'll want to point the -outputdirectory switch to $(solutionDir)\packages, which is the default configuration for NuGet to store packages relative to a solution. However, you can deviate from it if you want to. Just as with ASP.NET MVC, the NuGet team has been using a convention-over-configuration approach, allowing you to quickly benefit from the automation the tool provides without the need of having to configure a lot.

One of those conventions is that each package will be installed in its own subdirectory of the $(solutionDir)\packages directory. The subdirectory name equals the package ID followed by its version number, for instance, $(solutionDir)\packages\WebActivator.1.4\ would be used for version 1.4 of the WebActivator NuGet package. By doing so, NuGet allows you to use multiple versions of a package within the same solution. The binaries will not be overwritten on installation, as each package's contents will be contained within its own directory. Again, you can deviate from this default convention and instruct the NuGet command line to use only the package ID for its subdirectory names, without the version number added to it. Use the -ExcludeVersion flag to do so. For the given example using WebActivator, this would result in $(solutionDir)\packages\WebActivator.

If you need to install multiple packages at once, you probably don't want to go through them all one by one. A useful thing to do here is to target the packages.config file of the solution, as shown in Listing 2-3.

Listing 2-3. Installing the Latest Versions of All Packages in a Solution Using the NuGet Command Line

```
nuget install C:\src\sln\packages.config
```

You need to specify the full absolute path to the packages.config file, as shown in Listing 2-3. If the path contains spaces, you'll have to enclose it in quotes, for example, nuget install "C:\src\sln dir\packages.config".

Installing a Specific Version

Another useful option you can set when using the install command is the -version switch, shown in Listing 2-4. This allows you to install a specific version of a package from the command line.

Listing 2-4. Installing a Specific Version of a Package Using the NuGet Command Line

```
nuget install {packageId} -version {packageVersion}
```

Of course, all other command options remain valid for this scenario as well.

Configuring Package Sources

Because the NuGet command line does not have any toolbars to select from a list of package sources, you need to be aware of some convention here as well. By default, the NuGet command line will use all package sources as defined in the `nuget.config` file. This configuration file allows you to define package sources to be used system-wide by the NuGet command line.

■ **Tip** You can find the `nuget.config` file in your local application data folder, `%AppData%\NuGet\NuGet.config`.

If you emptied the `packageSources` section of the `nuget.config` file, the NuGet command line will fall back to the original NuGet feed URL. Most commands allow you to specify a package source; for instance, you can point the `install` command to a specific package source by using the `-Source` option. You can also list all configured package sources using the NuGet command line `sources` command.

Authenticating Package Sources

Some package sources require you to provide some kind of authentication before you can access them. The official NuGet feed doesn't require authentication for any operation that is consuming packages. However, when you want to push packages to the feed, you'll have to authenticate. For this, NuGet uses the concept of API keys. When you register yourself on `http://www.nuget.org`, you'll get an API key, which you can use to publish packages on the official NuGet feed. You can change this key at any point in time on the web site, but keep in mind that you'll have to update the usage of it in your commands as well.

MyGet, which will be discussed in Chapter 9, makes use of API keys, in addition to basic authentication. Whenever you need to authenticate while running an operation against a feed that has basic authentication enabled, the NuGet command line will prompt you for your username and password. Currently, there is no way to store them in the `nuget.config` file. However, nothing prevents you of creating your own preconfigured PowerShell commandlets for use in the Package Manager Console, or just from within PowerShell itself.

The NuGet command line is able to store a combination of URLs and API keys. To save an API key for a given package source URL, you can use the `SetApiKey` command in the NuGet command line, as shown in Listing 2-5.

Listing 2-5. *Storing an API Key for a Given Package Source Using the NuGet Command Line*

```
nuget setapikey {apiKey} -source {packageSourceURL}
```

If you want to set your API key for the official NuGet feed URL, you don't have to specify a package source. You can simply run the command as illustrated in Listing 2-6.

Listing 2-6. *Setting an API Key for the Official NuGet Feed URL Using the NuGet Command Line.*

```
nuget setapikey {apiKey}
```

Updating a Package

The NuGet command line allows you to update packages to a newer version. You can do so by using the update command (see Listing 2-7).

Listing 2-7. Updating All Packages in a Solution to the Latest Versions Using the NuGet Command Line

```
nuget update packages.config
```

or

```
nuget update solution.sln
```

The update command has various options allowing multiple update scenarios. For example, you can specify a list of package sources to be used using the -source switch, and you can specify a list of package IDs to update using the -Id switch.

You can also instruct NuGet only to consider *safe* packages using the -Safe flag. When you set this flag, NuGet will look for the highest available version of the package within the same major and minor version of the already- installed package.

If for some reason you want to deviate from the default Packages folder as the package repository path for your solution, you can specify another one using the -RepositoryPath option.

■ **Tip** The update command in the NuGet command line has another option that allows you to update the NuGet command line itself. To update the NuGet command line, execute nuget update -self.

Uninstalling a Package

The NuGet command line does not support uninstalling a package from a solution or project.

Managing Packages in a Solution

So far, we've shown you how you can add, update, and remove packages at the project level. In a lot of software development projects, multiple projects share the same dependencies. For example, multiple projects in a solution can have a dependency on Microsoft's Entity Framework (which is also on NuGet with package ID EntityFramework).

Both the NuGet Visual Studio Extension and the Package Manager Console support managing and updating packages across project boundaries. This enables you to have a consistent set of package dependencies in your solution, all having the same version and assemblies. Imagine if you had to update references manually in multiple projects!

Using a large Visual Studio solution, this section will show you how to install, update, and uninstall packages in multiple projects at once. As with installing NuGet packages at the project level, you'll find that right-clicking your solution in Visual Studio followed by clicking Manage NuGet Packages will allow you to perform some magic.

Installing Packages in Multiple Projects

In this section, we will add log4net, a logging framework, to some projects that require logging, and we'll use both the NuGet Visual Studio Extension and the Package Manager Console to do so.

Once you select a set of projects and the NuGet package to install, NuGet will download the selected package from its repository and install it into the selected projects. The same package installation steps will happen for each selected project:

1. The latest version of the selected NuGet package is downloaded from the Internet.

2. The required assemblies and other files are added to a folder under the solution root.

3. Assemblies in a NuGet package are referenced in all selected projects.

4. Optionally, configuration files and source files are added or transformed. This depends on the actual package contents.

Using the NuGet Visual Studio Extension

Right-click your solution in Visual Studio, and click Manage NuGet Packages. Notice that the exact same Manage NuGet Packages dialog is displayed as when you wanted to add a package reference to a single project. Figure 2-18 shows you what this screen looks like.

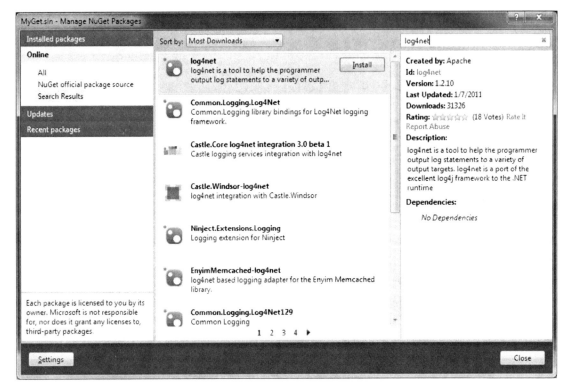

Figure 2-18. Searching for the log4net NuGet package

By now, you should be familiar enough with the Manage NuGet Packages dialog to search for the package log4net. If not, Figure 2-18 shows you what to look for. When you find the package, click the Install button next to it. Notice that, before the package is actually downloaded and installed, the NuGet Visual Studio Extension opens a dialog asking which projects to install the package to (see Figure 2-19). Select the projects to install log4net to, and click the OK button.

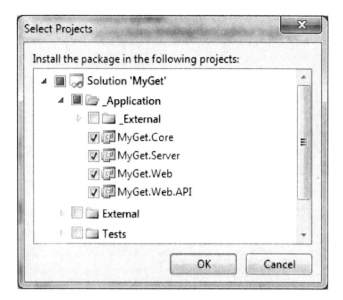

Figure 2-19. The Select Projects dialog when installing a NuGet package to multiple projects at once

Using the Package Manager Console

As with the NuGet Visual Studio Extension, the Package Manager Console is also able to install NuGet packages into multiple projects at once. Doing this requires you to sharpen your PowerShell scripting skills a little but enables you to do powerful things.

If we take the example of installing log4net into several projects at once, entering the following PowerShell command into the Package Manager Console should do the trick:

```
Get-Project MyGet.Core,MyGet.Server,MyGet.Web,MyGet.Web.Api | Install-Package log4net
```

If you prefer to install a package into every project (which is rare use case when solid architectural patterns are applied to a project!), issue the following command:

```
Get-Project -All | Install-Package log4net
```

As shown in Figure 2-20, the NuGet Package Manager Console runs through all project names specified and invokes the Install-Package command for each project.

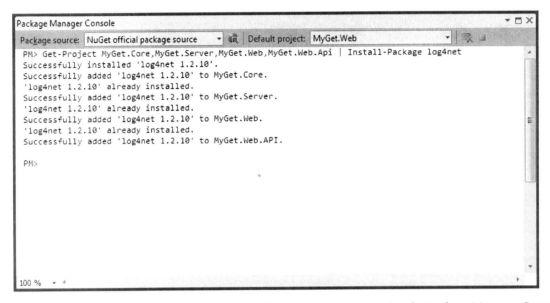

Figure 2-20. Installing a NuGet package into multiple projects at once using the Package Manager Console

Of course, you can also apply the commands learned earlier in this chapter to install a specific version of a NuGet package into multiple projects at once. The following example will install a specific version of log4net into multiple projects simultaneously:

```
Get-Project MyGet.Core,MyGet.Server,MyGet.Web,MyGet.Web.Api | Install-Package log4net↵
  -Version 1.2.10
```

░ **Note** The PowerShell command used actually consists of two commands. Get-Project retrieves a reference to one or more Visual Studio Projects specified as a parameter. Using the pipe symbol (|) tells PowerShell to loop the selection of projects and invoke the Install-Package command for every project. This very powerful concept enables you to chain multiple commands to do a lot of work using just a few keystrokes. This power is probably also the reason a lot of developers to prefer the Package Manager Console over the NuGet Visual Studio Extension.

Updating Packages in Multiple Projects

Updating packages in a solution to their latest versions can be done using both the NuGet Visual Studio Extension and the Package Manager Console. As with single-project updates, solution-wide updates also respect dependencies on other packages and may invoke additional downloads to ensure all package dependencies are met.

Using the NuGet Visual Studio Extension

Right-click your solution in Visual Studio, and click Manage NuGet Packages. After clicking the Updates pane, notice the exact same Manage NuGet Packages dialog that is displayed when you want to update a package reference in a single project. Instead of showing updates for a single project, this dialog displays a list of all packages used in a solution that have an updated version available. Figure 2-21 shows you what this screen looks like.

Figure 2-21. Updating NuGet Packages on a solution level

Once you select a package to update and click its Update button, the Select Projects dialog is presented (see Figure 2-22). It is important to note that the NuGet Visual Studio Extension will preselect all projects that currently have the old version of the selected NuGet package installed. If you wish to selectively update projects, this dialog allows you to cherry-pick the projects in which the selected NuGet package should be updated.

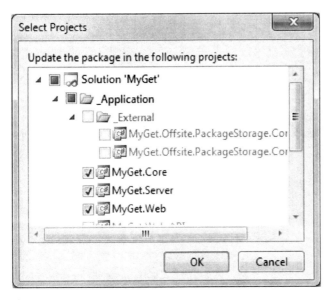

Figure 2-22. Selecting projects for which a package should be updated

Using the Package Manager Console

The Package Manager Console is also able to update NuGet packages in multiple projects simultaneously. Then too, it can also update all packages in all projects at once.

Using the same chained command used previously when installing a package into multiple projects at once, the following PowerShell command will update AutoMapper in multiple projects at once:

```
Get-Project MyGet.Core,MyGet.Server,MyGet.Web,MyGet.Web.Api | Update-Package AutoMapper
```

The NuGet Package Manager Console runs through all project names specified and invokes the Update-Package command for each project specified in the PowerShell command.

If you prefer to update all packages in all projects, you can issue the following command:

```
Get-Project -All | Update-Package
```

Of course, you can also apply the commands learned earlier in this chapter to update packages to a specific version instead of updating them to their latest available version.

Uninstalling Packages from Multiple Projects

In the event a package is obsolete, no longer supported by its author, or simply no longer needed in a project, it's perfectly possible to uninstall a package from several or all projects in a solution at once. Again, both the NuGet Visual Studio Extension and the Package Manager Console support this. As with single-project package uninstalls, solution-wide package uninstalls will also remove any dependencies that are no longer needed and will try to restore your projects to a state where no, or close to no, traces of the package are left behind.

Using the NuGet Visual Studio Extension

Right-click your solution in Visual Studio, and click Manage NuGet Packages. Here too, the exact same Manage NuGet Packages dialog is displayed as when uninstall a package from a single project (see Figure 2-23).

***Figure 2-23.** Uninstalling NuGet Packages on a solution level*

Once you select a package, the Manage button becomes visible. After clicking this button, you can select the projects from which a NuGet package should be removed.

Using the Package Manager Console

As you've seen previously, the Package Manager Console is able to manage NuGet packages in multiple projects at once. Using the following chained command, the log4net NuGet package will be removed from all projects in the open Visual Studio solution; Figure 2-24 shows you the output of this command:

```
Get-Project -All | Uninstall-Package log4net
```

Of course, you can also apply the commands learned earlier in this chapter to remove packages from only a few projects at once instead of removing them from all projects.

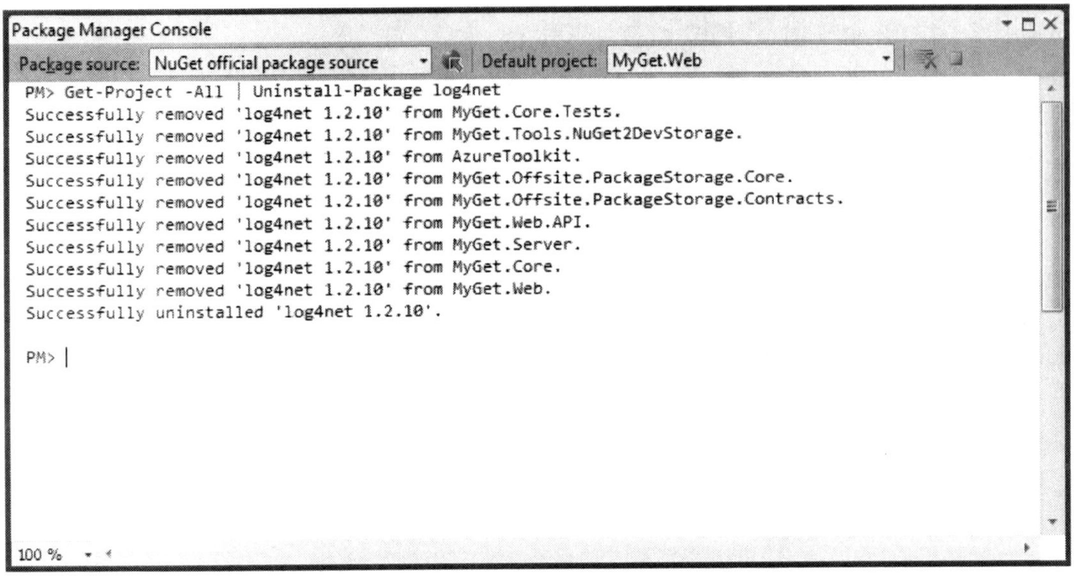

```
Package Manager Console                                                              ▼ □ ×
Package source: NuGet official package source  ▼  ⚙  Default project: MyGet.Web         ▼   ⚙ ⬚
PM> Get-Project -All | Uninstall-Package log4net
Successfully removed 'log4net 1.2.10' from MyGet.Core.Tests.
Successfully removed 'log4net 1.2.10' from MyGet.Tools.NuGet2DevStorage.
Successfully removed 'log4net 1.2.10' from AzureToolkit.
Successfully removed 'log4net 1.2.10' from MyGet.Offsite.PackageStorage.Core.
Successfully removed 'log4net 1.2.10' from MyGet.Offsite.PackageStorage.Contracts.
Successfully removed 'log4net 1.2.10' from MyGet.Web.API.
Successfully removed 'log4net 1.2.10' from MyGet.Server.
Successfully removed 'log4net 1.2.10' from MyGet.Core.
Successfully removed 'log4net 1.2.10' from MyGet.Web.
Successfully uninstalled 'log4net 1.2.10'.

PM> |


100 %  ▼ ◂                                                                             ▸
```

Figure 2-24. The result of uninstalling a NuGet package from all projects in a solution through the Package Manager Console

Visualizing Package Dependencies Using the Package Visualizer

In large projects, keeping track of all external package dependencies used in a solution can be difficult. Using the Package Visualizer that ships with the NuGet Visual Studio Extension, a graphical diagram of all projects in a solution and their package dependencies can be generated.

The Package Visualizer will be mainly used by technical project leads or architects to analyze which packages are referenced by which project and how a solution is structured.

■ **Note** The Package Visualizer depends on Directed Graph Markup Language (DGML) support in Visual Studio. Unfortunately, creating DGML diagrams is supported only in Visual Studio Ultimate. Viewing DGML diagrams is supported in Visual Studio Premium and higher.

Open a Visual Studio project that contains references to NuGet packages, and select Tools ➤ Library Package Manager ➤ Package Visualizer, as shown in Figure 2-25. After you click this menu option, a Packages.dgml file will be added to your solution.

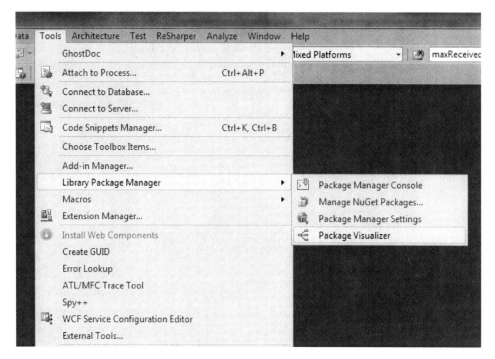

Figure 2-25. Finding the Package Visualizer menu option in Visual Studio

The Packages.dgml file automatically opens while generating the diagram, and Visual Studio opens a diagram that shows all projects in your solution on the left and maps all package dependencies (and their dependencies). Figure 2-26 shows an example of a project that depends on a large number of NuGet packages.

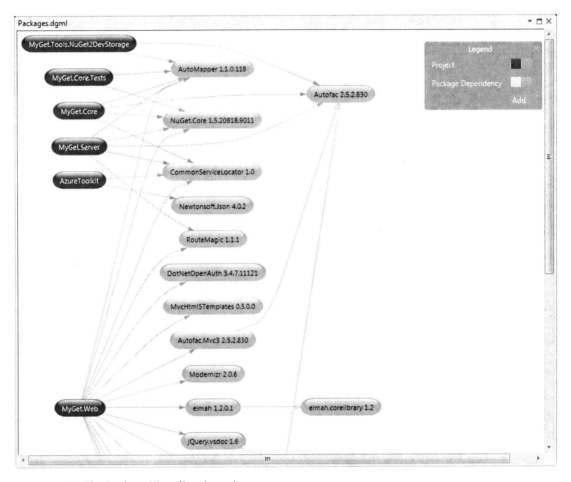

Figure 2-26. The Package Visualizer in action

The Visual Studio Directed Graph toolbar shows a series of options to display the diagram in a left-to-right, top-down, or clustered format. Dependency Matrix View is also one of the options; it's a useful matrix that enables you to analyze which NuGet packages are referenced by which projects, shown in Figure 2-27.

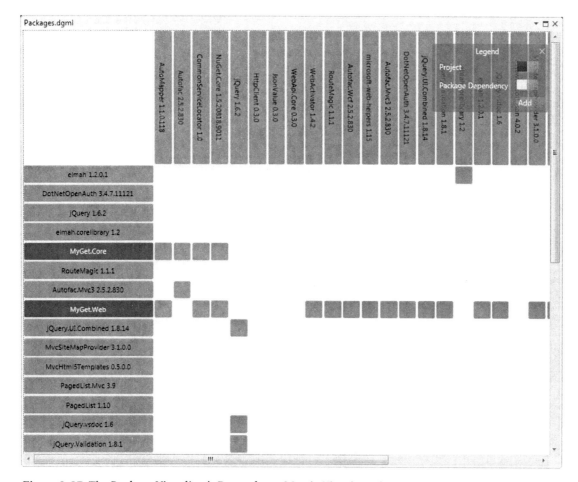

Figure 2-27. The Package Visualizer's Dependency Matrix View in action

Summary

In this chapter, we covered the basics of consuming NuGet packages. We showed you how you can consume NuGet packages in Visual Studio using different options, like the NuGet Visual Studio Extension and the Package Manager Console.

You learned how to perform basic operations using the NuGet command line and how package sources can be configured. We also explained what it means to perform a safe update of your packages and how you can install a specific version of a package.

We explored additional options for installing, updating, and uninstalling NuGet packages in your projects and how you can manage package references in multiple projects at once.

Finally, we demonstrated how you can analyze packages installed into a project and how they relate to your project and to each other, so you can quickly analyze interdependencies in a project.

CHAPTER 3

Creating Packages

In Part I of this book, we have introduced you to the concept of package management and how NuGet can help you when building software for the .NET Framework. We have also discussed how you can take immediate benefit from using NuGet by consuming packages in your projects. This chapter will change perspective and put you on the producer side of the package management flow.

Before we dive into how to create NuGet packages using the different tools available, we'll introduce you to some conventions and semantics that need to be respected by you, as a NuGet package producer, and as a result also by the packages you will be producing. Once you get yourself familiar with these basic conventions and how a well-designed NuGet package looks, we'll guide you through the process of actually creating those packages using both the NuGet command line and the Package Manager Console. We will take various approaches toward creating a package, starting from a convention-based working directory, and moving on to the NuGet manifest, Visual Studio projects, and finally compiled assemblies.

Finally, before publishing packages in the next chapter, we will show you how you can easily test your packages locally. Following the motto "eat your own dog food," you will consume your own packages and see if they work as expected.

Defining Package Conventions

NuGet uses a *convention over configuration* approach. These conventions are rather simple and easy to remember, but deserve special attention before we start creating our first packages. Many of these conventions will be described throughout this book as we dive deeper into more advanced topics, but you need to be aware of one set of conventions before creating your first NuGet package. These are defined in the NuGet package manifest, also known as a nuspec file.

The NuGet specification (nuspec) file is the one that is describing the contents and the metadata of your package. It is included in each NuGet package, or nupkg file, and it is also the file you'll need to create the actual package. In short, before you can create a package, you'll need to describe it.

Note Convention over configuration, also known as coding by convention, is a design paradigm that aims to decrease the number of decisions, and as such configurations, a developer needs to make. This results in increased simplicity without loss of flexibility.

Besides this package manifest, there's a second, more implicit package convention you need to take into account: the structure of a NuGet package. A NuGet package can contain different sorts of content, each having a different purpose. To indicate this, the NuGet package manager is not forcing you into providing an exhaustive settings file or any other type of configuration for that matter. Instead, you will be describing your content by the way you structure your packages using folders, which are named using a simple set of conventions.

Next to package content, metadata, and structure, a third convention should be taken into account: package versioning. Of all package conventions, this is probably the most important one because in package management, everything breaks or stands with proper package versioning. And this, again, is the responsibility of the package producer.

No need to worry; these conventions will feel very natural, and the NuGet Package Explorer will greatly assist you in setting up a correct NuGet package structure until you're ready to take matters into own hands and play with the underlying XML.

Creating a Package Manifest

All package meta-information is to be found in a package manifest, the nuspec file. This file provides information about the package's version, dependencies, contents, license, creators, and so on. The NuGet package manager uses this kind of information to automate dependency management in a smart way. Without exposing such critical information, automatically fetch any dependencies, or informing you about available updates, would be impossible.

The manifest contains *all* metadata of a given NuGet package. It informs NuGet where to find the contents, what it is supposed to do with them, and what extra steps should be triggered during a package's initialization, installation, or uninstall process. A NuGet package specification describes both its content and metadata in a predefined XML format. Because of the importance of these two aspects of package metadata, we'll handle both the pure metadata itself and the package contents as two separate topics.

The easiest way to create a nuspec manifest file is using the NuGet Package Explorer. When using the NuGet Package Explorer to create the nuspec file, you'll also notice that some defaults will be set, even when you didn't explicitly specify their values. The other way to create a nuspec file is simply by creating your own XML file that adheres to the nuspec.xsd format. The default nuspec file that the NuGet Package Explorer produces looks like Listing 3-1.

Listing 3-1. The Default NuGet Manifest File Created Using NuGet Package Explorer

```
<?xml version="1.0"?>
<package xmlns="http://schemas.microsoft.com/packaging/2010/07/nuspec.xsd">
  <metadata>
    <id>MyPackage</id>
    <version>1.0</version>
    <title />
    <authors>Xavier Decoster</authors>
    <owners />
    <requireLicenseAcceptance>false</requireLicenseAcceptance>
    <description>My package description.</description>
  </metadata>
  <files />
</package>
```

To create a nuspec manifest, you could also use the NuGet Command Line tool. Simply run the following command to create a default nuspec file in the current directory of the console prompt:

```
nuget spec
```

The default nuspec file created by the NuGet command line is slightly different from the one that NuGet Package Explorer will create, but both just serve as examples and need to be edited to suit your needs anyway. In short, it doesn't matter which one you start from. As you'll find out with NuGet in general, there's a lot of room for personal preferences, so use it the way you like most. In Listing 3-2, you'll find the default nuspec file created by the NuGet command line.

Listing 3-2. The Default NuGet Manifest File Created Using the NuGet Command Line

```xml
<?xml version="1.0"?>
<package xmlns="http://schemas.microsoft.com/packaging/2010/07/nuspec.xsd">
  <metadata>
    <id>MyPackageId</id>
    <version>1.0</version>
    <authors>Xavier Decoster</authors>
    <owners>Xavier Decoster</owners>
    <licenseUrl>http://LICENSE_URL_HERE_OR_DELETE_THIS_LINE</licenseUrl>
    <projectUrl>http://PROJECT_URL_HERE_OR_DELETE_THIS_LINE</projectUrl>
    <iconUrl>http://ICON_URL_HERE_OR_DELETE_THIS_LINE</iconUrl>
    <requireLicenseAcceptance>false</requireLicenseAcceptance>
    <description>Package description</description>
    <tags>Tag1 Tag2</tags>
    <dependencies>
      <dependency id="SampleDependency" version="1.0" />
    </dependencies>
  </metadata>
</package>
```

The preceding nuspec file could be considered a sample, guiding you in what metadata you preferably should provide with your packages. That's OK, especially for open source projects that will end up on the public NuGet.org gallery. For enterprise use, you'll probably end up with your own default XML template anyway, which might even be better in terms of consistency.

Exposing Package Metadata

Before we jump into the contents of a package and how they should be organized, we need to introduce you into the world of package metadata. The *metadata* element is a mandatory section within the package manifest. The metadata section itself also has a set of mandatory elements. These required elements must be specified before you can create a package based on the nuspec manifest. Here is the list of all required metadata fields:

- ID

- Version

- Description

- Authors

The first pieces of metadata your package exposes are the package ID and the package version. This pair of fields will uniquely identify your package on any NuGet feed. We'll come back to versioning later in this chapter with more in-depth guidance. Remember that these package IDs will be used in commands run by the Package Manager Console or the NuGet command line tool, so make sure you give your package a meaningful ID to ease discoverability of your package. In general, a package ID follows the same naming rules as namespaces in the .NET Framework: it cannot contain any spaces or characters that would be invalid in an URL. If you're not sure what to use, usually a dot-separated or dash-separated component or framework name will do, for instance SilverlightToolkit-Input or Glimpse.Mvc3.

The description field allows you to provide a few words that describe your package. This package description will be used by the Add Package dialog as well as by some commands in the Package Manager Console, for example, Get-Package. Next to the "description" field is an optional "title" field, which is meant to display your package in a more human-friendly way. If not specified, the package ID will be used as a title by default.

The last required metadata field is the "authors" field. This indicates the author or authors of the package code or contents. You can specify multiple authors using a comma-separated list. A related field is the "owners" field, which is optional. This field is intended to indicate the package owners, which are not necessarily the creators of its contents, although often the two are the same.

In addition to these required metadata elements and derived defaults, you can also specify more fine-grained information about your package, such as license information, release notes, package dependencies, required framework assembly references, tags, and more.

If your package concerns an open source project or requires some kind of license acceptance by the consumer, you can indicate as much using the licenseUrl and requireLicenseAcceptance elements. When the requireLicenseAcceptance element is set to true, the Add Package dialog will present you with a License Acceptance dialog during installation of the package, as illustrated in Figure 3-1. Notice the little link View License Terms, which will direct your browser to the license URL specified in the package.

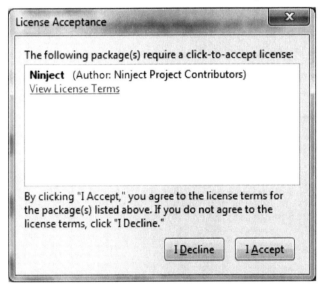

Figure 3-1. The License Acceptance dialog prompt appears during installation of a package that requires license acceptance.

Notice that the "title," "owners," and "requireLicenseAcceptance" fields in the metadata section have been provided with default values. Disregard the empty "files" section for now, as we will dive deeper into that element when we will discuss package contents. Use the "copyright" element to provide copyright information for the package.

In addition to these common metadata elements, some others provide metadata on how your package should be handled during the installation process. These additional elements give extra information about either the dependencies of your package or the dependencies of the target project of the installation process.

The first one of these elements is called `dependencies`. It's a straightforward list of package references, using their package ID and version (or version range). Combined, this list of packages indicates your package prerequisites. In other words, these packages must be installed prior to installing your own package and thus are to be considered as your package dependencies. An example of how to indicate your package dependencies in the manifest file is shown in Listing 3-3. Notice that there is no indication whatsoever about the origins or the location of these other packages. This will allow us to set up some more advanced scenarios later on in this book.

Listing 3-3. Listing Package Dependencies in the metadata Section of a nuspec Manifest

```
<?xml version="1.0"?>
<package xmlns="http://schemas.microsoft.com/packaging/2010/07/nuspec.xsd">
  <metadata>
    ...
    <dependencies>
      <dependency id="Some.Awesome.PackageId" version="1.0.0" />
      <dependency id="Some.Other.Awesome.PackageId" version="1.1.0" />
    </dependencies>
  </metadata>
  <files />
</package>
```

By default, all libraries contained in a package that match the targeted platform will be installed into the target project. If, however, you want to deviate from this behavior, you could use the `references` element in the `metadata` section. When using this element, you have to indicate explicitly which of the binaries in your package you want to be referenced in the target project after installation. Listing 3-4 shows you how you can specify explicit references in the `nuspec` metadata section. Files that are not explicitly indicated for treatment as references will be installed into the `Packages` folder of your solution but will not be added as references in the target project.

Listing 3-4. Listing Explicit References in the nuspec metadata Section

```
<?xml version="1.0"?>
<package xmlns="http://schemas.microsoft.com/packaging/2010/07/nuspec.xsd">
  <metadata>
    ...
    <references>
      <reference file="Some.Awesome.Library.dll" />
      <reference file="Some.Other.Awesome.Library.dll" />
    </references>
  </metadata>
  <files />
</package>
```

Notice that there is no need to specify any other information besides the full filename (including the extension). Be careful not to specify any path to the file, as this piece of metadata will be derived based on the target project and platform. NuGet will look into the correct place in your package to retrieve this file. More information on how this package can be structured is given in the next section in this chapter.

When it comes to dependencies and references, there's one thing we haven't mentioned yet. All .NET Framework projects depend on the .NET Framework itself. Occasionally, we might want to instruct NuGet to add some references to a .NET Framework assembly during package installation. When distributing a WCF contracts package, for instance, you'd probably want to add a reference to System.Runtime.Serialization. However, we don't want to distribute portions of the .NET Framework in all our NuGet packages every single time, over and over again—definitely not when these things are readily available in the Global Assembly Cache (GAC) on most development machines, as well as on build servers.

This is where the frameworkAssemblies element comes into play. This section instructs NuGet to add all listed framework assemblies as a reference into the target project during package installation, without the binaries being included inside the package. NuGet will pick them up directly from the GAC. Listing 3-5 shows you an example of how to define dependencies to framework assemblies.

Listing 3-5. Listing Required Framework Assembly References for the Target Project

```xml
<?xml version="1.0"?>
<package xmlns="http://schemas.microsoft.com/packaging/2010/07/nuspec.xsd">
  <metadata>
    ...
    <frameworkAssemblies>
      <frameworkAssembly assemblyName="System.Runtime.Serialization" />
      <frameworkAssembly assemblyName="System.Core" targetFramework="net40"/>
    </frameworkAssemblies>
  </metadata>
  <files />
</package>
```

Notice that this works for different versions and profiles of the .NET Framework and Silverlight. Each frameworkAssembly element within this section can have two attributes. The assemblyName attribute is required and obviously indicates the name of the framework assembly to be referenced. Optionally, you can add a targetFramework attribute, which dictates that this framework assembly will be referenced after installation only if the target project is targeting the specified target framework.

The example in Listing 3-4 used the value net40 to indicate that the .NET Framework 4.0 should be used as target framework in order to have the System.Core assembly referenced by the target project. If no targetFramework value is specified for the frameworkAssembly, the reference will always be added into the target project. The target framework of the project the package is installed into is irrelevant in this case.

After going through all these functional metadata fields, it's time to customize our package and add some branding and aesthetics. One thing you can do to make your package stand out is using a custom icon. This icon will then be used in the Add Library Package Reference dialog and on the NuGet Gallery web site. To specify a custom icon, you should use the iconUrl element in the package metadata, pointing to an image. This image should be a 32 × 32–pixel .png file with a transparent background.

A nicely chosen icon is not enough however. Your package needs to be easily discoverable as well. You can improve the discoverability of your package by tagging it with some relevant descriptive terms. That's why you should use the tags element in the metadata section with a space-delimited list of keywords you foresee will be meaningful. People looking for relevant functionality on NuGet will often search using such keywords. There are tons of hidden gems on the public feed because people don't know the name of those packages if yours are properly tagged people will find them with ease.

Especially when you expose open source packages on the public NuGet Gallery, you might consider adding a projectUrl to your package. This allows consumers to click trough to your online project page and provide feedback or report issues, or even better, submit patches!

Specifying the Package Contents

A NuGet package can be compared to an archive (e.g., a ZIP file). It's an archive of package contents and metadata. You can simply open any NuGet package in an archive tool or zip utility to inspect its contents. The first piece of content has already been discussed: it is the nuspec file. This manifest will always be part of any NuGet package. You don't need to do anything for that. When creating a NuGet package, you'll always start out of a nuspec file, and the file itself will be embedded in the root folder of the resulting package.

■ **Tip** You can simply open any NuGet package and inspect its contents using an archive tool or zip utility.

A NuGet package can have different kinds of content. They can be organized in libraries, content and tools:

- *Libraries*: Assembly files (.dll files) that will become references in target project

- *Content*: Content and source code to be injected into the target project

- *Tools*: PowerShell scripts and executables

We'll explain each of these in the next sections. If you want to create your own packages, you should do so starting from a convention-based working directory, containing the nuspec file, and any libraries, content, and tools you want to distribute with your package.

Libraries

The first thing you'll probably want to do when creating your first NuGet package is replace a library with a NuGet package that distributes this library. This is also the most common way of using NuGet: managing real software dependencies, or referenced assemblies, using NuGet packages as a means of distribution.

It is important to understand that a NuGet package can target multiple platforms or project types. As such, it is not necessary, or even desired, to create separate packages for all possible different framework versions (e.g., Silverlight 4, Silverlight 5, Windows Phone 7, and .NET Framework 4). You can achieve the same level of isolation with a single NuGet package because of the implicit package content conventions that you'll use to structure the package contents.

All binary files that should be installed into a consuming target project should be put inside the \lib folder of your package. The simplest package just puts all .dll files inside this platform-agnostic library folder. This indicates that you are not targeting any specific platform or framework version. However, if you package is built against version 4.0 of the .NET Framework, for instance, you might want to explicitly indicate that your package requires this. Actually, you should! To do so, you need to create a subfolder of \lib with a name that indicates the desired platform, version, and/or profile. Table 3-1 lists the supported conventions for these subfolders.

Table 3-1. Framework Profile and Version Specifications for NuGet Package Libraries

Framework name	Abbreviation	Supported profiles	Profile abbreviations
.NET Framework	net	Client Profile, Full Profile, Micro Framework, Compact Framework	client, full, mf, cf, compactframework
Silverlight	sl	Windows Phone	wp, windowsphone

NuGet is very flexible in how you use these conventions and allows you to be very specific in what you target. Targeting the .NET Framework version 4.0 would result in a folder called net40. Because the .NET Framework is the most commonly used target framework, you could even skip the framework name and only mention its version. This means that a folder named 40 would be treated as if it was called net40. NuGet will assume you meant the .NET Framework and use it as a default framework name. Libraries in your package that target the .NET Framework 4.0 should thus be put into the following folder structure: \lib\net40 or \lib\40.

In Table 3-2, you find a couple of examples on how you could combine the framework names, profiles, and versions based on the conventions from Table 3-1.

Table 3-2. Examples of Common Package Library Targets

Target	Libraries path	Supported alternative
.NET Framework 4.0	\lib\net40	\lib\40
.NET Framework 4.0 Client Profile	\lib\net40-client	
.NET Compact Framework 3.5	\lib\net35-cf	\lib\net35-compactframework
Silverlight 5.0	\lib\sl5	
Silverlight for Windows Phone 7.0	\lib\sl3-wp	\lib\sl3-windowsphone
Silverlight for Windows Phone 7.1 Mango	\lib\sl4-wp71	\lib\sl4-windowsphone71

Knowing all this, you can now very easily create a package that supports different frameworks and profiles. You can accomplish this by organizing your lib folder accordingly. Listing 3-6 shows an example of a package that targets the .NET Framework 4.0, Silverlight 4, and Windows Phone 7. Of course, the binaries inside those folders are built against those frameworks.

Listing 3-6. *A Multiplatform Package Library Structure*

```
\lib
    \net40
    \sl4
    \sl3-wp
```

NuGet will attempt to parse these folder names to `FrameworkName` object behind the scenes. Folder names are case insensitive, and the abbreviations listed in Table 3-1 are allowed. NuGet is open source, so you could dive into the codebase and find out how this got implemented. More information on the `FrameworkName` class can be found on MSDN, `http://msdn.microsoft.com/en-us/library/dd414023.aspx`.

Content

Besides binaries and libraries, you also can distribute content with your package, such as application configuration settings, images, JavaScript files, CSS, or even code files!

By convention, all these files should be put under the `\content` folder inside your package, or any subfolder of it. Notice that when you create a subfolder in `\content`, this folder will also be created inside the target project if it doesn't exist yet. All content under a subfolder will as such be placed in the same subfolder structure inside the consuming project. This means you'll have an exact content structure mapping between your package content folder and the consuming project. Think of the `\content` folder as the root folder of the consuming project, for example, `\content\scripts\filename.js` would map to `project\scripts\filename.js`.

So far, we have only mentioned copying files from within the package to the consuming project. You might be wondering now why we're not simply using a zip file or other type of archive containing these files. Let us introduce you to one of the neat features that NuGet supports out of the box: source code and configuration transformations. There might be occasions where you just want to inject some configuration settings or source code into the target project. If you haven't been using this functionality before, we invite you to explore this cool feature after reading this chapter, because it is straightforward and yet so powerful! It allows you to modify existing files in the target project to fit your requirements or create them if they don't exist already. This gives you tremendous flexibility to make it even easier for the consumer to install your package, without needing to touch a single file manually.

Configuration Transformations

If your package relies on certain configuration settings in the `app.config` or `web.config` file of the consuming project, you have a very good reason to modify this file during installation of your package. Before the existence of NuGet, people had to go through documentation, if any, and find out for themselves which settings or sections in the configuration files where required. Once they found that information, they still needed to discover how to use those settings and provide them with proper values for any specific requirements. As a package producer, you can now facilitate this yourself and provide the consuming project with whatever settings you require.

■ **Tip** You can check the Error Logging Modules and Handlers for ASP.NET (ELMAH) NuGet package for an example of adding an `httpModule` section to the `web.config` file.

The convention to be used to provide your package with an application or web configuration file transformation is the `.transform` suffix. In other words, if you add a file named app.config.transform or web.config.transform to the \content folder of your package, it will be picked up by NuGet during installation, and the transformation will be applied on the app.config or web.config file of the consuming project.

░ **Note** Between you and us, this works for *any* `*.config` file (except for configuration transforms such as `*.Debug.config` or `*.Release.config`). In fact, this works for *any file*, as long as its contents are XML and you use the `filename.ext.transform` convention. The only drawback is that you need to know the target filename upfront.

The `*.transform` file, or transformation file, is an XML file that includes only the sections to be merged into the target file that needs to be transformed. As a built-in safety precaution, only additions of sections, elements, or attributes are supported. These transformations are *merged* into the target file, as NuGet walks the XML tree of the target file and picks up any additions defined in the transformation file. This means you cannot use this feature to remove or modify existing elements or attributes of the target XML files. The reason is quite simple: there's no way NuGet would be able to restore the original state of the file after uninstalling the package. It would have to keep track of all changes it overwrites or removes and keep track of all changes to that file since installation, which is not the responsibility of a package management tool—not to mention to additional amount of complexity that doing so would bring to the tool.

EXAMPLE CONFIGURATION TRANSFORMATION

Let's say you have a Visual Studio web project containing a `web.config` file. This file already contains settings required by your application defined in the `AppSettings` section of the configuration file, as shown here:

```
<configuration>
  <appSettings>
    <add key="webpages:Version" value="1.0.0.0"/>
    <add key="ClientValidationEnabled" value="true"/>
    <add key="UnobtrusiveJavaScriptEnabled" value="true"/>
  </appSettings>
</configuration>
```

There is no way to change these settings using a transformation file during installation of a NuGet package. Only additions can be merged into the file.

Let's suppose we are installing a module that is configurable through a specifically named element defined in this `AppSettings` section. Our example module depends on one application setting named `OutputFormat`. The default value is *XML*. As a package producer shipping a product that depends on this application setting, it is desirable to inject this setting in the target project's configuration file, as well as setting the default value. In this scenario, our transformation file named `web.config.transform` would have the following contents:

```
<configuration>
  <appSettings>
    <add key="OutputFormat" value="XML"/>
  </appSettings>
</configuration>
```

The existing `web.config` file will be merged with this transformation file after installation of this package. Notice that NuGet has not changed any other elements, attributes, or values in the original configuration file. The resulting `web.config` file follows, with the changes highlighted in bold:

```
<configuration>
  <appSettings>
    <add key="webpages:Version" value="1.0.0.0"/>
    <add key="ClientValidationEnabled" value="true"/>
    <add key="UnobtrusiveJavaScriptEnabled" value="true"/>
    <add key="OutputFormat" value="XML"/>
  </appSettings>
</configuration>
```

Source Code Transformations

In addition to XML transformation, NuGet also supports source code manipulation, a feature that is very similar to Visual Studio project templating and very useful if you need to add some code to the target project. Typically, this additional code initializes or bootstraps the component or module you installed.

ASP.NET web applications are the most common type of projects that make good use of this feature because of the shared workflow these applications go through in Internet Information Services (IIS). The hookpoints in the life cycle of an ASP.NET web application are exposed in the `global.asax` code behind. This is the same for every ASP.NET web application. As such, during package installation, the producer could instruct NuGet to create this file, if it's not present, and inject custom startup or shutdown logic required by the package libraries. However, there's a better way for this specific scenario using WebActivator.

Tip A component that allows you to make very good use of this feature in ASP.NET web projects, is the WebActivator package, which you can find at http://nuget.org/List/Packages/WebActivator.

The WebActivator NuGet package allows other packages to easily inject startup and shutdown code into a web application. The convention is that you put your preprocessed code files in the `\content\App_Start` folder in your package. As such, all startup and shutdown logic of a web application can be installed into the project's `App_Start` folder. Don't forget to indicate that your package depends on the WebActivator package if you want to make use of this feature.

A code transformation file has a similar filename convention as for configuration transformation files: you need to append the .pp suffix to the filename of the code file you want to transform during installation, e.g. global.asax.cs.pp will be transformed into global.asax.cs.

Source code transformations can be specified by using Visual Studio project properties in the code files you inject in the consuming application. These properties are delimited with dollar signs ($). The most commonly used project properties are listed in Table 3-3. The most commonly used project property for source code transformations will definitely be $rootnamespace$, which gets replaced by the target project's default namespace.

■ **Tip** For more information and a full list of project properties, visit the following MDSN page at

http://msdn.microsoft.com/en-us/library/vslangproj.projectproperties_properties(VS.80).aspx.

EXAMPLE SOURCE CODE TRANSFORMATION

Let's say you want to a set of model classes injected in the target project's Models folder. It would make sense to have these models in the appropriate namespace. Since you don't know the target namespace up front, you could construct it using the target project's $rootnamespace$ property and append .Models yourself.

```
namespace $rootnamespace$.Models {
    public class Employee {
        public int Id { get; set; }
        public string Name { get; set; }
        public string ContractId { get; set; }
    }
}
```

If the target project's root namespace equals CompanyName.ProductName.Web, you'd get the following code file injected into the target project's Models folder:

```
namespace CompanyName.ProductName.Web.Models {
    public class Employee {
        public int Id { get; set; }
        public string Name { get; set; }
        public string ContractId { get; set; }
    }
}
```

Working with Tools

The \tools folder has a special purpose. It allows you to embed tools, binaries, scripts, and other useful files that should be used by the package manager but are not necessarily something that the consuming application should use, or even care about.

The most typical use case for having this folder is to hook into the package initialization, installation, and uninstallation processes. By convention, this can be achieved by providing PowerShell scripts with a filename indicating which hookpoint will execute the script. In other words, NuGet will automatically run these scripts based on their filename. NuGet supports three hookpoints:

- `Init.ps1`
- `Install.ps1`
- `Uninstall.ps1`

Nothing prevents you, of course, from importing other PowerShell modules or scripts or even calling executables embedded in your package. It is, however, important to know how and when these files are triggered by NuGet.

`Init.ps1` will be triggered the first time a package is installed into a *solution*. Installing the same package in a second project in the same solution will *not* trigger the `init.ps1` script. In addition, every time the solution opens, the `init.ps1` script, for each installed package that has one, will be executed. This is something you should be aware of when designing a package that needs additional initialization steps. This is also exactly what made it possible to extend the NuGet Package Manager Console (PMC) easily, as you will learn in Chapter 8.

`Install.ps1` runs when a package is installed into a *project*. This means that if you install the same package in multiple projects within the same solution, the `install.ps1` script will be executed during every single installation of that package. If you package also contains an `init.ps1` file, the `install.ps1` script will be executed after `init.ps1`. However, the `install.ps1` script will run only when there is actual content inside of the `\lib` or `\content` folder. The script is also ignored during updates (`Update-Package`).

■ **Note** A package that only contains a `\tools` folder does not have anything to install into a project. Such a package can, however, provide meaningful functionality and extend the NuGet Package Manager Console by adding custom cmdlets. If such package contains a `\tools\install.ps1` file, the script will be executed during installation in a solution.

`Uninstall.ps1` obviously runs every time the package is uninstalled from a project. If you need to perform any kind of cleanup or custom actions during the uninstall process of your package, this is the place where you could hook into the process.

At the top of each of these scripts files, you should add the following statement, which will give you access to some variables you might find useful:

```
param($installPath, $toolsPath, $package, $project)
```

These values are provided automatically by the NuGet Package Manager Console. Each of these parameters is described in Table 3-3.

Table 3-3. PowerShell Script Parameters Provided by the NuGet Package Manager Console.

Parameter	Description
`$installPath`	The path to the folder where the package is installed, by default, `$(solutionDir)\packages`.
`$toolsPath`	The path to the `\tools` directory in the folder where the package is installed, by default, `$(solutionDir)\packages\[packageId]-[version]\tools`.
`$package`	A reference to the package object.
`$project`	A reference to the target EnvDTE project object. This type is described on MSDN, `http://msdn.microsoft.com/en-us/library/51h9a6ew(v=VS.80).aspx`.
	The value will be null during `init.ps1` because there's not yet a reference to a particular project while you're initializing the package at the solution level.

Package Versioning

One of the first things you expose to any consumer of your package is the version number. This happens even before any other part of the package metadata is consumed. The version number is also the first piece of the contract between package producer and consumer. If done properly, a version number provides a lot of meaningful information. Versioning is critical in terms of dependency management, and as such also for package management.

Semantic Versioning

The most simple and pragmatic versioning pattern one could use is what is called semantic versioning. Semantic versioning consists out of a set of simple rules and requirements that dictate how a software assembly or package should be versioned and how you should increment this version for future releases.

■ **Tip** Visit `www.semver.org` for more detailed information and guidance on semantic versioning.

An assembly or package version consists out of maximum four numbers, out of which the first three are the most meaningful. You should read version information as: `major.minor.patch`. An explanation of the meaning of these different version numbers is given in Table 3-4. Semantic versioning (SemVer for short), allows you to use a fourth version part, the build number, to uniquely identify a given build. SemVer does not enforce the usage of the fourth number, but there might be use cases in favor of it, which is totally fine and not a violation of the SemVer rules.

Although NuGet supports SemVer quite well, the optional build number defined in the specification, came in too late in the NuGet v1.6 release process. Therefore, NuGet does not support the build number notation as defined in rule 11 of SemVer 2.0.0-rc.1. The rule says that a build number *may* be denoted by appending a plus sign (+) and a series of dot separated identifiers immediately following the patch version or pre-release version, e.g. v1.0.0-rc+2011.12.28.

Because NuGet does not support the build number notation using the plus sign, you'll have to come up with a different versioning scheme for your continuous integration and nightly builds. These are typical scenarios requiring a more fine-grained identification of the produced package.

Table 3-4. Semantic Versioning Explained

Version number	Usage
Major	Indicates a breaking change in the public API
Minor	Indicates a fully backward-compatible release containing public API additions, such as new features or functionality
Patch	Indicates a fully backward-compatible release containing hotfixes or internal changes that do not affect the public API at all

SemVer might sound very common sense and probably you are doing something close to this already. The problem is that close is not good enough! Let me be clear: NuGet as a tool will not enforce using this versioning pattern in any way, although it is optimized for it. The message here is that you, as a package producer, should be very clear in terms of the contract you'll expose to a potential consumer. If you tell the consumer you didn't create any breaking changes in your newest version, you'd better make sure you didn't. If you repeatedly break this promise, you'll end up with unhappy consumers of your packages, who then might choose to no longer use any of your packages at all! If you want to be considered a trustworthy package producer, you might consider sticking to semantic versioning. This is especially true for component vendors who want to use NuGet as a distribution channel and expose their component packages on a NuGet feed.

Prerelease Packages

Starting from version 1.6, NuGet also supports the concept of prerelease packages. Prerelease packages are indicated by a special tag trailing the patch number, separated with a dash sign (-), for example, v1.0.0-alpha. This format still is supported by SemVer, so nothing is preventing you from fully use semantic versioning as your standard.

Except for the build number: if you want to uniquely identify a given build, in a CI scenario for instance, you should, according to the SemVer 2.0.0-rc.1 specification, use a plus (+) character to indicate a build number. The easiest way is to increment the build number on each successful compilation, for example, v0.9.1-alpha+112 becomes v0.9.1-alpha+113.

NuGet does not support this build notation, so you'll have to come up with something different. The first thing that comes to mind to work around this issue, would be to add some dot separated information to the prerelease patch number, for example, v0.9.1-alpha.112. This, again, is fine with the SemVer specifications, but NuGet does not support this either. You'll need another workaround, while making sure that a new build (that incremented the version) is still considered a newer version by NuGet. Sadly enough, there is no *nice* solution at hand that doesn't mess up the package version ordering.

The order of precedence of prerelease packages is determined by lexicographic ASCII order. If this doesn't mean anything to you, no worries; we'll explain this by example. Consider the following prerelease packages, ordered by precedence (lowest to highest version):

- 0.9.1-alpha+1 (not supported by NuGet)

- 0.9.1-alpha+2 (not supported by NuGet)

- 0.9.1-alpha+10 (not supported by NuGet)

- 0.9.1-alpha

- 0.9.1-alpha2

- 0.9.1-beta

- 0.9.1-rc

- 0.9.1

- 0.10.0

- 1.0.0

Version Ranges

While discussing how to expose package metadata, and more specific package dependencies, we briefly mentioned you could denote package dependencies with a package ID and a package version. Although this is correct, there is more to know about this feature, which is very important when dealing with dependencies. After all, we want to keep you out of dependency hell, remember?

It is important to understand that, by simply specifying *a* version for the dependency, you are actually saying that *any* version is good, as long as it is equal to or higher than the specified version. A single version number is in fact a short notation for a version range with an inclusive lower boundary, and no upper boundary. Mathematically speaking, version 0.9.1 corresponds to $\geq 0.9.1$.

However, you might one day have a need to exclude some versions, or limit the range of allowed versions, or even explicitly set a version number while disallowing any other versions. If all package producers were properly using semantic versioning, version ranges wouldn't even be needed. The reality is different though, and there's a whole lot of legacy open source packages out there predating the SemVer guidelines. Some are even ignoring any other standards used in other, even non-.NET, communities.

NuGet supports interval notation for specifying version ranges, inspired by but not identical to the Maven Range Specification. Table 3-5 summarizes the various supported version range notations, where *x* stands for the packages that match the specified dependency.

Table 3-5. *NuGet version range notation.*

Version Range	Interpretation
`0.9.1`	$0.9.1 \leq x$
`(,0.9.1]`	$x \leq 0.9.1$
`(,0.9.1)`	$x < 0.9.1$
`[0.9.1]`	$x == 0.9.1$
`(0.9.1)`	*Invalid*
`(0.9.1,)`	$0.9.1 < x$
`(0.9.1, 1.0)`	$0.9.1 < x < 1.0$
`[0.9.1, 1.0]`	$0.9.1 \leq x \leq 1.0$
Empty	Latest version

Constraining Package Dependencies

On the other side of the feed, as a package consumer, you can also lock the versions of the dependencies you installed through the use of NuGet packages. When a NuGet packages gets installed into your project, an entry for that package ID and version is added into the project's `packages.config` file.

You might be wondering why one would want to look down a NuGet package dependency. When calling the `Update-Package` command (or through the dialog), you update your dependency for that package to the latest version. Because NuGet also supports updating all packages in a solution at once, this could become a very intrusive operation. Especially if you know upfront that your application is compatible with a newer version 2.x of a package, but not with version 3.x. This is a good reason to lock down those dependencies with a proper version range before performing any updates. Even when you're not planning any updates, it is a good piece of metadata indicating that your application has known incompatibilities with newer versions of certain dependencies.

Locking down package versions in the `packages.config` file must be done manually, as shown in Listing 3-7:

Listing 3-7. Constraining package dependencies in the packages.config file

```
<?xml version="1.0" encoding="utf-8"?>
<packages>
    <package id="SomePackage" version="2.1.0" allowedVersions="[2,3)" />
</packages>
```

Creating Packages Using the NuGet Command Line

Now that you know what the conventions for creating NuGet packages are and what a good package structure looks like, let's create one using the command line. This section will guide you through creating NuGet packages by using the NuGet command line; it starts off with the creation of a simple, Hello World–type package for NuGet.

After creating a simple package demonstrating the concept of creating a package from the command line, we'll guide you through some alternative methods of creating NuGet packages. Why craft everything yourself when nuget.exe provides a whole bunch of automation for you? We'll show you how NuGet creates the package manifest based on an assembly or Visual Studio project file and how you even can skip the process of creating a package manifest.

Creating a Package from Scratch

Creating a NuGet package from the command line is a very easy process which consists of three steps:

1. Create and modify a package manifest (a .nuspec file) containing all metadata for your NuGet package.

2. Create the package folder structure containing source code, assemblies, PowerShell scripts, and so on.

3. Package a combination of the package manifest and the folder structure.

Creating a fresh package manifest is probably the easiest task available in NuGet. Open a command prompt and navigate to an empty folder. Make sure the nuget.exe file can be found, and run the following command:

```
nuget spec HelloWorld
```

After you press the enter key, NuGet will greet you with a success message in the form of "Created 'HelloWorld.nuspec' successfully." When you check the folder in which you just ran this command, you'll find a file that looks, when opened in an XML editor, roughly the same as the code in Listing 3-8.

Listing 3-8. A Newly Created NuGet Package Manifest Using the NuGet Command Line

```xml
<?xml version="1.0"?>
<package>
  <metadata>
    <id>HelloWorld</id>
    <version>1.0</version>
    <authors>MBLRQ67</authors>
    <owners>MBLRQ67</owners>
    <licenseUrl>http://LICENSE_URL_HERE_OR_DELETE_THIS_LINE</licenseUrl>
    <projectUrl>http://PROJECT_URL_HERE_OR_DELETE_THIS_LINE</projectUrl>
    <iconUrl>http://ICON_URL_HERE_OR_DELETE_THIS_LINE</iconUrl>
    <requireLicenseAcceptance>false</requireLicenseAcceptance>
    <description>Package description</description>
    <copyright>Copyright 2011</copyright>
    <tags>Tag1 Tag2</tags>
    <dependencies>
      <dependency id="SampleDependency" version="1.0" />
```

```
    </dependencies>
  </metadata>
</package>
```

Note that NuGet adds some default values in the package manifest: The `id` element contains the name issued on the command line. The `version` by default is version 1.0. Both the `authors` and `owners` elements have been populated with your Windows username, if you have one. All elements in this file, like dependencies on other packages and dependencies on framework assemblies, are explained earlier in this chapter.

Modify the package manifest to something useful, like the package manifest in Listing 3-9.

Listing 3-9. The NuGet Package Manifest for the HelloWorld Package We Are Creating

```xml
<?xml version="1.0"?>
<package >
  <metadata>
    <id>HelloWorld</id>
    <version>1.0</version>
    <authors>Maarten Balliauw</authors>
    <owners>Maarten Balliauw</owners>
    <requireLicenseAcceptance>false</requireLicenseAcceptance>
    <description>This package provides a HelloWorld class, written in C#.</description>
    <copyright>Copyright Maarten Balliauw 2011</copyright>
    <tags>ProNuGet Apress HelloWorld Chapter Sample</tags>
  </metadata>
</package>
```

As discussed earlier, we have to create and/or add some package contents. To do this, create the folders required for your package:

- The `lib` folder can contain assemblies that should be added as a reference to a project when consuming the package.

- The `content` folder can contain configuration files, code, text files, images, any file you want to add as content in the project consuming the package.

- The `tools` folder can contain PowerShell scripts that are run on install or uninstall of the NuGet package.

Create a `lib` folder under the same folder as the .nuspec file just created.

For the `HelloWorld` package, find the sample Visual Studio 2010 solution `HelloWorld.sln` that comes with this book. It consists of a simple class, `HelloWorld`, which contains a method `Greet` that takes a string and returns a Hello World message. After compiling the project, copy the `HelloWorld.dll` into the `lib` folder created earlier.

The final step in the process is creating the NuGet package. To do so, copy the package manifest and package contents into a `.nupkg` file, in essence just a ZIP archive. Run the following command from the command line:

```
nuget pack HelloWorld.nuspec
```

`NuGet.exe` should greet you with a message similar to "Successfully created package 'C:\Temp\HelloWorld.1.0.nupkg'", as shown in Figure 3-2. Note that when the package folder structure is incorrect or package manifest information is missing, NuGet will provide a detailed list of errors found so you can easily fix those.

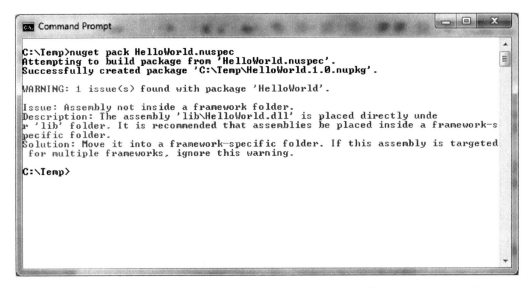

Figure 3-2. The NuGet.exe output after successfully packaging the HelloWorld NuGet package

The HelloWorld.1.0.nupkg file created by the NuGet command line can now be consumed using the NuGet Visual Studio extension, the NuGet Package Manager Console, or the NuGet command line. This chapter contains a "Testing Packages" section that covers how you can test your package in all of these tools. For now, just to verify the newly created package works as expected, run the following command:

```
nuget install HelloWorld -Source "c:\temp" -OutputDirectory "test"
```

When running this command, the NuGet command line will download the latest version of the HelloWorld package from the folder specified in the –Source switch, "c:\temp". It will extract the package to a subfolder called "test".

Congratulations! You've just created and consumed your first NuGet package.

Creating a Package Manifest from an Assembly

In the previous example, we used the nuget spec command, which resulted in a blank package manifest that you could modify and enrich. The NuGet command line offers some extra features with the nuget spec command. One of these features is generating a package manifest from an assembly.

Using the assembly created earlier, HelloWorld.dll, NuGet can look into the assembly details to generate the package manifest. This metadata about an assembly can be revealed by right-clicking the assembly and selecting Properties followed by Details. Windows will give you information similar to what's shown in Figure 3-3.

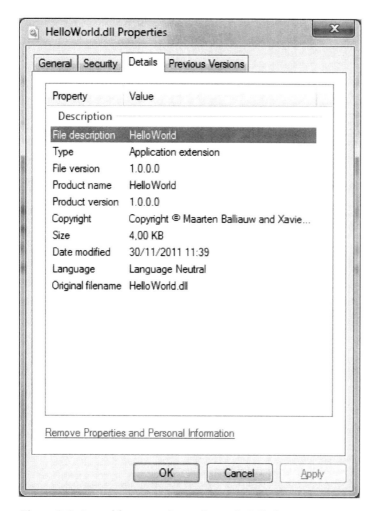

Figure 3-3. Assembly properties as shown by Windows

From the command line, issue the following command to create a package manifest based on this information:

```
nuget spec -a HelloWorld.dll
```

This command should complete very fast and create a file called `HelloWorld.nuspec`. The contents of this file are based on the assembly information retrieved from the assembly specified using the `-a` switch. Listing 3-10 shows you the contents of this file. Note the `id`, `version`, `authors`, and `owners` elements contain the information previously consulted through the Windows file property dialog.

Listing 3-10. The Package Manifest File Generated Using Assembly Information

```xml
<?xml version="1.0"?>
<package >
  <metadata>
    <id>HelloWorld</id>
    <version>1.0.0.0</version>
    <authors>Maarten Balliauw and Xavier Decoster</authors>
    <owners>Maarten Balliauw and Xavier Decoster</owners>
    <requireLicenseAcceptance>false</requireLicenseAcceptance>
    <description>Package description</description>
    <copyright>Copyright 2011</copyright>
    <tags>Tag1 Tag2</tags>
    <dependencies>
      <dependency id="SampleDependency" version="1.0" />
    </dependencies>
  </metadata>
</package>
```

Of course, this package manifest still requires some additional fine-tuning. For example, the copyright, tags, and dependencies elements still contain just sample data. After modifying the package manifest, a NuGet package can be created using the same technique as described previously. Run the following command to package the manifest and assemblies:

```
nuget pack HelloWorld.nuspec
```

The end result will be a NuGet package named HelloWorld.1.0.0.0.nupkg.

Creating a Package Manifest from a Visual Studio Project

In the previous example, we generated a package manifest from the metadata that is stored in an assembly, a great way to create package manifests from already compiled or even third-party assemblies. When you are in control of your own projects, there's an easier way to create a package manifest: create it using the information available in your .csproj or .vbproj.

Creating a package manifest from a Visual Studio project is as easy as running the following command in the same folder your project file resides. It will result in a HelloWorld.nuspec file:

```
nuget spec
```

Using the project file as the source for package manifest generation offers several advantages. First of all, you are not required to build the project first before generating the package metadata. The second advantage is that NuGet will add some so-called "replacement tokens" in your .nuspec file, as you can see in Listing 3-11.

Listing 3-11. The Package Manifest Generated Based on a Visual Studio Project File

```xml
<?xml version="1.0"?>
<package >
  <metadata>
    <id>$id$</id>
    <version>$version$</version>
    <title>$title$</title>
```

```
    <authors>$author$</authors>
    <owners>$author$</owners>
    <licenseUrl>http://LICENSE_URL_HERE_OR_DELETE_THIS_LINE</licenseUrl>
    <projectUrl>http://PROJECT_URL_HERE_OR_DELETE_THIS_LINE</projectUrl>
    <iconUrl>http://ICON_URL_HERE_OR_DELETE_THIS_LINE</iconUrl>
    <requireLicenseAcceptance>false</requireLicenseAcceptance>
    <description>$description$</description>
    <copyright>Copyright 2011</copyright>
    <tags>Tag1 Tag2</tags>
  </metadata>
</package>
```

Replacement tokens in the package manifest will be populated with project specific values retrieved from the `AssemblyInfo.cs` file at the moment the NuGet package is being created. Table 3-6 lists the replacement tokens that can be used in the package manifest as well as their sources.

If you're using replacement tokens, creating NuGet packages suddenly becomes more interesting: you can create a package manifest that contains all required metadata and replace some parts of the manifest with data coming from the Visual Studio project itself. This results in less maintenance of package manifests.

Table 3-6. *An Overview of the Available Replacement Tokens*

Token	Description
id	The assembly name of the project's output
$version$	The assembly version as specified in the assembly's `AssemblyVersionAttribute`
$author$	The company as specified in `AssemblyCompanyAttribute`
$description$	The description as specified in `AssemblyDescriptionAttribute`

Once the package manifest has been modified with the correct copyright notice, tags, logo URL, and such, it can be packaged. A NuGet package can be created using the same technique as described previously. Run the following command to package the project and the package manifest at once:

```
nuget pack HelloWorld.nuspec
```

The end result will be a NuGet package named `HelloWorld.1.0.0.0.nupkg`.

Packaging a Visual Studio Project

In the previous example, we generated a package manifest from a Visual Studio project and you saw that less maintenance of the package manifest is involved. If NuGet can create a manifest of a project, shouldn't it be possible to package a project without the intermediate step of creating a package manifest? The answer is yes.

Open a command prompt in the same folder where your `.csproj` or `.vbproj` file lives, and run the following command to package the project:

```
nuget pack HelloWorld.csproj
```

The end result will be a NuGet package named HelloWorld.1.0.0.0.nupkg. Unfortunately, the package metadata for this project is incomplete and only consists of the package identifier, its version, the authors, and a description—there are no traces of a copyright message, a logo URL, or a list of tags that the consumer of this package can use to search.

The reason for the absence of additional package metadata simply is the absence of that data: NuGet has no means of generating this information if you don't provide it. Therefore, it's always best to create a package manifest, ideally using replacement parameters to get the best of both worlds.

■ **Note** The NuGet pack command provides some additional command line switches. Noteworthy are the -Build switch, which will trigger a fresh build of the project when packaging; –Symbols, which creates an additional package containing all .pdb files for your project; and -Version, which overrides the version information listed in the package manifest. More NuGet pack switches are described in the NuGet documentation wiki at http://docs.nuget.org/docs/reference/command-line-reference#Pack_Command.

Generating the Dependencies Element

So far, all XML generated in the package manifest consisted of the package metadata such as the package identifier, version, and description. What is not generated is the dependencies element, which describes if the package requires other NuGet packages to be installed prior to installing it.

If you're creating packages from scratch, we're afraid we can't help you. You'll have to craft your own list of package dependencies and include that list in the package manifest. If you're creating packages using replacement tokens or when creating packages from a Visual Studio project file, things are different.

Many times, your project will have dependencies on other NuGet packages. These dependencies can be referenced using the Visual Studio NuGet Extension or the package manager console. Doing this generates a packages.config file contained in the Visual Studio project. The packages.config file contains a list of all dependencies for a project, including their package identifiers and versions (or a range of supported versions). Listing 3-12 shows the contents of the packages.config file for our HelloWorld project.

Listing 3-12. The packages.config File Containing a package Dependency on log4net Version 1.2.10

```
<?xml version="1.0" encoding="utf-8"?>
<packages>
  <package id="log4net" version="1.2.10" />
</packages>
```

Try using the technique described in "Creating a Package Manifest from a Visual Studio Project": generate a package manifest using the nuget spec command; update the package manifest; and package the project using either the nuget pack HelloWorld.nuspec command or the nuget pack HelloWorld.csproj command. The NuGet console will run this command and provide the output shown in Figure 3-4.

Figure 3-4. *NuGet.exe output when creating a package which consumes the packages.config for metadata*

Note the message "Found packages.config. Using packages listed as dependencies." The NuGet command line looks for a packages.config file present in the project and if it finds one, it will use the data as additional metadata and includes it in the package manifest. In the case of our HelloWorld project, NuGet lists *log4net* version *1.2.10* as a dependency and will make sure the consumer of our package is also required to install *log4net* in their project.

Creating Packages using NuGet Package Explorer

Creating NuGet packages is something currently best done by using a package manifest or by packaging your Visual Studio project. The reason for this is that artifacts are created in a reproducible way: the manifest is kept around; the project is kept around, and the same version of all code will always result in the same NuGet package. It can even be automated by creating a batch script that runs several NuGet.exe commands at once.

In many situations, for example when exploring what other people do in their NuGet packages or when creating a test package, a dedicated user interface to work with NuGet packages is preferable. For this purpose, Luan Nguyen (@dotnetjunky on Twitter) has created NuGet Package Explorer, a great tool to have in your developer tool belt. It allows you to open, edit, inspect, and validate NuGet packages from an easy-to-use graphical user interface.

As described in Chapter 1, NuGet Package Explorer (NPE) is a ClickOnce application that can be installed from inside your browser. Simply navigate to http://nuget.codeplex.com and find the Downloads page. You can install and run NPE by clicking the ClickOnce Installer download.

Figure 3-5 shows you the HelloWorld.1.0.0.0.nupkg created before, opened in NuGet Package Explorer. On the left-hand side, all package manifest metadata is displayed. The right-hand side shows the package's contents. Since we've only packaged some project output, the package consists of only a lib folder containing the HelloWorld.dll assembly.

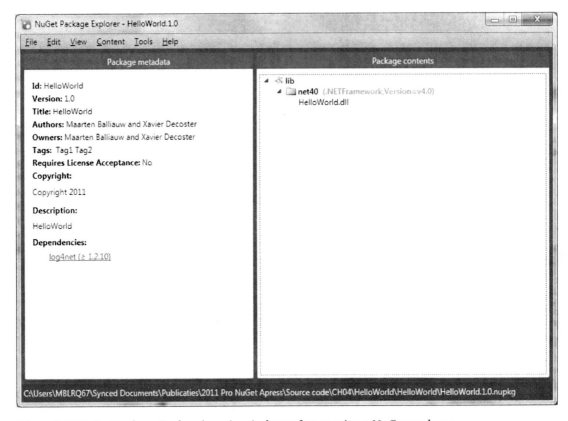

Figure 3-5. NuGet Package Explorer's main windows after opening a NuGet package

Browsing through the menus, you'll find a number of interesting options:

- Selecting File ➤ Export allows you to extract a package to disk.

- Clicking Edit ➤ Edit Package Metadata makes the left-hand screen editable, enabling you to modify the package manifest, add dependencies, and so on.

- By clicking Content ➤ Add, you open an interesting menu to add contents to the package. It enables you to add assemblies, framework folders, files in the tools folder, and so on.

- Finally, selecting Tools ➤ Analyze Package offers probably one of the most interesting menus: after clicking this option, NuGet Package explorer will scan the complete NuGet package for convention violations and provide warnings and errors when some rule has not been respected, as shown in Figure 3-6.

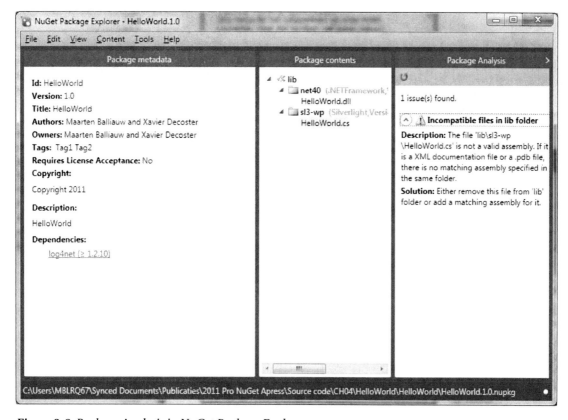

Figure 3-6. Package Analysis in NuGet Package Explorer

We often use NuGet Package Explorer to open up existing NuGet packages from the official NuGet package source, as many packages contain interesting hidden NuGet gems. For example, if you are wondering about how a Web.config transform has been created, simply find a package that applies this technique.

An interesting one, for example, is jQuery. Click the File Open from Feed menu, and search for **jQuery**. When you find it, double-click the package version you wish to load. Figure 3-7 shows the search we've done while writing this book.

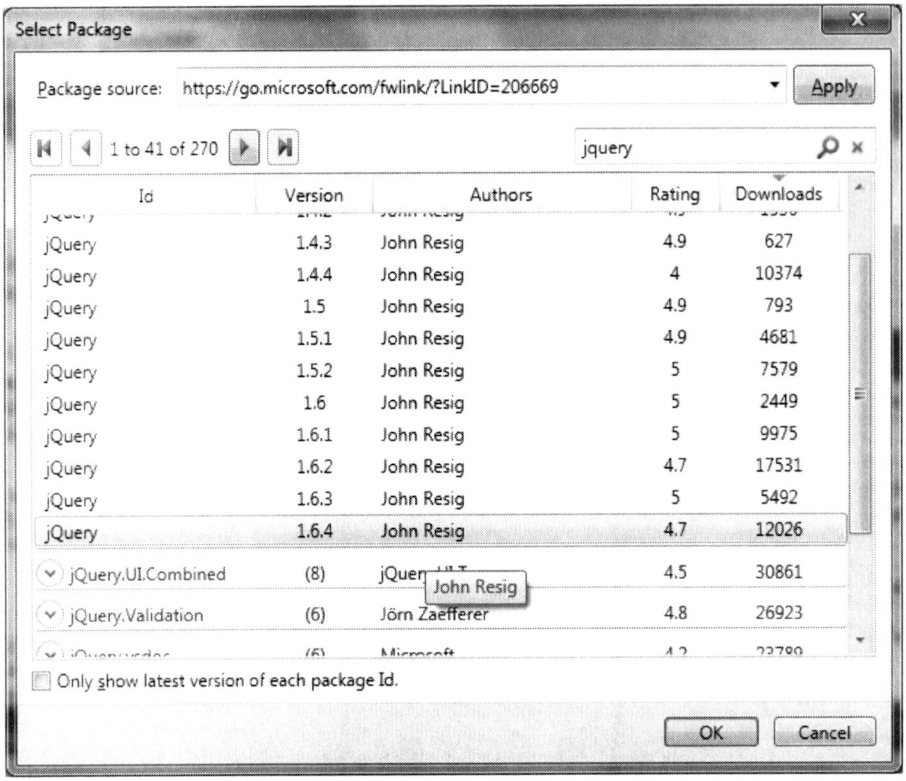

Figure 3-7. Searching for jQuery using NuGet Package Explorer

After opening the latest jQuery package, have a look at the package's contents. Of course, a content folder exists containing all JavaScript files related to jQuery. What is surprising, however, is that there is also a tools folder containing both the install.ps1 and uninstall.ps1 PowerShell scripts. The contents of install.ps1 are shown in Listing 3-13.

Listing 3-13. The install.ps1 PowerShell Script Contained in the jQuery NuGet Package

```
param($installPath, $toolsPath, $package, $project)

$extId = "JScriptIntelliSenseParaExtension.Microsoft.039ee76c-3c7f-4281-ad23-f6528ab18623"
$extManager = [Microsoft.VisualStudio.Shell.Package]::GetGlobalService(↵
    [Microsoft.VisualStudio.ExtensionManager.SVsExtensionManager])
$copyOverParaFile = $false
try {
    $copyOverParaFile = $extManager.GetInstalledExtension($extId).State -eq "Enabled"
}
catch [Microsoft.VisualStudio.ExtensionManager.NotInstalledException] {
    #Extension is not installed
}
```

```
if ($copyOverParaFile) {
    #Copy the -vsdoc-para file over the -vsdoc file
    #$projectFolder = Split-Path -Parent $project.FileName
    $projectFolder = $project.Properties.Item("FullPath").Value
    $paraVsDocPath = Join-Path $toolsPath jquery-1.6.4-vsdoc-para.js
    $vsDocPath = Join-Path $projectFolder Scripts\jquery-1.6.4-vsdoc.js
    Copy-Item $paraVsDocPath $vsDocPath -Force
}
```

If you read through this code, you may notice that it's being used to check if the JScriptIntelliSenseParaExtension Visual Studio Extension is installed and enabled. If that's the case, it copies an additional JavaScript IntelliSense file into the project consuming the jQuery package.

Of course, we don't expect you to grasp this entire script, nor do we expect you to write one. The point that we are trying to make is that you should open packages you find interesting using NuGet Package Explorer and look at how the package author accomplished certain installation steps. Steal with your eyes!

■ **Note** The *craziest* NuGet package we've found so far is Steve Sanderson's MvcScaffolding package. It is a NuGet package that contains a bunch of T4 templates (which are a means of code generation in Visual Studio). It also adds additional PowerShell commands to the NuGet Package Manager Console and enables you to do code generation in ASP.NET MVC. Find the package using NuGet Package Explorer, and see for yourself. And if you're interested in working with this package, a tutorial by the package author can be found at

http://blog.stevensanderson.com

/2011/01/13/scaffold-your-aspnet-mvc-3-project-with-the-mvcscaffolding-package/.

Testing Packages

So far, we've created a series of NuGet packages. One of the methods to test and consume those packages would be pushing these packages to the official NuGet package source. Chances are you don't want to do that: maybe the package you are creating is just a test package or isn't stable enough to be on the public package source. Maybe it even contains intellectual property that you don't want landing on the streets of the Internet, for everyone to use!

A solution to that would be to set up your own NuGet package source, which we will explain in Chapter 6 of this book. However, there's no need to set up a full-blown package repository when all you want to do is consume your freshly created NuGet package.

The easiest way to set up a test NuGet package source is by simply copying all your .nupkg files in a folder. For example, I have a folder on my drive where I copy packages that I want to test: C:\Sources\NuGet Repository. This folder can be specified as a package source for the NuGet command line, the NuGet Visual Studio Extension, or the package manager console. In Chapter 3 of this book, you learned how to configure each of these clients.

The NuGet command line does not have any toolbars to select out of a list of package sources. By default, the NuGet command line will use all package sources defined in the NuGet.config file, which can be found in %AppData%\NuGet\NuGet.config. You can change this file and add a permanent reference to the folder on your disk containing NuGet packages. Most commands, for example the install command, support a command line switch –Source, which uses the specified package source only for one action.

To configure package sources for the NuGet Visual Studio Extension or the package manager console, open Visual Studio and find the Tools ➤ Library Package Manager ➤ Package Manager Settings menu. To add a package source, provide a name and a path to the package source, and click the Add button. Figure 3-8 shows you a sample configuration of package sources.

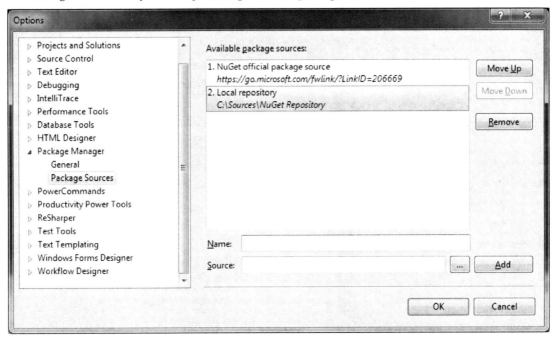

Figure 3-8. Configuring package sources in Visual Studio

From the moment a local package source has been configured, all that's left to do to test your packages is issue some commands on the command line or open a new Visual Studio project and add a package reference to it, making sure to select the package source containing your test packages.

Summary

In this chapter, you have learned that NuGet embraces the conventions over configuration principle, using a set of simple rules. You have been introduced to the NuGet package manifest, which contains all metadata and describes the package contents. This manifest and these rules deserve special attention by package producers, because both the package management tool and consumers are relying on them. This also explains why shipping a component or framework is more than just combining a set of library files in a ZIP archive.

We also explained to you how a good NuGet package should be structured—separating libraries from contents and tools. As such, a NuGet package can do more than add a reference to some assemblies by injecting content and code into the consuming Visual Studio project, or through the execution of custom scripts or executables during specific steps of the package management flow. This also opened the door to extensibility and automation of Visual Studio, the Package Manager Console, or NuGet itself. This extensibility is something we will come back to in Chapter 8.

In addition, we illustrated how you can easily create manifest files and NuGet packages using either the NuGet Command Line or NuGet Package Explorer. Creating your own manifest files gives you a lot of flexibility as a package producer and helps you to support various scenarios of package creation, both manual and automated, starting from an assembly, a Visual Studio project, or a convention-based working folder containing a NuGet manifest file.

Last but not least, we have shown you how you can easily test your own NuGet packages locally before pushing and publishing the package to a NuGet feed for consumption.

In the next chapter, we will continue with the next step in the process of shipping your own packages for consumption, by explaining you how you can push and publish a package to any NuGet feed or repository.

CHAPTER 4

Publishing Packages

In Chapter 3 of this book, we demonstrated you how you can create your own NuGet packages. It would be a shame if those packages weren't available to others, right?

This chapter will bridge the gap between package creation and package consumption. We'll show you how you can publish those precious packages to a NuGet feed, whether to the official NuGet package source available to everyone or to your own, private package feed. You'll learn that all this relies on three simple things: your NuGet package, a feed, and an API key.

We'll also explore how you can publish source code and debug symbols along with your binary NuGet package. This will enable consumers of your NuGet package to debug and step through your source code automatically from inside Visual Studio.

Creating a Sample Package

Let's start this chapter with creating a simple package that we'll deploy to the official NuGet package source. Feel free to create your own Visual Studio project containing code you wish to ship through the official NuGet package source, or use the project we'll create in this section. This section briefly covers creating a NuGet package. Refer to Chapter 3 for in-depth knowledge about creating NuGet packages.

Open Visual Studio, and create a new Class Library project titled **ProNuGetStringExtensions**, as shown in Figure 4-1.

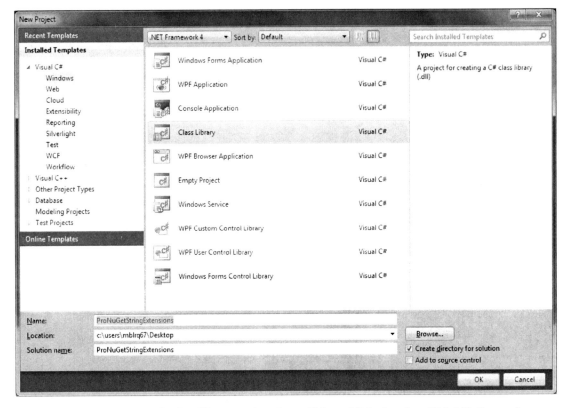

Figure 4-1. *Creating a sample class library project that will be published to the official NuGet package source*

By default, this new project will contain a file named Class1.cs. Since it's more fun to publish a useful NuGet package rather than a simple Hello World–style package, we'll provide some useful code. Remove this file and add a new class called StringExtensions. The code for this class can be found in Listing 4-1.

Listing 4-1. *The StringExtensions Class, which we'll push to the official NuGet Package Source*

```
namespace System
{
    public static class StringExtensions
    {
        public static string Truncate(this string input, int length)
        {
            return Truncate(input, length, "...");
        }

        public static string Truncate(this string input, int length, string suffix)
        {
```

```
        if (input == null)
        {
            return "";
        }
        if (input.Length <= length)
        {
            return input;
        }

        if (suffix == null)
        {
            suffix = "...";
        }

        return input.Substring(0, length - suffix.Length) + suffix;
    }
  }
}
```

The class that you have just added to this project will provide people with a useful extension method for strings: Truncate. For example, if you have a long string, you can use the Truncate extension method to truncate the string and add an ellipsis at the end. If we run Truncate(5, "...") on the current paragraph, the result would be "The c...".

■ **Note** An *extension method* is a language feature of C# and Visual Basic.NET that enables you to add methods to existing types without creating a new derived type, recompiling, or modifying the original type. This makes it possible to extend existing types such as System.String, even if the original source code is out of your control.

Try compiling the project (press Ctrl+Shift+B, or select Build ➤ Build Solution). If the project compiles correctly, it's time to create a NuGet package for this project. Open the folder where the ProNuGetStringExtensions.csproj file is located, and create a NuGet package manifest by running the nuget spec command from the command line A file named ProNuGetStringExtensions.nuspec should be created; modify its contents to something similar like the package manifest shown in Listing 4-2.

Listing 4-2. The Sample Package Manifest That Will Be Used Throughout This Chapter

```
<?xml version="1.0"?>
<package >
  <metadata>
    <id>$id$</id>
    <version>$version$</version>
    <title>$title$</title>
    <authors>Maarten Balliauw, Xavier Decoster</authors>
    <owners>Maarten Balliauw, Xavier Decoster</owners>
    <requireLicenseAcceptance>false</requireLicenseAcceptance>
    <description>Some useful string extensions for everyday use.</description>
    <copyright>Copyright 2011 Maarten Balliauw and Xavier Decoster</copyright>
    <tags>string extensions extension methods truncate</tags>
  </metadata>
</package>
```

As you've learned in the previous chapter of this book, packaging this project is now very straightforward: run the command nuget pack ProNuGetStringExtensions.csproj, and witness the NuGet package file ProNuGetStringExtensions.1.0.nupkg being created. We now have created the NuGet package that will be used throughout this chapter.

■ **Note** Feel free to test the ProNuGetStringExtensions.1.0.nupkg NuGet package using the approach described in the "Testing Packages" section found in Chapter 3 of this book.

Contributing to the Official NuGet Package Repository

Whenever you create a NuGet package, chances are that you want to publish this package on a NuGet feed. For example, you can publish your company's NuGet packages to a private NuGet feed, something we we'll continue to describe in the next chapter of this book. Another option is to publish a NuGet package to the official NuGet package source found at www.nuget.org.

The official NuGet package source is an online collection of NuGet packages available out of the box in Visual Studio after you install the NuGet Package Manager Extension. As Figure 4-2 shows, the Packages tab allows you to search for packages, inspect package information, consult package ratings, and find out the author of a NuGet package. It contains NuGet packages contributed by a variety of authors, including Microsoft, which is interesting: your NuGet package will be equally visible in these listings as, say, Microsoft's Entity Framework.

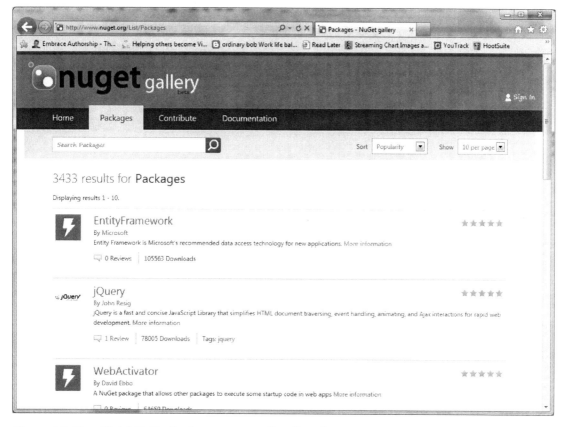

Figure 4-2. The official NuGet Packages source gallery found at www.nuget.org

Creating an Account

Before being able to publish a NuGet package on www.nuget.org, an account is required. Obtaining an account is a simple and short process in which you select a username and a password and provide your e-mail address. The account registration page for www.nuget.org can be found at www.nuget.org/Users/Account/Register.

After creating an account (and confirming it using the link sent to the e-mail address you provided), you can log on at www.nuget.org/Users/Account/LogOn. Log in, and find the My Account link on the top-right corner of the screen. This will bring you to an overview page of your account on www.nuget.org, as can be seen in Figure 4-3.

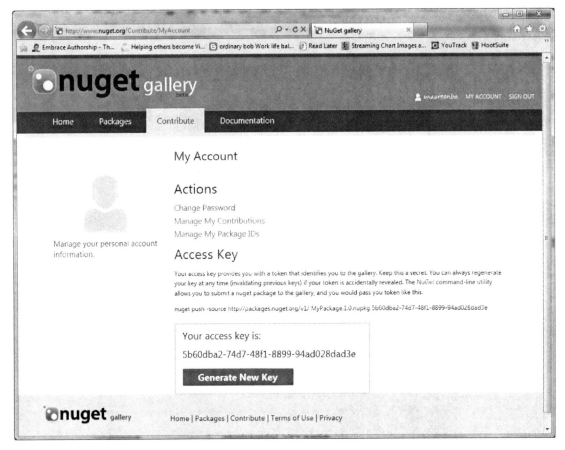

Figure 4-3. The My Account page on www.nuget.org *displaying a summary of all management options for a NuGet account*

NuGet.org's My Account page offers some management options related to your account on www.nuget.org. It allows you to change your password, manage your contributions, manage package IDs, and manage your API key.

The first option sort of speaks for itself: it allows you to change the password for your account. The second option, Manage My Contributions, is something we'll discuss in the next section of this chapter. Option three, Manage My Package IDs, allows you to reserve one or more package identifiers to ensure nobody else can register a package with the same identifier as your package. Finally, Generate New Key is an option we'll discuss in the "Obtaining an API Key" section of this chapter.

Publishing a NuGet package

The only way to let the world know about your package is to publish it to a NuGet feed. Publishing a package to the official NuGet package source can be done by anyone who has an account on www.nuget.org, like you now have since you are following the steps in this chapter of Pro NuGet. After signing in to www.nuget.org, click the Contribute link in the top menu. This should navigate you to the page shown in Figure 4-4.

Figure 4-4. *The first step of publishing a package to* www.nuget.org *after clicking the Contribute menu option*

Since what we want to do is add a package, click the Add New Package hyperlink. On the next page, you will be presented with two options for handing over your NuGet package to the official NuGet package source. You can either upload a package from your local computer or specify a URL to a package hosted somewhere else. Select the first option, and browse for the ProNuGetStringExtensions.1.0.nupkg file located on your computer. Next, click the Upload button, and wait until the NuGet package has been uploaded to www.nuget.org. After uploading the NuGet package, you will be presented with the screen shown in Figure 4-5.

Figure 4-5. Verify the details of your contribution to the official NuGet package source.

On this page, you can verify and modify the details of your NuGet package. All data shown comes directly from the package manifest, which was embedded in the NuGet package file. What can not be changed are the package ID and the package version. Other information like the package title, description, and authors can be changed at will. Verify the information is correct, and click the Next button at the bottom of this page. This will present you with the screen shown in Figure 4-6.

Figure 4-6. Add a logo and/or screenshots to your package submisison.

This page allows you to either upload a logo from your computer or specify a link to the logo for your NuGet package if you so desire. This logo will be displayed on the www.nuget.org web site as well as in the Visual Studio Package Manager Extension. Additionally, screenshots of your NuGet package in action can be added to the submission as well; this is very useful if you have a package that, for example, adds functionality or visual elements to a Visual Studio solution. Screenshots can, in those, situations be used to attract more people to your NuGet package as well as give people an idea of what to expect after installing your package.

To finalize the addition of your NuGet package to the official NuGet package source, click the Finish button. After a short time, usually less than a minute, you should be able to find your freshly submitted NuGet package in the official NuGet package source.

■ **Note** This section demonstrated the happy path of submitting a NuGet package. It is important to know that from the moment you upload a package on `www.nuget.org`, it will be available under the Manage My Contributions page under the Unpublished Packages listing. From there, you can either delete a pending package submission or continue editing the submission before publishing it to the official NuGet package source.

Managing Published Packages

After a few submissions of a package on the official NuGet package source, chances are you want to manage all of your submitted packages. Also, if you've previously started submitting a package to `www.nuget.org` but weren't able to complete the publishing process, you may want to either finalize or abandon the unpublished package.

Log in at `www.nuget.org` using your account and find the Manage My Contributions page. It can be found through the Contribute menu or by navigating directly to `www.nuget.org/Contribute/MyPackages`. This page will show an Unpublished Packages list, if any exist, as well as a list of submissions that have been published to the official NuGet package source. Figure 4-7 shows you what this page may look like (we admit, we're addicted to publishing NuGet packages).

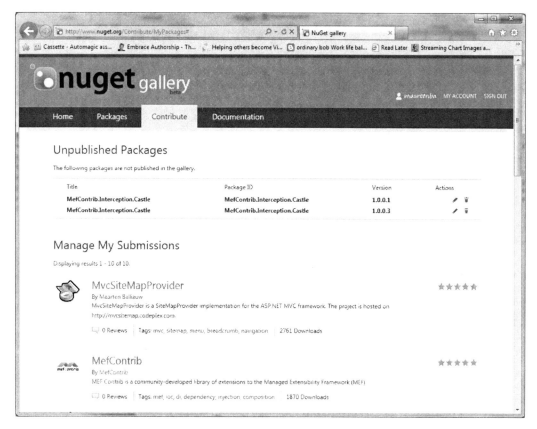

Figure 4-7. *Overview of unpublished packages and published packages on the official NuGet package source*

In addition to being able to finalize a package submission from the Unpublished Packages list, you can also edit or delete existing packages published on the official NuGet package source. Also reviews and ratings for a package can be edited, which is useful if someone posts an inappropriate review or rating. Do note that this should not be used for censorship!

■ **Caution** While, in theory, the official NuGet package source allows package authors to remove their package from www.nuget.org, we encourage you not to do so. People may depend on your NuGet package and may even depend on a specific version you've published. This puts you in a powerful position: you have the ability to break people's development process by suddenly removing one of their dependencies. You are responsible for software builds worldwide! Be nice, and keep every package version you publish on the official NuGet package source, even if it is buggy or outdated.

Obtaining an API key

Since you created an account on www.nuget.org earlier in this chapter, the My Account page (refer to Figure 4-3) showed the existence of something known as an API key. This API key (sometimes also referred to as an access key) provides you with a token that identifies you to a NuGet feed. An API key is not required to work with the official NuGet package source through www.nuget.org in a web browser, as you will always have to log in using your account's username and password combination. However, when you're publishing a NuGet package using the NuGet command line or NuGet Package Explorer, the API key will be used to authenticate you.

All NuGet server implementations in the wild, such as the official NuGet package source, MyGet.org, and the NuGet.Server package have a notion of an API key.

On the My Account page, you can easily find your API key to publish packages to the official NuGet Package source gallery. It also features a Generate New Key button, which you can use to generate a new API key and invalidate your current one, something we did after writing this chapter to ensure that you, dear reader, cannot publish NuGet packages under our NuGet.org account—just to be on the safe side.

In the next sections of this chapter, the API key listed under the My Account page will be used. Most examples will use the key shown in Figure 4-3: 5b60dba2-74d7-48f1-8899-94ad028dad3e.

Publishing Packages Using the NuGet Command Line

While there's no doubt it is useful to be able to publish a NuGet package to the official NuGet package source using your browser, it is not the most convenient way to publish NuGet packages, not to mention the fact that you can't automate this process. Also, publishing a package through your web browser probably takes more time than doing so using a command line tool. This section will show you how you can use the NuGet command line to publish packages to *any* NuGet feed.

Publishing a Package to a NuGet Feed

To get you started quickly, issue the following command on a console using the NuGet command line:

```
nuget push ProNuGetStringExtensions.1.0.nupkg
```

As you can see in Figure 4-8, this command fails, because no API key was specified to authenticate you to the official NuGet package source and to identify you as the package owner.

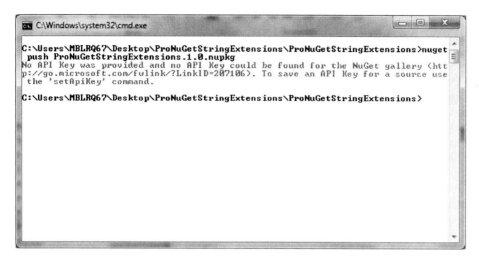

Figure 4-8. Pushing a NuGet package to the official NuGet package source fails because no API key was specified.

To overcome this failure, specify the API key retrieved earlier in this chapter in the command. Let's retry using the following command:

```
nuget push ProNuGetStringExtensions.1.0.nupkg 5b60dba2-74d7-48f1-8899-94ad028dad3e
```

Figure 4-9 shows you the result of specifying the API key when publishing our NuGet package—a successful publication. After approximately a minute, the ProNuGetStringExtensions package should be visible on the official NuGet package source at www.nuget.org.

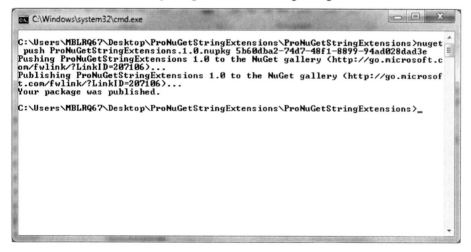

Figure 4-9. The result of a NuGet push command publishing a package to the official NuGet package source

■ **Note** As Figure 4-9 shows, publishing a NuGet package consists of two steps: pushing the package and publishing the package. The first is similar to starting package submission through your web browser: The package will be uploaded to www.nuget.org and kept the package under the Unpublished Packages list. The second is similar to clicking the Finish button when publishing through www.nuget.org: NuGet finalizes the submission and makes sure the package you submitted is listed in the official Nuget package source.

If you want to only push a package and not publish it, use the -CreateOnly switch on the nuget push command, for example:

```
nuget push ProNuGetStringExtensions.1.0.nupkg 5b60dba2-74d7-48f1-8899-94ad028dad3e -CreateOnly
```

Most NuGet commands, including the nuget push command, support the -Source switch and support pushing packages to feeds other than the default official NuGet package source. The following command pushes our package to the pronuget feed on www.myget.org:

```
nuget push ProNuGetStringExtensions.1.0.nupkg 82bccc78-c428-42c6-a568-42760994b077⏎
    -Source http://www.myget.org/F/pronuget
```

■ **Note** You may notice the API key used in this command is different from the API key used earlier in this section. The reason for this is that, since we are pushing to a NuGet feed other than the official NuGet package source, the API key for that other repository will be different.

Managing API Keys

As you've seen in the previous section, all NuGet server implementations out there, such as the official NuGet package source, MyGet.org, and the NuGet.Server package, have a notion of an API key. This API key is used to authenticate you and to identify you as the rightful owner of a package published on a NuGet feed.

The NuGet command line features a setApiKey command, which is used to store API keys in a central location in an encrypted manner. Doing so makes publishing packages easy, because you only have to specify the API key once. Open a console, and use the NuGet command line to store the API key for the official NuGet package source:

```
nuget setApiKey 5b60dba2-74d7-48f1-8899-94ad028dad3e
```

The preceding command stores the API key for the official NuGet package source in the NuGet.config file, described in Chapter 2 of this book. You can have a quick look at it by opening it from %AppData%\NuGet\NuGet.config.

As with most NuGet commands, the setApiKey command also makes use of the –Source command line switch to specify the NuGet feed for which you're specifying the API key. For example, we've created a pronuget feed on www.myget.org, on which Maarten is identified through the API key 244e9ea0-737e-

48cd-9c51-9426365d0362. Here's how to store the API key for our pronuget feed using the setApiKey command:

```
nuget setApiKey 244e9ea0-737e-48cd-9c51-9426365d0362 –Source http://www.myget.org/F/pronuget
```

Note There is no common best practice in using API keys. Some prefer specifying the API key on every command, as shown earlier in this section. Others prefer storing the API key using the setApiKey command. We recommend storing the API key on your local development computer, as this makes it easier to work with. To push NuGet packages from a build server or a different machine, it's probably safer to specify the correct API key, as well as the package source to be used, on every command.

Publishing Packages Using NuGet Package Explorer

In the previous chapter of this book, we showed you that you can use both the command line and a GUI-based tool called NuGet Package Explorer (NPE) to create NuGet packages. The same is true for publishing NuGet packages: NPE contains all tools to publish NuGet packages directly from its user interface.

As explained in Chapter 1, NuGet Package Explorer is a ClickOnce application that can be installed from inside your browser. Simply navigate to http://nuget.codeplex.com, and find the Downloads page. You can install and run NPE by clicking the ClickOnce Installer download.

Open NuGet Package Explorer on your system, and open the package we created in this chapter, ProNugetStringExtensions.1.0.nupkg. Figure 4-10 shows you what this should look like.

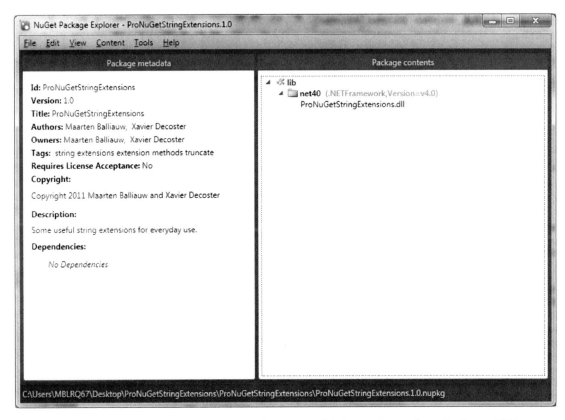

Figure 4-10. The ProNuGetStringExtensions package opened using NuGet Package Explorer (NPE)

From the File menu, the Publish menu item will do what you would expect: publish the package that is currently open to a NuGet feed. Figure 4-11 shows you the Publish Package dialog.

Figure 4-11. The Publish Package dialog in NuGet Package Explorer

The Publish Package dialog contains no rocket science options: it asks for the Publish Url, which, by default, points to the official NuGet package source. Next, it requires you to specify the Publish key, the API key provided by the My Account page on www.nuget.org. There's also a check box that enables you to only push your NuGet package to the feed, resulting in an additional entry in your Unpublished Packages list.

As with the nuget push command you saw earlier, the Publish button will perform the actual work and make sure your NuGet package is pushed directly to the destination feed from the graphical user interface. The ProNuGetStringExtensions package should be visible on the official NuGet package source at www.nuget.org after about a minute.

Note We typically use the NuGet package Explorer (NPE) tool while developing a NuGet package. Since it allows you to open a package directly from a NuGet feed, as shown in Chapter 3, and since it allows you to push a package directly to a feed, as shown in this section, NPE serves as a handy small NuGet package development interface that allows for an easy NuGet package development workflow.

Publishing a Symbol Package

We have all had the experience of debugging an application in Visual Studio that contains external libraries. Usually, you don't have the debugging symbols or the original source code for those dependencies at hand. It's often difficult to obtain all of those, let alone to hook them up in your Visual Studio and step through the external sources.

A symbol server can provide relief there: symbol servers host the .pdb files related to an assembly referenced in your project. Ever since Visual Studio 2005, a symbol server could be referenced in the

Visual Studio settings to retrieve debugging symbols and source code for external assemblies directly from such symbol server.

Users of Microsoft Team Foundation Server (TFS) can make use of the built-in symbol server and index their sources during builds. This is a configurable setting in the default Team Foundation Server build definition template. When using this feature, and Visual Studio is configured correctly, you can still benefit from stepping through the source code directly from TFS Source Control while inheriting all built-in security and permission checks on these sources. However, not everyone is using TFS, and NuGet is meant to be Version Control System (VCS)-agnostic. That's where SymbolSource.org comes in.

This section will show you how to configure Visual Studio to consume the symbol server for the official NuGet package source hosted on SymbolSource.org and how you can provide debugging symbols and source code to consumers of your NuGet packages.

Configuring Visual Studio

NuGet has teamed up with SymbolSource.org to provide a symbol server for all NuGet packages hosted in the official NuGet repository. As a package consumer, using the symbols hosted on SymbolSource.org is a one-time action that consists of adding the correct URL to the symbol server in Visual Studio. This section will take you through the required Visual Studio configuration steps.

First of all, Visual Studio typically will only debug your own source code—the source code of the project or projects that are currently opened in Visual Studio. To disable this behavior and to instruct Visual Studio to also try to debug code other than the projects that are currently opened, open the Options dialog (under the Tools ➤ Options menu). Find the Debugging node on the left, and click the General node underneath. Turn off the option Enable Just My Code.

In the same dialog, turn on the option "Enable source server support." This usually triggers the warning message shown in Figure 4-12. It is safe to just click Yes and continue with the settings specified.

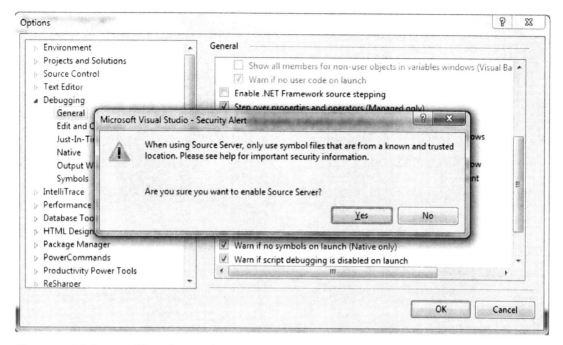

Figure 4-12. When enabling the use of a Source Server, a warning is displayed.

Keep the Options dialog open, and find the Symbols node under the Debugging node on the left. In the dialog shown in Figure 4-13, add the symbol server URL for the official NuGet package source: `http://srv.symbolsource.org/pdb/Public`. After that, click OK to confirm configuration changes and consume symbols for NuGet packages.

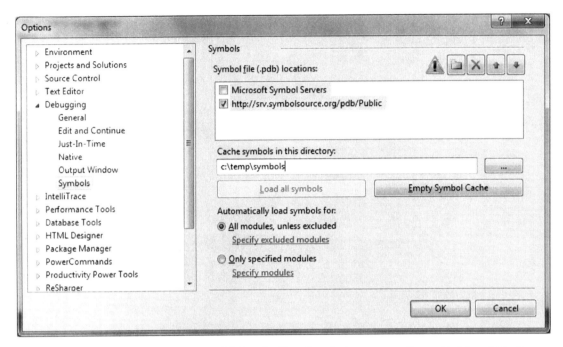

Figure 4-13. The NuGet symbol server added to the list of symbol servers configured in Visual Studio

---

■ **Tip** Did you know most assemblies of the Microsoft .NET Framework also provide their debugging symbols from a symbol server? For example, you can debug your ASP.NET MVC application and step into Microsoft's code to see what happens inside those System.* assemblies. To do so, add the open the Options dialog, and then open the Debugging node, and click Symbols. Add the Microsoft symbol server, located at http://msdl.microsoft.com/download/symbols. Some Visual Studio installations will already have the Microsoft Symbol Server listed. In those versions, just enabling it through the dialog mentioned earlier in this note is enough to step into any core .NET assembly.

Consuming Symbols for NuGet Packages

While technically not in the scope of this book, we do want to demonstrate you how you can consume symbols for NuGet packages from Visual Studio. Create a new project in Visual Studio, a console application, and install the ProNuGetStringExtensions package into it using either the NuGet Visual Studio Extension or the Package Manager Console (Install-Package ProNuGetStringExtensions will do the trick). In the Program.cs file, add the code from Listing 4-3.

Listing 4-3. *A Simple Console Application Consuming the Truncate() Method from the*
ProNuGetStringExtensions Package

```
using System;

namespace ConsoleApplication1
{
    class Program
    {
        static void Main(string[] args)
        {
            string longString = "This is a long string that I'll truncate later.";
            string shortString = longString.Truncate(5, "...");

            Console.WriteLine(shortString);
            Console.ReadLine();
        }
    }
}
```

The code fragment shown creates a long string and then uses the Truncate() method from the
ProNuGetExtensions package created earlier in this chapter. Add a breakpoint on line 10 (string
shortString = longString.Truncate(5, "...");). Run the application by pressing *F5* and step through
the source code.

As you can see in Figure 4-14, Visual Studio downloads the symbols package from the symbol server
we've added to the Visual Studio configuration. You are now able to step through this code and debug it
as if it were your own source code.

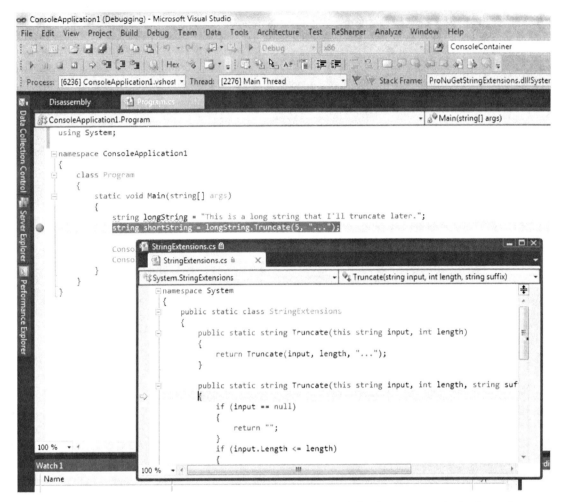

Figure 4-14. Visual Studio has downloaded the debugger symbols for the ProNuGetStringExtensions package.

Publishing Symbols for Your Own NuGet packages

NuGet has teamed up with SymbolSource.org to provide a symbol server for all NuGet packages hosted in the official NuGet repository. With almost no additional effort, package authors can publish their symbols and sources, and package consumers can debug into them from Visual Studio.

Before you can publish a symbols package for a NuGet package, the symbols package has to be created first. As you learned in Chapter 3, creating a symbols package can be done using the nuget pack command, specifying the –Symbols switch. Run the following command to create a symbols package for ProNuGetStringExtensions:

```
nuget pack ProNuGetStringExtensions.csproj -Symbols
```

On your file system, two NuGet packages should now be created:

- ProNuGetStringExtensions.1.0.nupkg: The NuGet package that will be published to the official NuGet package source

- ProNuGetStringExtensions.1.0.symbols.nupkg: The NuGet package containing debugging symbols (.pdb files), which will be published to the symbol server at SymbolSource.org

Assuming the API key for publishing to the official NuGet package source is 5b60dba2-74d7-48f1-8899-94ad028dad3e, the following command will publish these two packages in one go:

```
nuget push ProNuGetStringExtensions.1.0.nupkg 5b60dba2-74d7-48f1-8899-94ad028dad3e
```

If you wish to just push the symbols package, the following command can be used to achieve that goal:

```
nuget push ProNuGetStringExtensions.1.0.symbols.nupkg 5b60dba2-74d7-48f1-8899-94ad028dad3e
```

Summary

In this chapter, we've shown you how you can publish packages created on a NuGet feed. We've demonstrated how to use www.nuget.org, how you can use your web browser to publish your NuGet package to the official NuGet package source, and how to list your NuGet packages among other packages offered through that feed.

Next, we've shown you how to use the NuGet command line to do the same using the nuget push command. We've touched the notion of API keys (or access keys) that are used to authenticate against a NuGet feed and to identify who owns the package being pushed. The nuget setApiKey command proved helpful when working with the NuGet command line to push packages.

NuGet Package Explorer (NPE) again proved itself as a useful tool by providing a graphical user interface to do common tasks like publishing a NuGet package. It can also be used to ease the NuGet package development workflow by opening a package from a NuGet feed directly, modifying the contents, and publishing it back to the NuGet feed.

Finally, we've demonstrated how you can consume and publish symbol packages. With almost no additional effort, package authors can publish their symbols and sources, and package consumers can debug them from Visual Studio.

The next chapter will show you how you can set up your own NuGet feed using different approaches, and we will explain you why you might want to do so even though there's an official NuGet package source.

CHAPTER 5

Hosting Your Own NuGet Server

In Parts 1 and 2 of this book, we have introduced you to package management with NuGet. By now, you know everything you need to know to get started with NuGet and consume or produce packages. In Chapter 4, we demonstrated how you can easily publish those packages onto *any* NuGet server.

Based on this knowledge, we will now start with the fun part! So far, we have mainly been targeting the official NuGet Gallery. The public NuGet feed is aimed at the distribution of open source libraries and components. We really want to encourage you all to share your cool projects and contribute to those projects and libraries you really enjoy! Contributing is a wonderful learning experience, and before you know it, you will be able to call yourself an active member of the community.

While the NuGet model is very interesting, the team behind NuGet realized that not everyone is developing open source software for a living and wants to contribute their valuable in-house software packages to this official NuGet package source. Many companies eventually might want to set up their own package repositories, preferably using NuGet, to escape from dependency hell and overcome common package management issues.

This chapter will dive a bit deeper in why you may want to host your own NuGet feed and what it takes to set up your *own* NuGet repositories. That's right; after reading this chapter, you can set up your own NuGet repositories!

Why Host Your Own NuGet Feed?

A good place to start this chapter is with one of the "W" questions: why host your own NuGet feed? To be honest, there are many valuable reasons to do this, reasons that we'll touch on briefly in this chapter and that will become more clear in the next chapters, for example, when we explain continuous package integration.

The first and obvious reason to host your own NuGet feed is simple. By default, your NuGet world consists of only the official NuGet package source. Anyone can post packages to this, and all packages are public. A big consequence of this is that to distribute your company's internal application framework using NuGet, your only option would be to publish it to the official NuGet package source. Are you sure you want to submit all your in-house–developed intellectual property and make it public? Probably not. Your own, private NuGet feed would come in handy in such situation.

Maybe you do want to push packages to either the official NuGet package source or to your own feed. And maybe you want to do that from your build server. Why not first push those packages to your personal NuGet feed before doing the actual push to the target feed? This workflow ensures you can safely validate packages published before submitting them officially.

Another reason for setting up a personal NuGet feed may be the fact that you only want to provide your developers access to "approved" packages, that is, packages that have been tested and validated for use in your company's software projects. The easiest way to do this is setting up your own NuGet feed and "mirroring" specific packages from the official NuGet feed. Resultingly, your feed will be limited to only packages that you as a team lead approve.

Hold on; there are more reasons for setting up your own NuGet feed. Good reason number three is simply the fact that the official NuGet package source is growing every hour. What if you are only interested in packages related to Silverlight? Or only packages meant to be used with Windows Phone 7 development? This problem can easily be solved by creating a feed that contains just packages of interest, with no packages related to technologies you're not even using in your projects.

Packages on the official NuGet package source are maintained by their respective package authors. This means that whenever a package author updates a NuGet package or when the package is removed from the official NuGet package source, your developers may have difficulties consuming existing NuGet package references. It may be a good idea to mirror these packages and host your own NuGet feed simply to make sure packages that are being used are always available, regardless of what the package author decides to do with it.

Yet another reason to set up a personal NuGet feed is security: NuGet feeds can prompt users to authenticate to consume packages listed on such feed. Combine that fact with your corporate Active Directory or LDAP account, and you'll notice that it becomes very easy to authenticate users to a private feed using their corporate credentials. What if you want some users to just consume packages while others are permitted to publish them? You can do all of this on your private NuGet feed!

Another reason for hosting your own NuGet feed may be your network connection. Maybe the official NuGet package source has a high latency where you are located, or a corporate firewall prevents you from connecting there. A solution to that can be to host your own NuGet feed within your firewall and keep both speed and security high.

■ **Note** The reasons we've listed here are based on our own experience at customers and at our employers. There are probably a number of other reasons to host your own NuGet feed.

Setting Up a Simple NuGet Package Repository

The easiest and fastest way of setting up your own NuGet package repository is by setting up a simple network share to act as the physical repository. A folder containing a bunch of NuGet packages (.nupkg) will be treated as a NuGet package source. This is a very cheap way of getting started with NuGet today with almost no effort! No matter what type of NuGet repository you will end up with later, they all have one thing in common: under the hood, simple BLOB-storage (Binary Large Object) is used. A network share is a good starting point, as we will show you later in this chapter, because you can easily extend it with more advanced NuGet server functionality. It all builds on top of a simple package repository. Before spending much effort in a full-fledged NuGet server, we strongly suggest you to get started with this minimal setup and get familiar with the concepts while taking immediate benefit from NuGet's package management.

Figure 5-1 illustrates a network share acting as a NuGet package repository in Windows Explorer. You can simply host your packages in a central folder on any network attached storage (NAS) device or server.

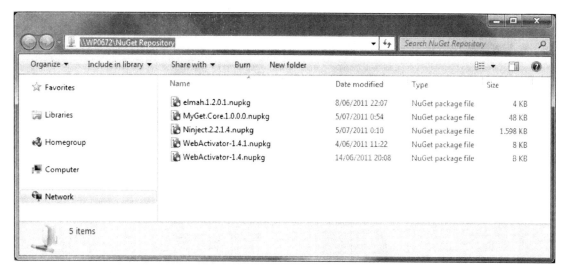

Figure 5-1. *A Windows Explorer view on a network share acting as a NuGet package repository*

■ **Tip** If you are the only person who will be using a simple package repository, you can achieve the same results by using a local folder instead, as we showed while testing your packages in Chapter 3.

To start using this network share as a NuGet package source, you'll need to configure the NuGet Visual Studio Extension to use it. To do so, click Tools Options, and navigate to the Package Manager Package Sources tab (see Figure 5-2). For network shares, you can provide the UNC path to the shared folder. The only thing left to do is to communicate this package source setting to your fellow team members. Congratulations! You have just created your *own* private NuGet package repository!

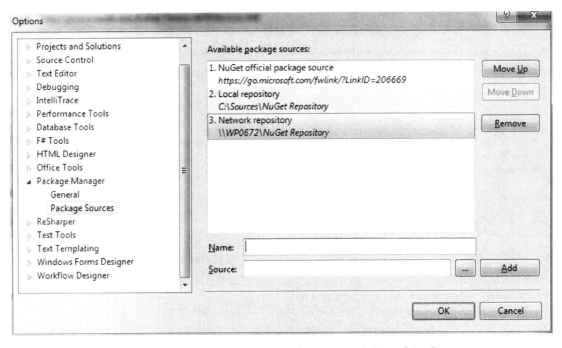

Figure 5-2. Configuring a network share as a NuGet package source in Visual Studio

Creating a Basic NuGet Server

The NuGet team realized people would need to set up a NuGet server with support for API keys, an OData feed on top of the physical package repository, and maybe some web interface as well. We've also explained that NuGet itself is fully open source, so you can grab the bits and pieces and tweak it to your needs. However, you might want to make sure your NuGet server implementation can evolve together with the public one and consider building on top of the released versions instead of extending the sources directly.

NuGet is really well designed in terms of extensibility. There are two main components that make a NuGet server: NuGet.Core and NuGet.Server. Of course, using the open source mantra that "it doesn't exist unless it's on NuGet," these two components are available as NuGet packages.

Since we want to host a NuGet *feed*, we will need a simple web application that can serve as a basic NuGet server. We will choose for an ASP.NET MVC web application, but know that it would work as well for the more classical ASP.NET web forms approach. Let's get started and create an empty ASP.NET MVC web application in Visual Studio through the well-known File New Project dialog, where you select ASP.NET MVC 3 Application in the Web category, as shown in Figure 5-3.

■ **Tip** If you are unfamiliar with ASP.NET MVC, we recommend reading *Pro ASP.NET MVC 3 Framework* by Adam Freeman and Steven Sanderson—also known as the creator of the MvcScaffolding package—published in the same Apress series as this book.

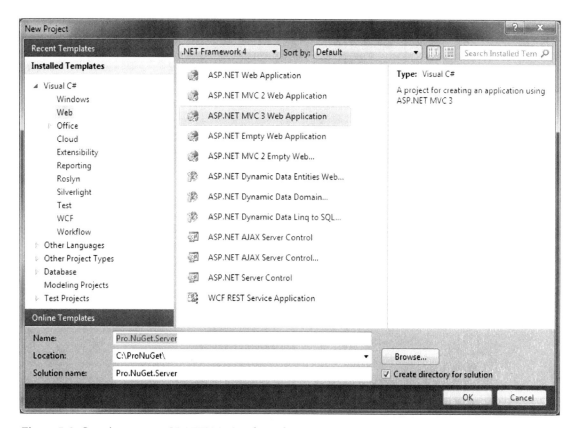

Figure 5-3. Creating a new ASP.NET MVC web application project in Visual Studio 2010.

Choose a location for your project, and give it a meaningful name. We have chosen `Pro.NuGet.Server` for the example in this book. After clicking the OK button, you'll be prompted by a dialog to choose the desired *recipe* for your ASP.NET MVC web application. You can choose an empty project, an Internet application, or an intranet application. If you feel like building everything from scratch, you should pick the Empty option. If you want to get a template for an Internet application, preconfigured with Forms Authentication, the Internet Application recipe will be most suitable for you. For the purpose of this book, we want to build a NuGet server hosted on the corporate intranet, which is most likely to be the most realistic scenario for a custom NuGet server implementation. Hence we will continue our sample using the Intranet Application recipe, as illustrated in Figure 5-4.

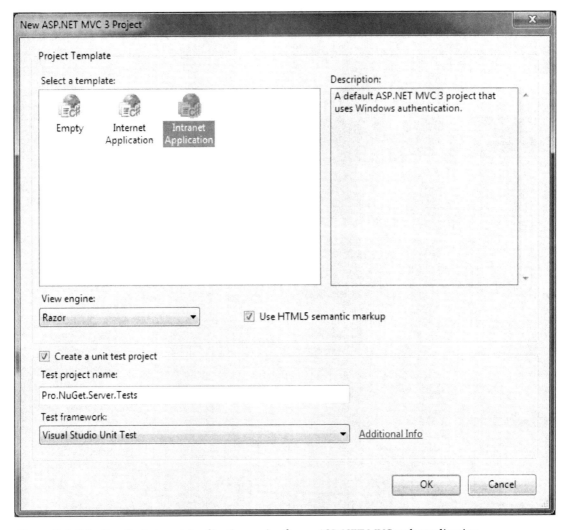

Figure 5-4. Selecting the Intranet Application recipe for an ASP.NET MVC web application

CONFIGURING INTRANET AUTHENTICATION

The Intranet Application recipe comes preconfigured for Windows Authentication, and the `readme.txt` will be opened by default, providing you with detailed instructions on how to configure authentication on Internet Information Services (IIS) or IIS Express.

To use the Intranet Application template, you'll need to enable Windows Authentication and disable Anonymous Authentication. For detailed instructions (including instructions for IIS 6.0), please visit `http://go.microsoft.com/fwlink/?LinkID=213745`. To guide you through this process, we provide you some instructions for IIS7 and IIS Express.

IIS 7

1. Open IIS Manager, and navigate to your web site.

2. In Features View, double-click Authentication.

3. On the Authentication page, select Windows Authentication. If Windows Authentication is not an option, you'll need to make sure Windows Authentication is installed on the server. To enable Windows Authentication

   a. In Control Panel, open "Programs and Features".

   b. Select "Turn Windows features on or off".

   c. Navigate to Internet Information Services ▸ World Wide Web Services ▸ Security, and make sure the Windows Authentication node is checked.

4. In the Actions pane, click Enable to use Windows Authentication.

5. On the Authentication page, select Anonymous Authentication.

6. In the Actions pane, click Disable to disable anonymous authentication.

IIS Express

1. Right-click the project in Visual Studio, and select Use IIS Express.

2. Click your project in the Solution Explorer to select it.

3. If the Properties pane is not open, make sure to open it (F4).

4. In the Properties pane for your project

   a. Set Anonymous Authentication to Disabled.

   b. Set Windows Authentication to Enabled.

You can install IIS Express using the Microsoft Web Platform Installer.

For Visual Studio, visit `http://go.microsoft.com/fwlink/?LinkID=214802`.

For Visual Web Developer, visit `http://go.microsoft.com/fwlink/?LinkID=214800`.

If all went well, you should now have a standard ASP.NET MVC intranet web application, fully running with Windows Authentication. Pressing F5 (or selecting Debug ▸ Start Debugging) in Visual Studio should give you the result shown in Figure 5-5.

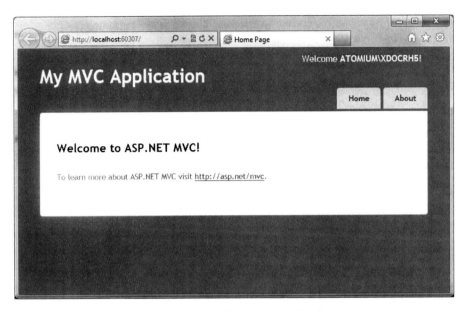

Figure 5-5. *First run of the ASP.NET MVC intranet application*

With minimal effort, you managed to create a nice-looking, fully functional intranet application. If you look closely at what's included in this Intranet Application recipe, you'll notice something very cool: this project template already is consuming NuGet packages!

░ **Tip** Creating an ASP.NET MVC recipe of your own is a very interesting approach in an enterprise scenario. It's an easy way to quickly start new projects or solutions, preconfigured, for instance, to consume specific NuGet packages, such as default company design theme, corporate frameworks, and so on.

Although this is not an ASP.NET MVC book, we highly value the importance of its early adoption of NuGet and the way it opens up possibilities to quickly set up a fully functional web application by selecting the building blocks you want.

If we want to turn this web application into a NuGet server, we need to install some additional building blocks. As you, by now, are getting familiar with the NuGet package manager, you might have guessed those building blocks could be found on the official NuGet feed. You would have guessed right! The very building blocks of NuGet itself are available on the official NuGet feed. We mentioned earlier you'd need the NuGet.Core and NuGet.Server packages, so let's go ahead and install those into our web application project. Run the following command from within NuGet Package Manager Console, targeting the web project:

```
Install-Package NuGet.Server
```

Installing the NuGet.Server package will add a set of packages to your project, including the NuGet.Core package because NuGet.Server depends on it. After installation, you'll notice that

Default.aspx and some other files were installed into your project. Because the NuGet.Server package is targeting an ASP.NET web forms application, we'll manually adjust the Home view to contain the contents from Default.aspx. To do so, open the Views\Home\Index.cshtml file, and paste the markup code of Default.aspx. After adjusting the Home view, your file should look similar to Listing 5-1.

Listing 5-1. Default Home Page for NuGet.Server in a MVC Web Application

```
@using System.Configuration
@{
    ViewBag.Title = "Home Page";
}
<h2>@ViewBag.Message</h2>
<div>
    <h2>
        You are running NuGet.Server v@(typeof(NuGet.Server.DataServices.Package)↵
.Assembly.GetName().Version)</h2>
    <p>
        Click <a href="@VirtualPathUtility.ToAbsolute("~/nuget/Packages")">here</a> to view
        your packages.
    </p>
    <fieldset style="width: 800px">
        <legend><strong>Repository URLs</strong></legend>In the package manager settings,
        add the following URL to the list of Package Sources:
        <blockquote>
            <strong>@Helpers.GetRepositoryUrl(Request.Url, Request.ApplicationPath)</strong>
        </blockquote>
        @if (String.IsNullOrEmpty(ConfigurationManager.AppSettings["apiKey"]))
        {
            <text>To enable pushing packages to this feed using the nuget command line tool
            (nuget.exe). Set the api key appSetting in web.config.</text>
        }
        else {
            <text>Use the command below to push packages to this feed using the nuget↵
command line tool (nuget.exe).</text>
        }
        <blockquote>
            <strong>nuget push {package file} -s @Helpers.GetPushUrl(Request.Url,↵
Request.ApplicationPath) {apikey}</strong>
        </blockquote>
    </fieldset>
    @if (Request.IsLocal) {
    <p style="font-size: 1.1em">
        To add packages to the feed put package files (.nupkg files) in
        the folder "@NuGet.Server.Infrastructure.PackageUtility.PackagePhysicalPath".
    </p>
    }
</div>
```

> ■ **Note** If you are familiar with ASP.NET MVC, you obviously could plug in these changes anywhere in your application that you want. This sample page contains both the physical and virtual paths to the NuGet package source. It also contains instructions on how to configure Visual Studio to use your brand new NuGet repository.

Configuring the Packages' Location

You now have set up a basic NuGet server, preconfigured with a NuGet OData feed and a default package location. Any .nupkg file that you put in the packages' location will be immediately picked up by the OData feed the moment you query it for packages.

Go ahead and copy a few packages into the {applicationPath}\packages folder. You should see your packages listed when navigating to the OData feed located on {applicationUrl}/nuget/packages using a browser such as Internet Explorer.

> ■ **Tip** You could change the location of the packages—by default, it is located under {applicationPath}\packages—by configuring a virtual directory in Internet Information Services (IIS) to point to any path you want. It doesn't even have to be on the same machine. Just make sure you configure security permissions accordingly.

Starting from NuGet.Server version 1.5, you can also point the application to a specific location for packages by setting the packagesPath application setting in web.config, as shown in Listing 5-2.

Listing 5-2. Setting the packagespath Configuration Setting for NuGet.Server v1.5

```
<appSettings>
    <!-- Set the value here to specify your custom packages folder. -->
    <add key="packagesPath" value="C:\MyPackages" />
</appSettings>
```

If you start the application now, you should see something similar to the page shown in Figure 5-6.

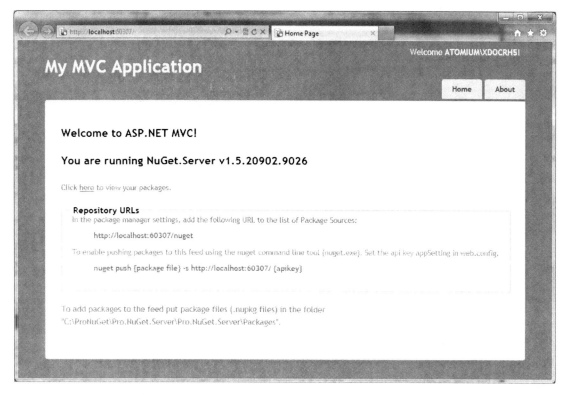

Figure 5-6. First run of the NuGet server implementation

In order for your team members to start using this NuGet feed, they need to add the package source to the NuGet configuration in Visual Studio. The NuGet.Server package has configured the *routing* of your application for you and located the NuGet repository URL under {applicationUrl}/nuget. This is the package source URL you'll need to configure in Visual Studio.

You now have everything in place to start building a fully fledged NuGet server in ASP.NET MVC. Instead of manually placing packages into the packages' folder, you could build a complete package management user interface where you could upload packages, for instance. We'll leave it up to you to build it, because these needs are most likely to be different for each organization. If your organization wants to use multiple package repositories and feeds, you'll need to deploy and configure this web site multiple times as well, because the NuGet.Server package only supports a single feed per web application.

In short, the NuGet.Server package is very useful if you only have basic requirements or if you want to build the web application hosting the NuGet feed completely from scratch. If you want something more feature-rich and don't want to develop everything yourself, you might consider the Orchard-based NuGet Gallery implementation we'll discuss in the next topic.

Setting the API Key

You can still use the NuGet.exe command-line tool to push and publish packages to your own feed. To enable this functionality, you'll need to configure your server with an API key. This is done through another application setting in your server's web.config file, as shown in Listing 5-3.

Listing 5-3. Setting the Packages' Path Configuration Setting for NuGet.Server v1.5.

```
<appSettings>
    <!-- Set the value here to allow people to push/delete packages from the server.
        NOTE: This is a shared key (password) for all users. -->
    <add key="apiKey" value="" />
</appSettings>
```

When the key is omitted or empty, which is the case by default, pushing packages to the feed is disabled. Note that this API key is shared among all users of your private NuGet feed. In other words, everyone who's using your feed will need to use the same key when pushing or publishing packages to your repository. By setting the API key through a setting in the configuration file, this also means that you can't change this as easily as a registered user on http://nuget.org could do. Changing this setting requires access to the web.config file.

As we will explain later in this chapter, MyGet has the concept of an API key per user, which allows unique permissions on such feed on a per user basis. If you're fine with a shared API key for the entire feed, a NuGet.Server based implementation is probably good enough to suit your needs.

NuGet Gallery

If you like the look and feel of the official NuGet gallery on http://nuget.org, you might be very pleased to learn that you can actually host the exact same web application yourself. The NuGet Gallery is built using ASP.NET MVC and can be installed on your own web server as well as on Microsoft's cloud computing platform, Windows Azure.

This section will show you how you can download, compile, and deploy the NuGet Gallery source code to your own web server.

Downloading the Source Code

The NuGet Gallery has to be compiled and installed from its source code. There are two options to obtain the source code for the NuGet Gallery:

- If you are familiar with the Git version control system, you can easily clone the NuGet Gallery Git repository using the git clone git@github.com:NuGet /NuGetGallery.git command. This will download the latest source code version from GitHub to your local disk.

- A ZIP file containing the exact same source code can be downloaded by browsing to https://github.com/NuGet/NuGetGallery/zipball/master. This URL will trigger a download of the latest version of the NuGet Gallery source code. You can save and extract the ZIP file to your local disk.

Make sure the source code is extracted on your local disk. We'll use these extracted sources to compile and deploy the NuGet Gallery.

Creating a SQL Server Database

Many applications, including NuGet Gallery, require a SQL Server database to store their data. NuGet Gallery can make use of SQL Server and SQL Server Express, a free version of which can be downloaded from www.microsoft.com/sqlserver/en/us/editions/express.aspx.

The NuGet Gallery database has to be created on a SQL Server instance. Once you are connected to the SQL Server instance of your choice—we use our local SQL Server instance represented by the dot (.) notation—you can right-click Databases in the Object Explorer window, and select New Database from the contextual menu, as shown in Figure 5-7.

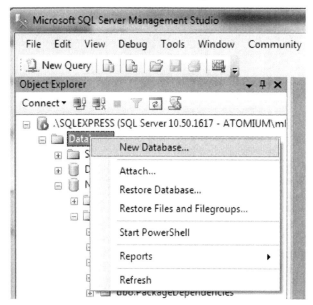

Figure 5-7. *Creating a new SQL Server database using SQL Server Management Studio*

We will call our database NuGetGallery, but this name can be anything you find meaningful.

Configuring NuGet Gallery

The folder where you initially extracted the NuGet Gallery source code will contain a folder named Website. This folder contains a Web.config file, which you should edit and update according to your situation. Open this file in Visual Studio (or your XML editor of choice), and update the appSettings and connectionString section accordingly. Table 5-1 lists the available configuration keys and their description.

Table 5-1. Overview of Possible NuGet Galery Configuration Settings

Setting name	Required?	Description
GalleryOwnerEmail	Yes	The e-mail address of the NuGet Gallery owner. Update this to your own e-mail address.
Gallery:ReleaseName	No	The release name for the NuGet Gallery. This is only used at www.nuget.org and displayed in the footer.
Gallery:ReleaseSha	No	The release hash for the NuGet Gallery. This is only used at www.nuget.org and displayed in the footer.
Gallery:ReleaseBranch	No	The release branch name for the NuGet Gallery. This is only used at www.nuget.org and displayed in the footer.
Gallery:ReleaseTime	No	The release time for the NuGet Gallery. This is only used at www.nuget.org and displayed in the footer.
Configuration:SiteRoot	Yes	The site root of the NuGet Gallery. This should be updated to the same root URL as where you will be installing NuGet Gallery. For example, if you are installing NuGet Gallery on the domain name nuget.mycorp.com, this setting must be updated to http://nuget.mycorp.com/.
NuGetGallery connection string	Yes	This connection string is used to connect to the SQL Server database created earlier. Update the connection string to reflect the connection details for your SQL Server database.

After updating the Web.config file, you are ready to compile NuGet Gallery.

Compiling NuGet Gallery

Before being able to deploy and use the NuGet Gallery server, you will have to compile it. In the source code folder for the NuGet Gallery, there is a PowerShell script called Build-Solution.ps1. This script can be run from a PowerShell console and will download all dependencies required to compile the NuGet Gallery (using NuGet, of course). It will also run all unit tests and compile the NuGet Gallery source code to a web application, which you can deploy on your web server.

To compile NuGet Gallery, open a PowerShell console (by selecting Start All Programs Accessories Windows PowerShell Windows PowerShell), navigate to the folder on your local disk where the NuGet Gallery sources have been extracted, and run the command .\Build-Solution.ps1. Figure 5-8 shows you a part of the output of this compilation process.

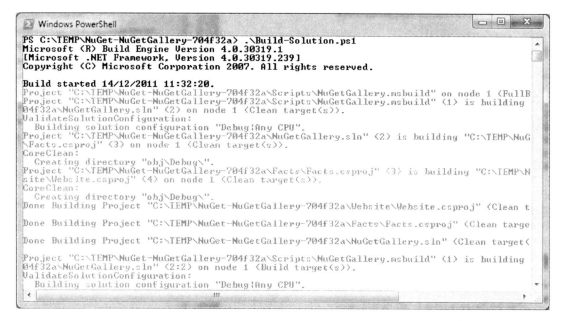

Figure 5-8. The build script output for NuGet Galler's Build-Solution.ps1 script

After this script has been run, the folder where you initially extracted the NuGet Gallery source code will contain a folder named Website. This is the actual application you'll have to deploy to your server in order to run your own NuGet feed.

Finalizing your NuGet Gallery Installation

After you have deployed the NuGet Gallery to your web server, navigate to the URL where the NuGet Gallery web site can be found. We have installed NuGet Gallery on a local IIS server available at http://localhost:55880/. You will be greeted by a similar web site to www.nuget.org (in fact, www.nuget.org runs on the same code you have just deployed).

Since you are installing NuGet Gallery, chances are you will be the administrator for the installation as well. To enable the administration user interface, you will have to register on your NuGet Gallery first. Click the Register link in the top-right corner of NuGet Gallery, and specify the username and password you would like to use. Figure 5-9 shows you this registration page in action.

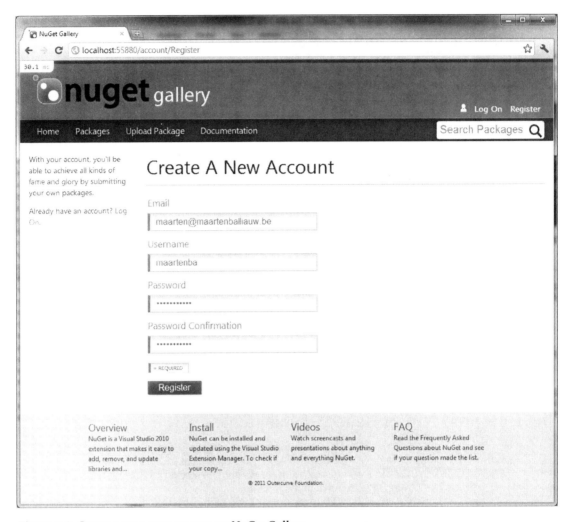

Figure 5-9. Create a new account on your NuGet Gallery.

Since this is the first user being created and settings, like the mail server to use, have not yet been updated, NuGet Gallery creates a registration e-mail in the `Website\App_Data\Mail` folder. Open this folder, and double-click the e-mail message generated after registering your username. The e-mail you can see in Figure 5-10 is a confirmation e-mail containing a URL that is used to validate the registration. Navigate to this link, and validate your registration.

Figure 5-10. NuGet Gallery registration confirmation e-mail located in the Website\App_Data\Mail folder

After confirming your registration, you are a regular user of your NuGet Gallery. This means you can create and upload NuGet packages just like anyone else would do it.

To become the administrator of your NuGet Gallery, you will have to upgrade your account to an administrator account. To do so, connect to the NuGetGallery database you've created on SQL Server and run the following query:

```
INSERT INTO [dbo].[UserRoles] ([UserKey],[RoleKey])
    VALUES ( (SELECT TOP 1 [Key] FROM [dbo].[Users]), 1)
```

This query adds the first user in your NuGet Gallery (which should be your newly created account as you are the only user at this time) and assigns it the Admins role. From now on, you'll be able to manage the database directly from the URL http://localhost:55880/dbadmin/. The first thing you may want to do is update mail server settings in http://localhost:55880/dbadmin/GallerySettings/Edit?Key=1.

Congratulations, you are now running your own version of www.myget.org!

Orchard Gallery

If you are using Orchard, a free, state-of-the-art modular open source content management system (CMS), you may be interested in the fact that a NuGet repository implementation built on Orchard exists. The Orchard-based NuGet Gallery allows you to create a dedicated Orchard installation or extend an existing Orchard installation with all the tools and features required for serving NuGet feeds.

In this section, we'll guide you through the process of setting up such a NuGet gallery. For starters, we assume you have some experience with Mercurial source control, setting up and deploying web sites under IIS, managing SQL Server databases, and have some experience with managing Orchard.

The fastest and easiest way to set up an Orchard-based NuGet Gallery is by simply cloning the Mercurial repository from Codeplex and deploying it on your server. You'll need to have the Mercurial tooling installed on your machine in order to do so. Preferably, you clone the repository on your local development machine and copy the bits over to the web server that will host the NuGet Gallery application. No need to install any source control tooling on your web servers!

If you don't have any Mercurial tooling installed on your system, we suggest you install the latest version of TortoiseHg, which you can download from `http://mercurial.selenic.com/`. TortoiseHg is a Windows shell extension and a series of applications for the Mercurial distributed revision control system. After installing TortoiseHg, you'll have access to the `hg` command-line tool from any command prompt, or you could use the Explorer Shell integration for a visual experience.

To clone the NuGet Gallery repository, simply run the following command using the `hg` command-line tool in a command prompt, while making sure you are in the directory where you want to clone the remote repository.

```
hg clone https://hg01.codeplex.com/nugetgallery
```

You achieve the same using the graphical user interface by navigating to the desired clone directory (e.g., `C:\nugetgallery\`) using Windows Explorer, right-clicking and selecting TortoiseHg ➤ Clone from the contextual menu, as shown in Figure 5-11.

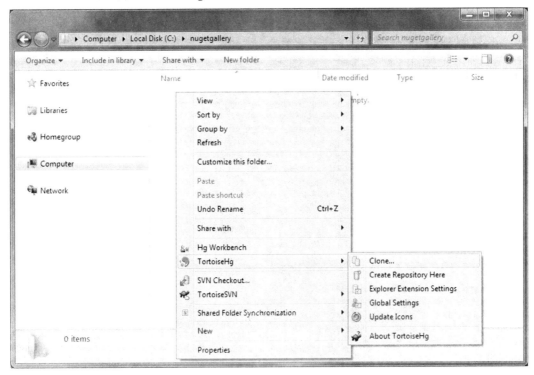

Figure 5-11. Using the TortoiseHg shell integration in Windows Explorer

A dialog will open allowing you to specify the source and destination to be used for the clone operation. Simply fill-in these details, and click the Clone button shown in Figure 5-12, and a repository clone operation will be initiated.

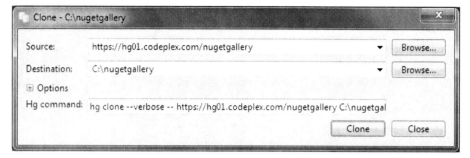

Figure 5-12. Clone a remote Mercurial repository using TortoiseHg in Windows Explorer.

Your computer will now spend some CPU cycles on fetching all changesets from the remote repository, but upon successful completion of the operation, you should end up with a local repository containing everything you need to get started with your own local NuGet Gallery implementation.

Configuring IIS and Permissions

Next, you'll need to configure IIS to run the services and web site. We'll guide you through the process of doing so. The Orchard-based NuGet Gallery is a two-tier application, meaning it has a separate backend containing services and a frontend consuming those and using them in a web application.

If you look closely to the cloned repository of the Orchard-based NuGet Gallery, you'll notice a \Services folder and a \Website folder. You'll have to use these and configure them as separate IIS web sites:

- Create an IIS website pointing to the \Services\GalleryServer\src\Gallery.Server folder. We will refer to this tier of the application in this chapter using the term *backend*.

- Create an IIS web site pointing to the \Website\src\Orchard.Web folder. We will refer to this tier of the application in this chapter using the term *frontend*.

Also make sure the application pool for these two web sites is running in .NET 4.0 Integrated Mode, as shown in Figure 5-13.

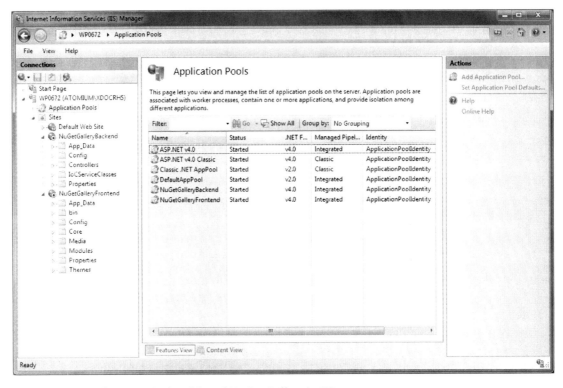

Figure 5-13. *Configure an Orchard-based NuGet Gallery in IIS.*

Next step is to grant the application pool identity write permissions to the App_Data directory for these applications. If the App_Data directory is not yet present, now would be a good time to create one. To set permissions on these directories, right-click the App_Data folder, and select Edit Permissions, as demonstrated in Figure 5-14.

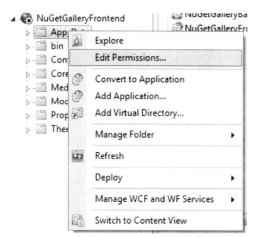

Figure 5-14. Edit permissions on App_Data folders in IIS.

When you click Edit Permissions, you'll be presented with the classic Windows Explorer folder permissions dialog. Navigate to the Security tab, and click Edit. In the newly opened dialog, you can now click Add to add the IIS_IUSRS group to the list. This special user group contains the IIS application pool identities for the local machine. Select the IIS_IUSRS group in the list, and make sure the Write permission is checked in the list "Permissions for IIS_IUSRS," as illustrated in Figure 5-15. You can now close all dialogs by clicking the OK button and repeat these steps for the other tier of the NuGet Gallery applications. Both the backend and the frontend need to be configured this way, so make sure both of them have an App_Data folder with the same permissions explained in this paragraph.

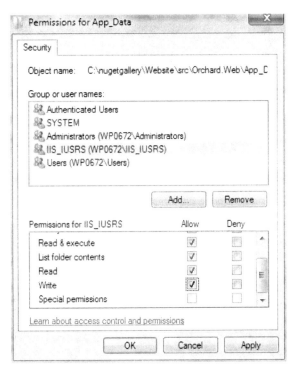

Figure 5-15. Give the IIS application pool identity group write permissions on the App_Data folder.

Finally, the frontend needs one additional security configuration: the application pool identity needs write permissions on the \Media folder as well.

Configuring Databases

While reading the previous section, you might have been thinking about data storage when we said you should create an App_Data folder if not presented, as this would be the default location for an ASP.NET application to store its data.

The Orchard-based NuGet Gallery is configurable in such way you can choose where you want to store its data. As such, you can create the required databases in a location of your choice, for instance on one of the dedicated database servers within your organization.

You will need to create two SQL Server databases, one for the frontend and one for the backend. Once you are connected to the SQL Server instance of your choosing—we use our local SQL Server instance represented by the dot (.) notation—you can right-click Databases in the Object Explorer window, and select New Database from the contextual menu, as shown in Figure 5-16.

■ **Tip** If you want to set up this NuGet Gallery on your local machine (to impress your manager and convince him of the usefulness for instance), and you don't have Microsoft SQL Server installed on your system, you can download the free SQL Server Express Edition from www.microsoft.com/sqlserver/en/us/editions/express.aspx.

Figure 5-16. *Create a new database in Microsoft SQL Server.*

We will call our frontend and backend databases NuGetGalleryFrontend and NuGetGalleryBackend respectively, similar to the name of our application pools. Don't forget to create a SQL Server login for the application pool identities and grant them the dbowner role for their respective databases, as shown in Figure 5-17.

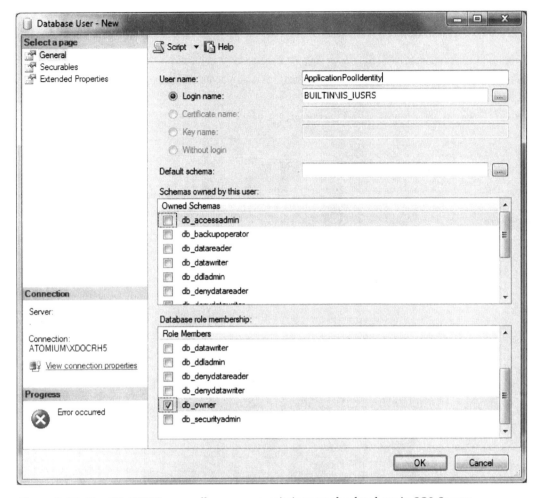

Figure 5-17. Give IIS_IUSRS group db_owner permissions on the database in SQL Server.

Build and Configure

We now have set up the web server and database storage for our advanced NuGet Gallery, but we still can't run the application. We first need to make sure that our web application is aware of the location you choose for data storage, both for the frontend and backend services.

Let's start with the backend. If you've used SQL Server and deployed the frontend to http://localhost:80, you don't have to change any application settings, because these defaults are supported out of the box. Otherwise, you'll have to manually adjust the Config\AppSettings.config.default file to reflect your needs:

- Make sure the FrontendWebsiteRoot key has a value equal to the URL (including a trailing slash!) of your frontend deployment. In our case, we used http://localhost:80/, or http://localhost/ which is the default setting.

- Make sure the MigratorProvider is set to either SqlServer when using SQL Server databases, or SqlServerCe for SQL Server CE databases.

Still on the backend, you'll have to tell it where to find its database. And where else would you define this than in the Config\ConnectionStrings.config.default? As such, make sure the connection string points correctly to your backendDb. In our sample, we created the NuGetGalleryBackend database on our localhost, so our connection string looks like Listing 5-4.

Listing 5-4. *Setting the Backend Connection String for the Orchard-Based NuGet Gallery Services*

```
<connectionStrings>
  <add name="GalleryFeedEntities"
      connectionString="Data Source=(local);Initial Catalog=NuGetGalleryBackend;Integrated↵
Security=SSPI"
      providerName="System.Data.SqlClient" />
</connectionStrings>
```

Now, the NuGet Gallery backend services are fully configured and ready to be built. Navigate to the directory where you cloned the entire remote repository, and find the ClickToBuildRelease.bat file in the \Services folder. Double-click it, and after successful completion of the command, you can test the backend by navigating to the FeedService, and query it for Packages. If the batch file did not work as expected, you might need to verify whether the MSBuild command is defined in the PATH environment variable. If you have Visual Studio installed, this should be the case. If you're running this on the server, you might want to build it locally and copy it over to the server when you're finished, unless you are fine with having MSBuild on your web server.

In our sample, the backend was deployed on the localhost on port 180, so the FeedService is located at the following location: http://localhost:180/FeedService.svc/Packages. Note that the first hit might take a minute or two as it is populating the database. Testing the backend FeedService packages query should give you the result shown in Figure 5-18.

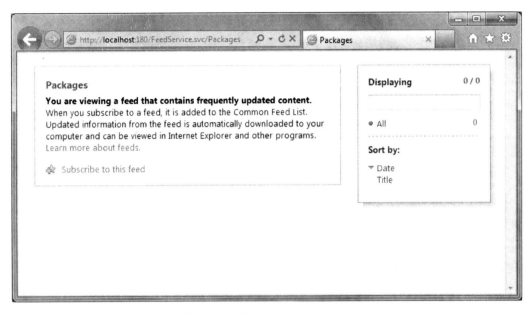

Figure 5-18. Testing the advanced NuGet Gallery backend

Next up, the frontend! If you followed the instructions for the backend carefully, you already created a frontend database and SQL Server login that has the db_owner role on that database. Great! So let's build this application as well, by double-clicking the ClickToBuild.cmd listed in the \Website folder of your local clone directory. After a couple of minutes, the command should complete, and we can go on with the next phase of the frontend setup.

Navigate to the frontend URL, http://localhost/ in our case, and you should be presented with an Orchard setup screen, as shown in Figure 5-19. Provide a username and password to be used as administrator account, and make sure you provide the connection string to an existing SQL Server frontend database, NuGetGalleryFrontend in our sample. Click Finish Setup, and wait for the Orchard setup process to complete.

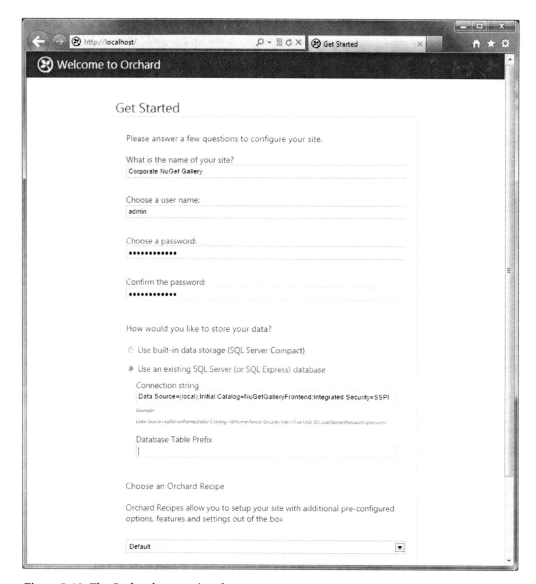

Figure 5-19. The Orchard setup wizard

After completing the setup process, you'll be automatically redirected to the Orchard home page, as shown in Figure 5-20.

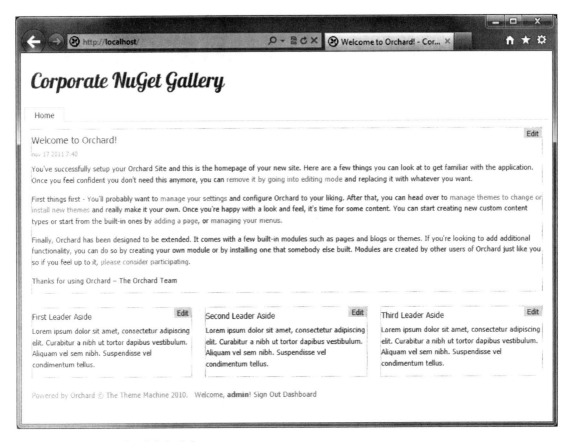

Figure 5-20. The Orchard default home page

The next step is to go to the management section of your brand new Orchard installation. To do so, click the Dashboard link at the bottom of the page. Click the Users tab, and edit the administrator user you just created during the setup process by clicking "edit" next to the username. You can now provide the user with a valid e-mail address, as shown in Figure 21, and save the account information by clicking the Save button.

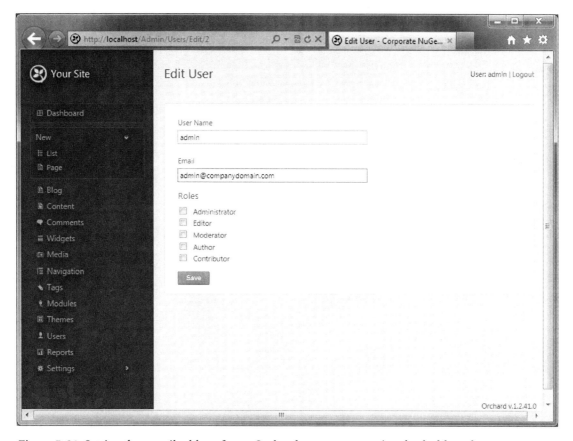

Figure 5-21. Setting the e-mail address for an Orchard user account using the dashboard

Next, you need to navigate to the Modules tab and enable the Orchard.Gallery module in the Features section (see Figure 5-22). You'll find this feature under the Packaging section. Click the "enable" link to enable this feature and its dependencies.

Packaging

Gallery	Disable	Orchard.Gallery	Enable	Package Updates	Disable
Depends on: Packaging commands		Depends on: Email Messaging, Lucene, Profile, Reviews, Search,		Depends on: Gallery	

Packaging	Disable	Packaging commands	Disable
		Depends on: Packaging	

Figure 5-22. Enabling the Orchard.Gallery feature in the Orchard Modules administrative section

If all went well, you should see a list of green notifications at the top of the page, indicating which modules got installed and enabled, as shown in Figure 5-23.

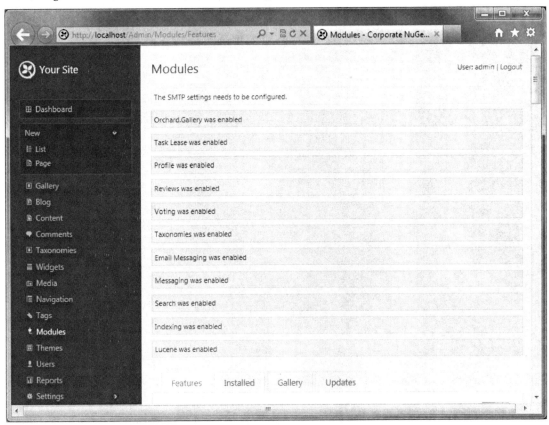

Figure 5-23. Enabling the Orchard.Gallery feature completed successfully

This is an excellent illustration of the true power of a content management system (CMS) such as Orchard. It comes with a very easy-to-use dashboard, providing you with tons of options and numerous features and configuration options. There's no need to dive into code (although you still can of course); just pick the modules you want from the Orchard gallery, enable them, and start using them immediately.

While you are getting the hang of using Orchard, let's do something about that default home page, which probably isn't what you expected when we referred to http://nuget.org as an example. Again, all you need to do is select a *theme* (a design template for the entire application). Navigate to the Themes section of the dashboard, and find the NuGetGallery theme (see Figure 5-24). Click the Set Current button to activate this theme and apply it to your entire application.

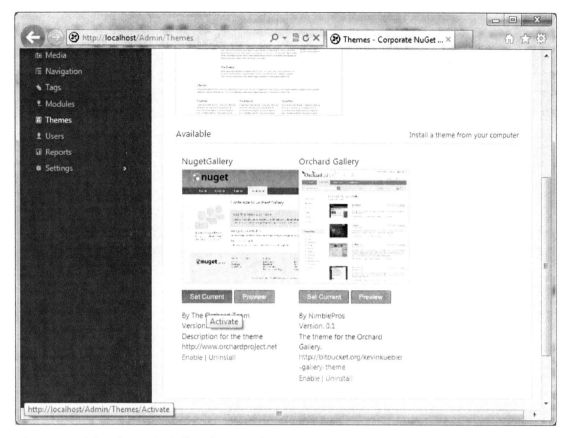

Figure 5-24. *Select the NuGetGallery theme and activate it.*

If you now navigate to the application's home page, you should see the same look and feel as if you were on the official NuGet Gallery itself. This is illustrated in Figure 5-25.

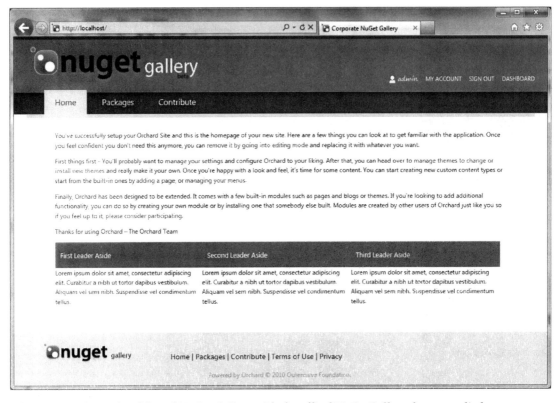

Figure 5-25. The Orchard-based NuGet Gallery with the offical NuGetGallery theme applied

Great! We are almost there! All that's left now is to hook up the NuGet Gallery backend with our brand new Orchard frontend. To do so, navigate to the dashboard, and find the Settings ➤ General page, where you will see various configuration options for the Gallery Server.

This is where you'll need to define the Gallery Server service root, by providing it with the backend URL, in our case `http://localhost:180/` (note the trailing slash!). Additionally, you'll also need to provide the Gallery Feed URL, in our case `http://localhost:180/FeedService.svc`.

Below those settings, you'll also find some extra tweaking points for your NuGet Gallery setup, such as expiration dates for preregistered package IDs. A preregistered package ID is automatically created the moment you push a package to the feed, before you publish it. Therefore, you reserved that specific package ID for your pushed package, once you decide to publish it. By default, you can have an unlimited set of preregistered package IDs for an unlimited amount of time, but if you want, you can limit this and even specify a number of days a user should receive a warning prior to package expiration. Don't forget to save your settings. The Gallery Server settings screen is shown in Figure 5-26.

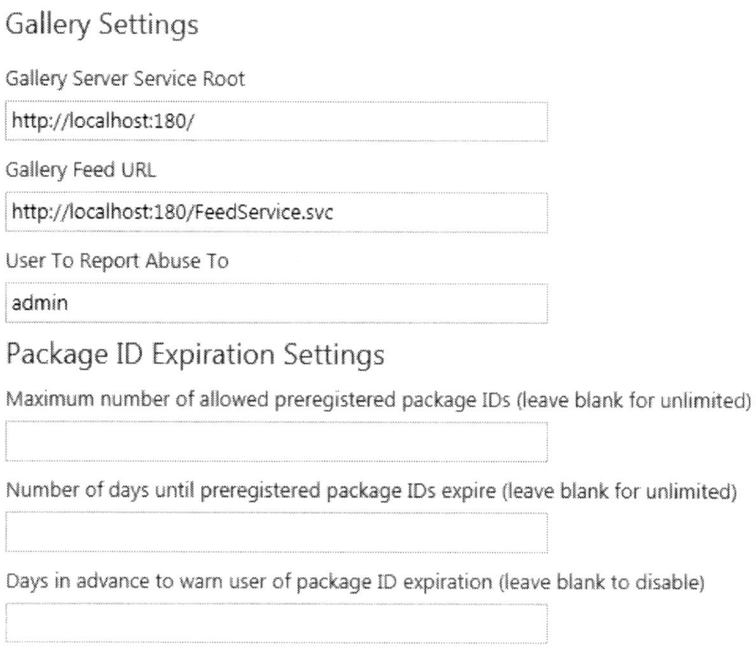

Gallery Settings

Gallery Server Service Root

```
http://localhost:180/
```

Gallery Feed URL

```
http://localhost:180/FeedService.svc
```

User To Report Abuse To

```
admin
```

Package ID Expiration Settings

Maximum number of allowed preregistered package IDs (leave blank for unlimited)

Number of days until preregistered package IDs expire (leave blank for unlimited)

Days in advance to warn user of package ID expiration (leave blank to disable)

Figure 5-26. Configuration options for the Orchard-based NuGet Gallery Server

There you are, running a fully featured corporate NuGet Gallery, at no development cost and with minimal setup effort. Once you configure SMTP settings and user registration options through the dashboard, users can register themselves and receive e-mail notifications from the application.

And the best part is that you have the source code: you can tweak and adjust in every possible way to make the application suit your needs and requirements.

However, while this NuGet Gallery is feature rich, you are still limited to a single feed. There are numerous reasons to host your own NuGet feed, so many that there are plenty enough reasons to host *multiple* NuGet feeds.

NuGet As a Service: MyGet

So far, you've learned how to set up a NuGet server based on a local directory or a file share, as well as using an open-source NuGet server implementation. But why do everything yourself if someone else can do it for you? At least, that's what we thought when creating MyGet.

MyGet is our attempt to create a hosted private NuGet feed. It offers everyone the possibility to create their own, private, filtered NuGet feeds for use in the Visual Studio Package Manager. It can contain packages from the official NuGet feed as well as private packages. In short, it supports all usage scenarios we've mentioned at the start of this chapter (in the "Why Host Your Own NuGet Feed?" section). And it's easy to set up. Plus, it's free.

This section will take you through some characteristics of MyGet and show you some features that you would have to develop yourself when using one of the solutions mentioned earlier in this chapter. But let's start with the beginning: where do you find MyGet and how can you create a NuGet feed?

Creating a NuGet feed on MyGet

Before being able to create a NuGet feed, you have to sign in to MyGet. The MyGet web site can be found at www.myget.org. If you navigate to this web site using your browser of choice, you'll be greeted with the MyGet front page shown in Figure 5-27. Because we envisioned MyGet to be easy to use, we have chosen not to provide a user registration page. Locate the Sign In link in the top-right corner, or find the big green "Get started for free" button to log in to MyGet.

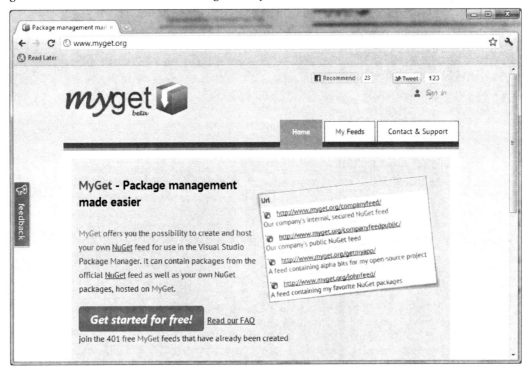

Figure 5-27. The MyGet front page after navigating to www.myget.org

The sign-in page does not require you to have a login for MyGet. Instead, it cleverly uses one of many external identity providers, such as Windows Live ID, Google Accounts, Facebook, Yahoo!, and OpenID. Simply click the logo of your identity provider of choice, and you will immediately be signed in to MyGet.

At your very first login, you will be prompted for some additional information, as shown in Figure 5-28. MyGet will ask you for your name, e-mail address, and a username/password combination. We advise you to immediately choose a username and password on this page, as that combination will be used to authenticate against your private NuGet feeds when working with the NuGet Visual Studio Extension or the Package Manager Console.

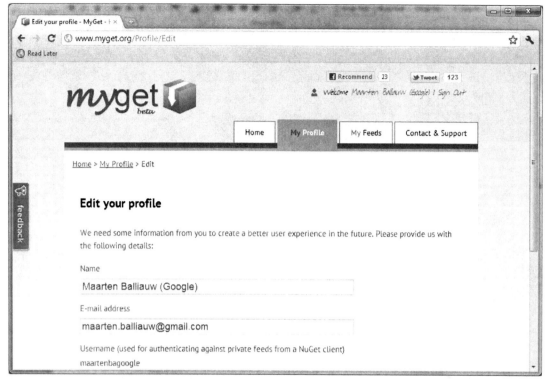

Figure 5-28. Some additional profile information is asked for the first time you sign in to MyGet.

After updating and saving your profile, you're ready to go. Creating a NuGet feed using MyGet can be done through the My Feeds tab that you can find in the top menu of the web site. After clicking it, you will be taken to a list of feeds you own or have access to. Of course, this list will be empty initially.

You can create a feed using the "Create a feed" button. This will take you to the page shown in Figure 5-29. A feed, of course, requires a name, which has to be unique across MyGet. Popular feed names like myget, nuget, and pronuget (the name of our book) may be taken by someone else, just as is the case with domain names on the Internet. Name your feed carefully: you cannot change the feed name later. The second piece of information asked for is a short description for the feed. This can be anything you want to identify the feed in your list of feeds.

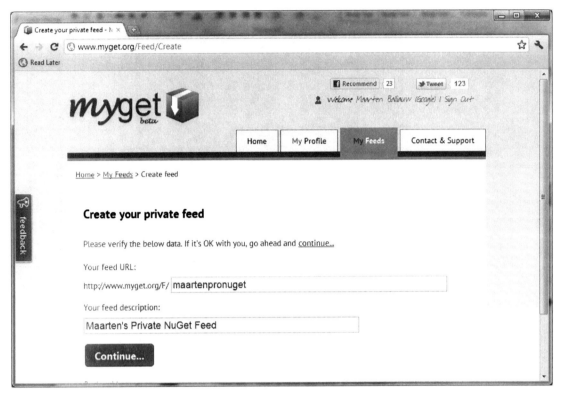

Figure 5-29. Create your own NuGet feed.

After clicking the "Continue" button, you'll be taken to the list of packages hosted in this feed. As Figure 5-30 shows, this page contains three tabs (Packages, Feed details, and Feed security).

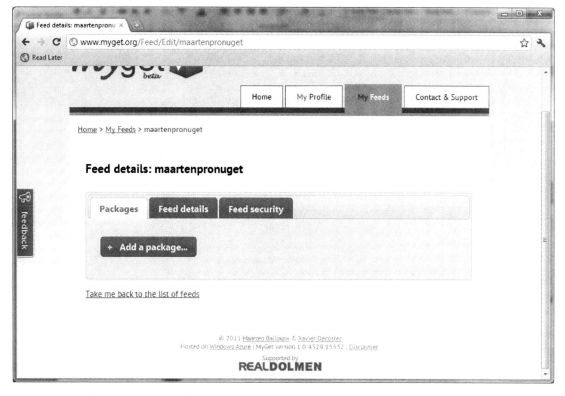

Figure 5-30. The overview page of your newly created NuGet feed

The Packages tab contains the list of packages you are hosting on this feed. Obviously, this list is empty when you've just created a new feed. The "Feed details" tab contains all details about your feed: the feed URL that you can add to the list of package sources in Visual Studio, your API key (which can be used to push packages from the NuGet command line or from NuGet Package Explorer), and some other information. The last tab, "Feed security," contains all settings related to who may access your feed and what privileges one has on the feed.

On the "Feed details" tab, find the URL to your NuGet feed. My feed URL is
http://www.myget.org/F/maartenpronuget/. As shown in Figure 5-31, you can simply register this feed in the NuGet Visual Studio Extension's list of available package sources. After doing so, you can consume your own NuGet feed in the same manner as you would any other NuGet feed: search packages, install and uninstall packages, and so on.

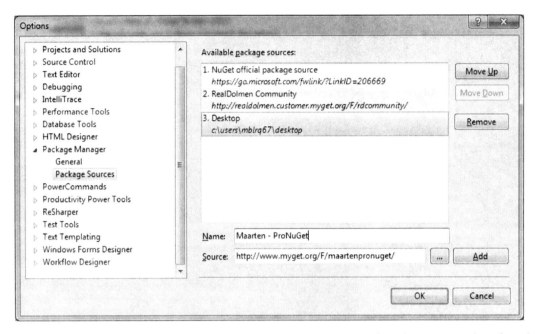

Figure 5-31. Adding a NuGet feed hosted on MyGet to the NuGet Visual Studio Extension list of available package sources

Congratulations, you've now created your first NuGet feed using MyGet!

Mirroring Packages from the Official NuGet Package Source

When we first developed MyGet, our idea was nothing more than a web application that enables you to mirror packages from the official NuGet package source. There are plenty of reasons for doing this: it allows you to essentially filter the official NuGet package source and only displays packages you've selected to be on your feed. If you want to provide your developers access to approved packages that have been tested and validated for use in your company's software projects, it's easy to create a NuGet feed containing only those packages.

Packages on the official NuGet package source are maintained by their respective package authors and not by Microsoft or any other party. This means external people have control over dependencies used in your software projects! Whenever a package author updates a NuGet package or when the package is removed from the official NuGet package source, your developers may have difficulties consuming existing NuGet package references. The easy way to solve this is to mirror packages from the official NuGet package source. And that's what we'll do in this section.

After logging in to your MyGet account, navigate to the list of packages in a feed you've created. If you haven't created a feed yet, start by creating one using the steps outlined in the previous section of this chapter. After clicking the "More" button next to your MyGet feed, you'll see the list of packages on your feed under the Packages tab. Obviously, there will be no packages to list when you have an empty feed.

Clicking the "Add a package" button will take you to the screen shown in Figure 5-32. This screen has several options to add packages to your MyGet feed. We'll be using the From NuGet option, which allows you to add a package from the official NuGet package source. The other options, "From an uploaded package" and "From packages.config," will be demonstrated later in this chapter.

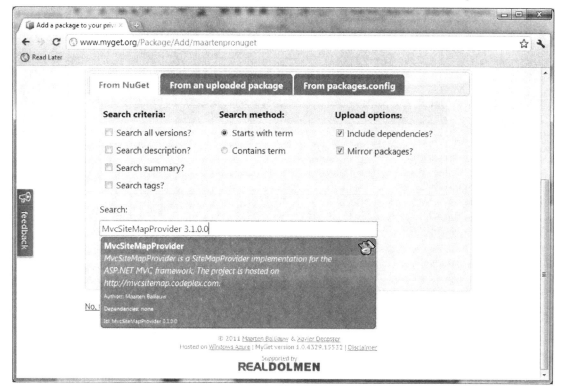

Figure 5-32. Adding a package from the official NuGet package source

■ **Note** The "From packages.config" tab allows you to upload the `packages.config` file from a project you've created and will add multiple packages from the official NuGet package source at once. This is by far the quickest way to mirror a series of packages that are required in your project(s).

The From NuGet tab offers a rich search interface: packages from the official NuGet package source can be searched for using a number of criteria. For example, you can choose to search only in the latest versions of packages or in earlier versions. You can search in title, summary, and tags, as well as define how the search should be performed ("Starts with term" or "Contains term").

In the Search box, start typing a keyword related to the package you want to mirror onto your MyGet feed, or simply enter the package identifier if you know it. After a second, search results will come in, and you'll be able to select a package to add to your MyGet feed. Make sure to check the "Mirror packages" check box and click the Add button to add a package to your MyGet feed. In Figure 5-32, we've searched for the package identifier `MvcSiteMapProvider` and clicked the Add button.

■ **Warning** By default, the "Mirror packages" check box is unchecked. This means that the package metadata, but not the package itself, will be added to your MyGet feed. To ensure the package itself is copied onto your MyGet feed, we recommended checking the "Mirror packages" check box. This ensures a package author deleting a package from the official NuGet package source does not affect your MyGet feed.

In the previous chapter, we showed you how to contribute and publish packages to the official NuGet package source. While doing so is interesting for open source projects, you may not want to publish the frameworks developed by your company or other intellectual property to the official NuGet package source. Everyone can consume packages from that feed, which means your intellectual property would be on the streets.

A solution to that would be hosting your own NuGet feed, something we've described throughout this chapter. Using MyGet, you can combine mirrored packages from the official NuGet package source with your own NuGet packages. All gathered in the same NuGet feed, *your* NuGet feed.

As with the official NuGet package source, adding packages to a feed can be done using a web interface and the NuGet command line. The next section will show you how to do this.

Adding Custom NuGet Packages Through the MyGet Web Interface

Just like adding a package from the official NuGet package source to your MyGet feed, adding a custom NuGet package is done through MyGet's web interface at www.myget.org. After logging in to your MyGet account, navigate to the list of packages in a feed you've created. You'll see the list of packages on your feed under the Packages tab.

Click the "Add a package" button to go to the screen where packages can be added. Navigate to the "From an uploaded package" tab, and you'll see the screen shown in Figure 5-33.

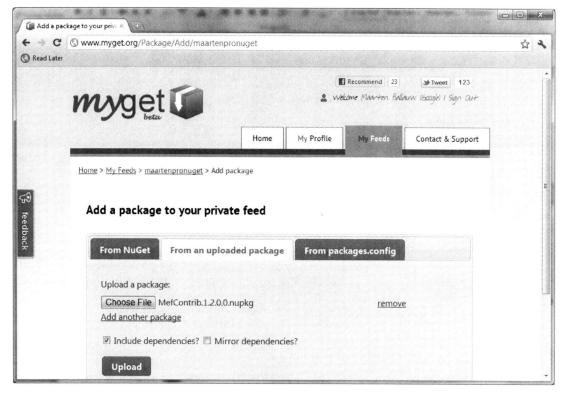

Figure 5-33. Adding a custom package to a MyGet feed using the web interface

This screen allows you to select one or multiple packages from your local hard disk. Optionally, dependencies can be included as well as mirrored. For example, if you create a package that depends on one or more packages from the official NuGet package source, checking the "Include dependencies" check box will add those packages to your MyGet feed, next to the packages you are uploading. Optionally, these packages can also be mirrored, as we explained in the previous section of this chapter.

Clicking the Upload button will send the packages you've selected to upload to your MyGet feed. When the upload succeeds, your feed will show all packages you've added previously as well as the any packages just uploaded.

Adding Custom NuGet Packages Using the NuGet Command Line

When doing a lot of work with NuGet, you may prefer to use the NuGet command line to push packages to your MyGet feed. Also, when automating package creation and publishing, for example, on a build server, using the NuGet command line may come in handy. This section will show you where to find the MyGet API key and how to push a package to a MyGet feed using that key.

The first step in pushing a NuGet package to your MyGet feed using the NuGet command line will be obtaining an API key. After logging in to MyGet and navigating to the "Feed details" tab, as shown in Figure 5-34, you'll find all your feed details: the URL to add in the NuGet Visual Studio Extension and your MyGet API key. By the time this book is in your hands, this tab will also display all information related to integrating MyGet and SymbolSource.org (refer to Chapter 4 to learn more about SymbolSource).

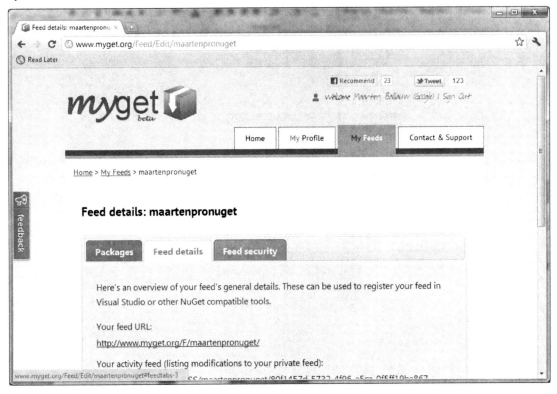

Figure 5-34. *The Feed Details tab displaying all sorts of integration information*

The API key displayed on the "Feed details" tab is 82bccc78-c428-42c6-a568-42760994b077 (in our case—yours will be different). As you saw in Chapter 4, most NuGet commands support the -Source switch. The nuget push command supports this switch as well and supports pushing packages to feeds other than the default official NuGet package source. The following command pushes a package named ProNuGetStringExtensions to the pronuget feed on MyGet, using the API key obtained from the "Feed details" tab:

```
nuget push ProNuGetStringExtensions.1.0.nupkg 82bccc78-c428-42c6-a568-42760994b077 -Source
http://www.myget.org/F/pronuget
```

Obviously, this API key can also be used in the NuGet Package Explorer (NPE) to publish NuGet packages directly from the user interface to any MyGet feed on which you are allowed to publish packages.

Applying Different Security Settings to Your Feed

One of the reasons for setting up your own NuGet feed listed at the beginning of this chapter was security. "Security" is a large word with many nuances and possible scenarios, many which are supported by MyGet. For example, some users can manage users and packages, while some can only manage packages, and others can only consume packages. This section will guide you through MyGet's security model and show you how to set up security and permissions in MyGet.

MyGet's Security Model

MyGet features a rich security model for your feeds. You, as a feed owner, always have the richest set of permissions possible. You can assign privileges to specific users also known on MyGet as well as to the anonymous Everyone user. Table 5-2 lists all possible permissions and what they mean.

Table 5-2. MyGet's Permissions Explained

Permission	Description	Requires a MyGet Account?	Requires Username/Password to Consume the Feed?
Owns this feed	This privilege can only be assigned to the feed owner, who can manage the feed, users and packages in the feed.	Yes	No*
Can manage users and all packages for this feed	This privilege can be assigned to any user registered on MyGet and allows the user to manage all packages and all user permissions on the feed.	Yes	No*
Can manage all packages for this feed	This privilege can be assigned to any user registered on MyGet and allows the user to manage all packages on the feed.	Yes	No*
Can contribute own packages to this feed	This privilege can be assigned to any user registered on MyGet and allows the user to publish packages on the feed. Users with this privilege will only be able to manage their own packages. This security setting is identical to the security settings on the official NuGet package source.	Yes	No*
Can consume this feed	This privilege can be assigned to any user registered on MyGet and to anonymous users. It allows the user to consume packages.	No	No*

Permission	Description	Requires a MyGet Account?	Requires Username/Password to Consume the Feed?
Has no access to this feed	This privilege can be assigned to any user registered on MyGet and to anonymous users. It denies access to the feed.	Not applicable	Yes

Unless Everyone is assigned the "has no access to this feed" privilege

All of these privileges can be combined at will to create your unique security configuration. A common scenario is the so-called "private feed" scenario. You want to create a private feed to which only you can add and consume packages. Configuring this one is easy and consists of the following list of privileges configured:

- You: Owns this feed (this cannot be changed)
- Everyone: Has no access to this feed

Now, imagine you want to keep these settings and give some colleagues the privilege to consume packages after logging in using their MyGet usernames and passwords. The following configuration should do the trick:

- You: Owns this feed (this cannot be changed)
- Colleague X: Can consume this feed
- Colleague Y: Can consume this feed
- Everyone: Has no access to this feed

If you want to allow Colleague X to manage all packages on this feed, you can assign that user the "can manage all packages for this feed" privilege. Optionally, the "can manage users and all packages for this feed" privilege will enable thus user to manage user permissions as well.

Another interesting scenario may be mimicking the official NuGet package source: everyone can publish and manage their own packages on the feed, while everyone can consume every other user's packages. This can be easily configured using the following permission set:

- You: Owns this feed (this can not be changed)
- Everyone: Can contribute own packages to this feed

Inviting Other Users to Your Feed

To give other users certain privileges, they have to be invited to your MyGet feed. This can be done in the "Feed security" tab for your feed. This tab lists all users that currently have access to your feed as well as a list of pending users, that is, users who have been invited to your feed but haven't confirmed yet. An example of the "Feed security" tab is shown in Figure 5-35.

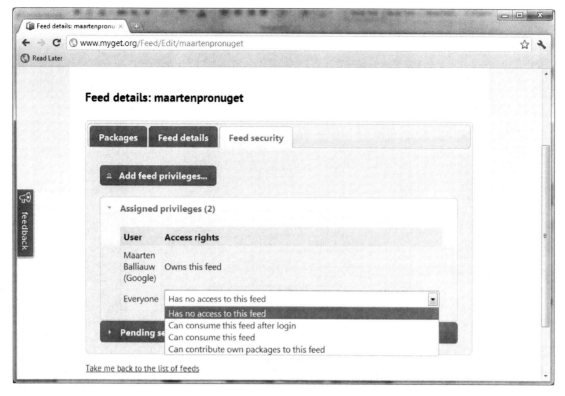

Figure 5-35. The Feed security tab enables you to assign specific privileges to other users

The "Add feed privileges" button will open a dialog that allows you to invite a user to your feed by entering an e-mail address. You can immediately assign the correct privilege to this user to ensure the correct privilege will be assigned once the user confirms the invitation. Figure 5-36 shows an invitation for maarten@maartenballiauw.be to whom, once the invitation is confirmed, the "can manage all packages for this feed" privilege will be assigned.

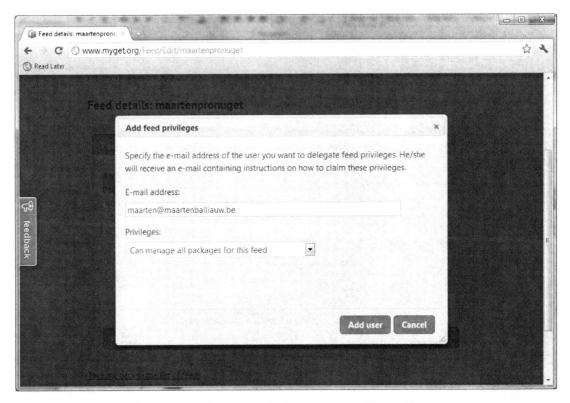

Figure 5-36. Inviting other users to a feed and assigning them a specific privilege

Once you've clicked the "Add user" button, an e-mail will be sent to the e-mail address provided. The user being added to your feed will receive this e-mail and can choose to claim the privileges you've assigned or to simply ignore the invitation. An example of such e-mail is shown in Figure 5-37. Once the user confirms this e-mail by clicking the link provided in the e-mail body, the user will be granted access to your feed with the privileges chosen in the "Add feed privileges" dialog.

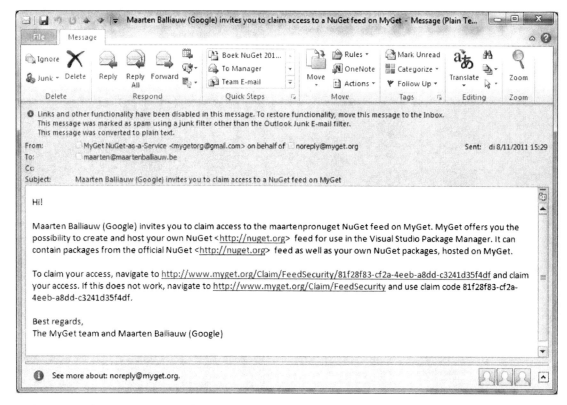

Figure 5-37. *The invitation e-mail sent to a user whenever you grant specific privileges on your private feed*

Managing User Permissions

After inviting a user to your feed, you can change the privileges previously assigned. For example, a user who could previously only consume packages may now be granted the privilege of contributing packages to your feed. Also, a user who could previously manage all packages on the feed can be locked down into a privilege where only consuming packages, not managing them, is permitted.

The "Feed security" tab for your feed lists all users that currently have access to your feed as well as a list of users that have been invited to your feed but haven't confirmed their privileges yet. The drop-down list next to a user's name allows you to modify the currently assigned privilege (see Figure 5-38).

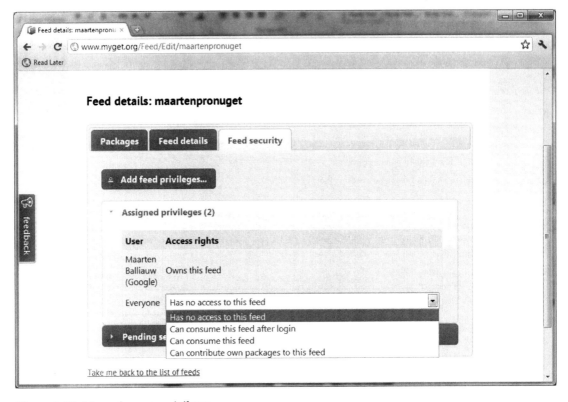

Figure 5-38. Managing user privileges

■ **Note** When you're assigning the "has no access to this feed" privilege to a certain user, the user will be removed from the list of users. If, afterward, you want to assign a different privilege to this user, the user should be sent a new invitation using the "Add feed privileges" button.

Summary

In this chapter, we've gone further than simply consuming packages and publishing packages to the official NuGet package source. We've shown you a variety of reasons to why you may want to have *your own* NuGet feed.

The reasons for hosting your own NuGet feed were as simple as filtering the official NuGet package source and mirroring packages from it and as complex as advanced scenarios like security, privacy, and protecting intellectual property.

We've covered several options of creating your own NuGet feed. The easiest solution was using a folder or network file share to distribute packages. The NuGet.Server package, the NuGet Gallery, and the Orchard Gallery allowed you to expose NuGet feeds and packages through a URL and allow you to expose your own NuGet feed to the Internet or intranet if you want.

Finally, you've seen how MyGet, a hosted private NuGet feed solution, allows you to set up your own NuGet feed in seconds and provides a rich set of security options to configure your feed according to your needs.

In this chapter, the fun began—we've gone beyond consuming and creating packages into hosting your own NuGet feed. The next chapters will go even further and explore some scenarios for integrating NuGet in your software development process as well as how to leverage NuGet in other scenarios than pure package management.

CHAPTER 6

Continuous Package Integration

Having read the previous chapters of this book, you have now reached the point where you can start supporting processes in your development environment using NuGet. You know how to create and publish packages and you have also learned how to set up your own NuGet feeds. Great! Now, let's fit the pieces together and streamline our development processes, because from a business point of view, that's one of the main reasons to introduce a package manager into a development organization.

You may already be using some common concepts and techniques to mitigate the risks of development, such as continuous integration and unit testing, perhaps even integration testing and automated deployments, or maybe a fully streamlined continuous delivery process. If you don't do any of these already, now would be a very good time to start.

This chapter will demonstrate how you can use NuGet in your development environment to support these processes. We'll focus primarily on supporting good practices for the application life cycle. We'll discuss whether or not NuGet packages belong in source control and look at the options available to facilitate both scenarios. Ensuring packages flow from development to release without modification or rebuild is a typical scenario that deserves some attention as well; we'll call it *package promotion* later in this chapter.

Using a No Commit Strategy

When it comes to source control, it is very interesting to see how development teams approach external software dependencies, or software dependencies in general. Many of us use a dedicated folder to store them in source control, often called `ReferencedAssemblies`, `References`, `Lib`, or similar. This is a well-known strategy for keeping solution-level software dependencies close to the source code.

Many developers have been applying this good practice for years, yet there is no single convention on how the folder should be named or structured or where it should be located. This kind of information is typically defined in the corporation's naming conventions and guidelines documentation. It is strange to see a multitude of different guidelines, often with variations in underlying reasons, solving a common problem we all share. NuGet offers an opportunity to have a standardized location and name for those references by using the default `$(SolutionDir)\Packages` folder. Even though this default can be overridden, it is a step into a common direction.

In addition to this rather cosmetic annoyance (something many developers experienced when trying to figure out conventions while onboarding a new project or team) you might also experience issues with your version control system. Team Foundation Server (TFS) is a common victim of rants against its merging behavior for binary files. Ever had the task of upgrading a dependency and trying to check it into TFS source control, only to be prompted by a dialog stating that TFS did not see any changes and leaving you with no other option but to undo your pending changes for that binary file?

Although blaming a tool is always easier than questioning the process, you have to realize that a version control system is not designed to version binary files but rather to track textual files such as source code. Even though some distributed version control systems (DVCSs) are capable of doing so, a developer should be annoyed by such behavior because he's using a different source control system.

The bigger issue that comes with storing all those software dependencies in source control is the amount of disk space required to store all those files, which are often duplicated in multiple project repositories. What's the point in storing NHibernate version 2.2.0 in source control, next to all of your 37 solutions? All of them are the same. What kind of history will you keep in your version control system for these files? You won't change them yourself, so all you keep track of is that, at a certain point in time, you added, removed, or changed the version of a dependency. The amount of useful information, in bytes, is almost nil compared to the amount of storage required for the dependency itself. Also, do the binaries for these external dependencies belong in your source code repository? Is the actual binary a requirement for your software? Or would an identifier for it, such as a name and version number, be enough to rebuild a specific version of your software?

In NuGet terms, all you need is a package ID and a package version. The information stored in the packages.config file in your project contains everything you need to manage your dependencies. You store it in a version control system (VCS) after all.

Does this mean that you can choose to no longer commit packages into your VCS? Yes! But before you do, you need to put in place a good process supporting this scenario. It's not a lot of work; it's not over-complicated, and it's quite fast to set up.

Keep in mind that we don't want to break any other established good practices by banning NuGet packages from source control. If you want to keep storing those packages next to your sources, that's fine. It's your choice. We don't want to force you in any way. But if you do want to get out of the comfort zone and gain insights into an alternative approach, you might want to give it a try and see for yourself. In fact, we want to make sure that every single build you do, based on a given revision or changeset of your sources, *even without* the required NuGet packages in source control, always produces the same output. The end result of building with or without NuGet packages in source control must be the same. The no-commit strategy outlined in the following sections explains how to achieve this while not storing those dependencies in source control.

Source Control Layout

As stated before, NuGet has a default setting as to where packages are being located relative to the Visual Studio solution. Depending on the VCS tool you use, there are various ways to keep out NuGet packages from your source control repository. We'll stick to the default package installation directory of $(SolutionDir)\Packages. Conceptually, all you need to do is to ignore the entire directory, except for the repositories.config file.

The next sections will describe ignoring the $(SolutionDir)\Packages directory for some popular VCS tools such as Mercurial, Git, Subversion, and TFS.

Using Mercurial

When using the Mercurial (HG) source control system, you can add this directory to your ignore file. The Mercurial system uses a file called .hgignore in the root directory of a repository to control its behavior when it searches for files it is not currently tracking. More information about its syntax can be found at the following URL: http://www.selenic.com/mercurial/hgignore.5.html.

■ **Tip** If you're not familiar with this file, you can easily install a base `ignore` file for each of your projects by using NuGet (what else?). Simply install the HgIgnore NuGet package by running the `Install-Package HgIgnore` command in the NuGet Package Manager Console.

A good baseline for a `.hgignore` file when doing .NET development looks as follows:

```
syntax: glob

TestResults/*
*[Bb]in/
*[Dd]ebug/
*[Oo]bj/
*[Rr]elease/
*_[Rr]e[Ss]harper.*/
*.docstates
*.user
*.suo
*.xap
```

The preceding default is the one that is contained in version 1.4 of the HgIgnore NuGet package. However, this one still keeps track of the NuGet packages installed into the $(SolutionDir)\Packages folder, which is the default location defined by NuGet.

To make sure you only track the $(SolutionDir)\Packages\repositories.config file and no NuGet packages, you should add the following to your `.hgignore` file:

```
syntax: regex
^packages/(?!repositories.config)
```

Another way is to use the HgIgnoreNuGet package we created for you, available on the ProNuGet MyGet feed of this book. Install it by executing the following command in the NuGet Package Manager Console:

```
Install-Package HgIgnoreNuGet –Source http://www.myget.org/F/pronuget
```

Using Git

Git has a very similar concept for ignoring files and folders in source control by using a `.gitignore` file. You can define ignore settings globally, on a per-repository basis, or even on the folder level. Detailed information about how Git handles the `.gitignore` file can be found at the following URL: `http://help.github.com/ignore-files/`.

To ignore NuGet packages from being tracked by the Git VCS, you should put a `.ignore` file in the $(SolutionDir)\packages folder with the following contents:

```
# ignore everything in this folder
*

# do not ignore the .gitignore file
!.gitignore

# track the repositories.config file as well
!repositories.config
```

Using Subversion

Subversion (SVN) also supports ignoring files. However, it does not use any ignore file to achieve this. Instead, SVN works with *ignore lists* and SVN properties, which makes ignoring the $(SolutionDir)\packages folder, except the repositories.config file, a bit more cumbersome. We will use TortoiseSVN in our example, because it is the most popular SVN utility out there.

TortoiseSVN has Windows Explorer shell integration. When you open a local source folder with an SVN repository, you'll have SVN functionality readily available in the right-click contextual menu in Windows Explorer. When using SVN, you have to reverse your logic a bit. Instead of ignoring, we'll be adding only the files we want to the repository. To track the $(SolutionDir)\packages\repositories.config file, you simply right-click the $(SolutionDir)\packages folder in Windows Explorer and choose the Add option in the contextual menu that appears, as shown in Figure 6-1.

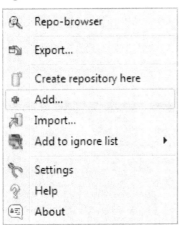

Figure 6-1. Adding an item to the SVN repository using TortoiseSVN

After doing so, you'll be prompted with a dialog where you'll have more options to specify what exactly you want to track in your SVN repository, as shown in Figure 6-2.

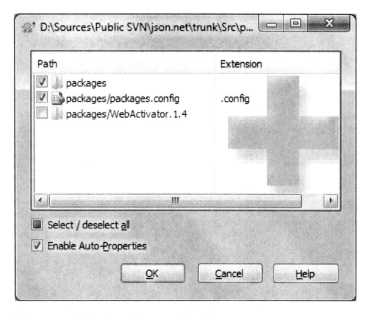

Figure 6-2. Selecting what to add to the SVN repository using TortoiseSVN

By only selecting the `$(SolutionDir)\packages` folder and the `repositories.config` file, we are not keeping track of everything else inside the package installation directory. All other contents will be treated as *unversioned*.

Using Team Foundation Server

TFS does not deal with ignore files as such. You have to think in terms of *workspaces* and *cloaking*, which might make you feel a bit like Darth Vader designing the Death Star. It is, however, quite easy to achieve the same result once you know where to look.

The no-commit strategy tells you not to commit any NuGet packages into your VCS, but as most people using TFS have mapped the entire branch to their workspace, this causes issues. Whenever we install a package through Visual Studio into a mapped workspace folder, Visual Studio tells TFS to add these files to source control. We want to keep track of the `repositories.config` file but not of the actual packages, which are, by default, being installed into the same `$(solutionDir)\packages` folder. Respecting NuGet's convention-over-configuration approach, we want to keep these defaults.

The workaround is actually pretty simple, albeit not that straightforward given the lousy UI that the workspace mapping dialog provides. If you thought you could only map folders, think again! You can map single files as well! Knowing this is half of the work, the other part is just setting the correct workspace mapping, as shown in Figure 6-3.

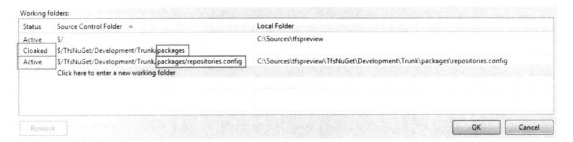

Figure 6-3. Cloaking the packages folder (except repositories.config) in a TFS workspace mapping

Trade-offs

The no-commit strategy is a specific approach to dealing—actually, to *not* dealing—with NuGet packages in source control. You might be wondering what the trade-offs are for this approach, or which benefits you get versus what kind of drawbacks to expect. As with everything, criticism is justified. Every approach has its benefits and its drawbacks. It's only a matter of picking the approach that works best for you in your situation.

Let's discuss the aspect of storage. One could say that *disk space* is cheap nowadays. And as a matter of fact, that is very true! If you have abundant storage, and you have no issue in duplicating those references over and over again, one could very easily agree with you. However, when you do care about disk space usage, which always is limited. Even when space is abundant, you might consider a no-commit strategy in any case. There is, however, one thing that is not cheap, and most likely will never be. It's usually left out of the picture in these kind of discussions—*time*. Time is expensive. In fact, we often find ourselves lacking time. Duplicating your binaries in source control not only requires disk space but relies on processing power as well. What happens if you branch your project? Are those binary files copied into the new branch? Or is your VCS only tracking the delta of those files? Do you know the answer to this question with absolute certainty, without looking it up on the Internet? As usual, it depends. It depends on the source control system you are using. Distributed version control systems (DVCSs), such as Git or Mercurial, tend to behave very different and centralized version control systems, such as TFS. The way your VCS will deal with those binaries during a branch (or merge) operation heavily depends on its (in)capability of tracking history on those files. For instance, TFS cannot track any differences for a .dll file, hence it cannot calculate its delta between two changes. Because of that, it will do a full copy of this file when it is branched. On the other hand, it will most likely not be able to merge changes for those files as well. You'll have to choose between the server version and your local version. This, again, takes time—time from the CPU tracking your sources, as well as time from the developers dealing with this kind of problem. Did we mention the time needed to perform backups of your source repository? Extrapolate the impact of time on your operational *costs*, and you might have found another compelling argument to convince your manager to consider another approach. Also, bear in mind that you don't want to track history on the actual content of those binary files, especially for external dependencies. What you really want to track is its metadata: the package ID and version information.

What would you say if centralizing your dependencies could save you time? Some teams already took a similar approach in the pre-NuGet era. They usually dedicated some network share to store all binary references and pointed all their projects to reference assemblies directly from that location. And the funny thing is, that, most of them are complaining about the time it takes to build. A significant delay is experienced when building your projects referencing binaries located somewhere on the network. This is obviously caused due to the amount of network traffic required to fetch those binaries during the build process.

NuGet, however, has built-in support for *caching* of NuGet packages. By default, every new package you fetch from a NuGet feed is cached on the local machine. This is true both for your development machine and for any build server that fetches a NuGet package. This is a significant benefit over the custom solution of referencing binaries directly from a network share. Instead of downloading the binaries upon every single compilation of your project, you now only need to download them once. Every subsequent build of your project referencing those exact same packages will not experience the delay caused by network traffic and will fetch those packages from the local cache.

In addition to the caching optimization, NuGet packages are also *compressed*. As we mentioned earlier, a NuGet package is an archive file, which you can uncompress using any popular archive tool out there, such as our favorite, 7Zip (`www.7-zip.org`). This is another optimization to increase the speed at which packages are downloaded, or in other words, decrease the amount of time required to fetch those NuGet packages.

So far, the trade-offs give the no-commit strategy the benefit of the doubt. A centralized location for your references, less disk space required to store them, and less time spent on tracking changes, dealing with conflicts, or across the wire generating unnecessary amounts of network traffic.

There is, however, one subtle dependency for this approach, which, at the same time, is its major drawback: a *network connection* to the package source is required. When the package source cannot be queried for the necessary packages required to build your project, compilation will fail—obviously because of the missing references. Note that NuGet only requires a connection to the package source when it can't find one of the referenced NuGet packages in its local cache. If we analyze the impact of this drawback, it is rather limited.

A build server needs a connection to your source repository as well, so on that level, your build server and source control repository share the same risk. If the package repository is on a different server than your sources, you just added another point of failure, because you now have two different connections that can fail. You have various options, though, for hosting your package repository: on the same server as your sources, on the build server (if you only have one), or even in the cloud (MyGet).

Your development machines share the exact same drawback as the build server. If a developer cannot build the solution because his laptop cannot connect to the NuGet repository, he has an issue. Developers don't like issues. Developers like good (or better) practices. The developer's workstation does *not* need to be connected with the NuGet package repository all the time though. As with the build server, the connection is only required if the developer is performing operations against the NuGet repository. The actions a developer typically performs against a NuGet repository are limited as well:

- Updating a NuGet dependency to a newer version

- Installing a new NuGet dependency

- Fetching a NuGet package that is not yet available in the local cache

- Pushing or publishing a package to the NuGet repository (shouldn't this be done as part of the release process, through an automated build for instance?)

If you analyze the use cases in the preceding list, you should notice that none of those actions a developer performs everyday. Preferably, these actions are well planned and at least have some kind of standardized process. Updating a NuGet dependency or installing a new one should not be an ad hoc decision. Neither is releasing a package to the repository, ready for consumption by everyone pointing to it. This is not something you will do when working on the train home.

The use case of fetching a NuGet package that is not yet available on the local cache of the developer's workstation, however, is one to keep in mind, because it might happen more often than you think. Imagine that someone else in your team upgraded a NuGet dependency or installed a new package, and you just got the latest version out of your VCS, eager to continue coding on that same train home. If you did not build your solution and fetched those new NuGet packages before leaving the office, you'd be in for a frustrating ride.

As such, we want to introduce a good practice: whenever you fetch the latest sources from your VCS, rebuild your solution, and make sure you have all packages required for compilation to succeed. There's an even better approach: *communicate* changes in project dependencies to the team! Make it part of the process of updating or installing new dependencies. If you don't have a process, then this *is* the minimum. Communication is key!

NuGet in its most *pure* form, the command line and its packages, do not rely on Visual Studio or PowerShell. If you check in the installed NuGet packages into your VCS, not a single developer is required to have any NuGet tooling installed on his system. That is good! We don't want to break this by requiring all developers to have this tooling installed on their systems. Even though it is very easy to get up and running fast, we consider it clean. When applying a no-commit strategy, we need to respect that. You'll read later on in this chapter how to do so.

Tracking Package Metadata

In a nutshell, all we want to have in our VCS is a trace of which dependencies we have and which versions we depend on. In NuGet terms, we're talking about package IDs and package versions. This happens to be exactly what is being stored into the `packages.config` files that NuGet produces when managing NuGet packages in a project or solution. Next to that, there's also the `repositories.config` file, by default located under the `$(solutionDir)\packages` folder. The `repositories.config` file, as its name suggests, keeps track of the different NuGet repositories that your solution projects rely on and is thus pointing to all `packages.config` files for a given solution. This is the kind of metainformation we want to keep track of.

The information contained within these files is everything you need to fetch the required NuGet packages before building your project. This form of tracking your dependencies is very elegant. Every VCS is able to deal with XML files, which are just simple textual files, so we benefit from the comparison and tracking capabilities. The few merge conflicts you might encounter on these files will be very easy to resolve, as you'll be able to actually compare the contents of these files.

The main reason that we do want to track this information lays in one of the most important principles behind the continuous integration process: *a given changeset in your VCS must always produce the same build output.* This effectively means there is no room for tampering with any file you get from source control before unleashing the compiler on it to produce its build output.

Another key practice is to only use *trusted sources* when continuously integrating your product on the build server. That's the only way to ensure that no one else has modified any input to the build server. The need for this practice is very obvious for your source code files, which are being tracked in your VCS: you can easily view the history of your sources and track changes made it to your build server. This is less obvious but equally as important for NuGet packages that come from outside your VCS. Make sure you can *trust* the NuGet package source you are using for your builds. This could result in limiting write permissions on the package source you are using, for instance a network share, an internal NuGet server, or a secured MyGet feed. This could also mean you want to track who modified what in your NuGet repository, through RSS activity feeds, for instance, or custom logging you implemented in your NuGet server. In addition, this could even mean that every project has its own NuGet repository, which again is very easy to achieve using MyGet.

■ **Tip** If you experience issues connecting to an internal VCS and an external NuGet repository, or vice versa, whether on the build server or local machine, you might need to add both of them to the Trusted Sites list in Internet Options. This is definitely the case when your development workstation or build server is behind a corporate proxy.

Another great opportunity resides in the fact that software dependencies are now easily discoverable in these XML configuration files. Any decent software factory wants to know the answers to the following questions at any time:

- Who is using version X of component Y?

- Which versions of component Z are in use (and which not)?

- What dependencies does application A have and to which versions?

Answering these questions typically requires someone to maintain a spreadsheet with dependency matrixes. What if you could just analyze these files with a tool and automate the generation of a *package dependency matrix?*

■ **Tip** In an attempt to automate dependency matrices, Xavier has built a proof-of-concept NuGet command line extension that allows you to analyze a TFS or filesystem repository for NuGet package dependencies. It is open source and available on GitHub (patches and feedback are much appreciated):

`https://github.com/xavierdecoster`
`/NuGet.Analyze.`

Try it out using the following commands in the NuGet Package Manager Console:

```
Install-Package NuGet.InstallCommandLineExtension
Install-CommandLineExtension NuGet.Analyze
```

Enabling Package Restoration

To perform continuous integration on your sources that depend on NuGet packages that are not in your VCS, we need restore those packages before building. This is what we call *continuous package integration.*

Up to version 1.5 of NuGet, this could be achieved using David Fowler's NuGetPowerTools package (`Install-Package NuGetPowerTools`), which you can find on the official NuGet.org gallery feed. Because of the success of this approach, the NuGet team decided to integrate this functionality in NuGet 1.6, making it unnecessary for you to reinstall the NuGetPowerTools NuGet package for every single solution.

An example process flow for continuous package integration can be found in Figure 6-4.

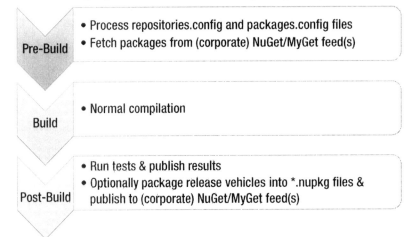

Figure 6-4. A basic continuous package integration process flowchart

The *enable package restore* feature built into NuGet 1.6 and above allows you to very easily set up the prebuild part of the workflow. To do so, right-click the solution node in Visual Studio's Solution Explorer, and click the Enable NuGet Package Restore option. Note that you need to have the NuGet Visual Studio Extension installed on your system. If you do, and you still don't see this menu item appear, you either already enabled this option, or you have a folder named .nuget in your solution directory. Figure 6-5 illustrates this option.

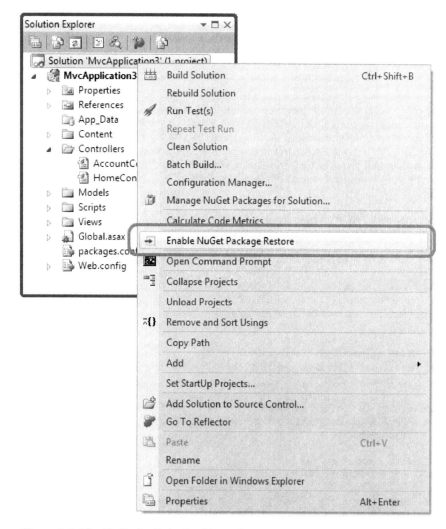

Figure 6-5. The NuGet built-in Enable Package Restore option in Visual Studio's Solution Explorer

You're now all set. If all went well, you can now delete all subfolders of your package installation directory, by default $(SolutionDir)\packages, except for the repositories.config file, and your solution should still compile properly. During compilation, you should see NuGet installation traces in the Visual Studio output window, and you should see the required NuGet packages reappear in the package installation directory as well.

Although it is very easy to set this up, we encourage you to read further and get to know the details of how this works. If you ever run into issues, due to a merge conflict for instance, and notice strange behaviors, it helps you a lot if you know what is going on.

After enabling NuGet package restore, you'll notice a .nuget folder in your solution directory, containing both the NuGet command line (nuget.exe) and an MSBuild file called NuGet.targets.

■ **Caution** Do not forget to check in the .nuget folder into your VCS, because your solution now depends on it to be able to compile successfully.

Again, if you know that your Visual Studio project files are MSBuild files as well, you conceptually already know what's going on. What happens is that, when enabling NuGet package restore, the NuGet Visual Studio Extension will iterate over all your solution's Visual Studio projects that contain NuGet package dependencies and add an import statement in the project file. The import statement will import the NuGet.targets MSBuild Task. It will also add a RestorePackages property to your project and set it to True. Listing 6-1 shows you the most meaningful parts of the NuGet.targets task, allowing you to understand what's going on.

Listing 6-1. Partial NuGet.targets MSBuild Task Used for Package Restoration

```xml
<?xml version="1.0" encoding="utf-8"?>
<Project ToolsVersion="4.0" xmlns="http://schemas.microsoft.com/developer/msbuild/2003">
    <PropertyGroup>
        <SolutionDir Condition="$(SolutionDir) == '' Or $(SolutionDir) ==↵
  '*Undefined*'">$(MSBuildProjectDirectory)\..\</SolutionDir>
        <NuGetToolsPath>$(SolutionDir).nuget</NuGetToolsPath>
        <NuGetExePath>$(NuGetToolsPath)\nuget.exe</NuGetExePath>
        <PackagesConfig>$(ProjectDir)packages.config</PackagesConfig>
        <PackagesDir>$(SolutionDir)packages</PackagesDir>
        <PackageOutputDir Condition="$(PackageOutputDir) ==↵
  ''">$(TargetDir.Trim('\\'))</PackageOutputDir>

        <!-- Package sources used to restore packages. By default will use the↵
  registered sources under %APPDATA%\NuGet\NuGet.Config -->
        <PackageSources>""</PackageSources>

        <!-- Enable the restore command to run before builds -->
        <RestorePackages Condition="$(RestorePackages) == ''">false</RestorePackages>

        <!-- Property that enables building a package from a project -->
        <BuildPackage Condition="$(BuildPackage) == ''">false</BuildPackage>

        <!-- Commands -->
        <RestoreCommand>"$(NuGetExePath)" install "$(PackagesConfig)" -source↵
  $(PackageSources) -o "$(PackagesDir)"</RestoreCommand>
        <BuildCommand>"$(NuGetExePath)" pack "$(ProjectPath)" -p↵
  Configuration=$(Configuration) -o "$(PackageOutputDir)" -symbols</BuildCommand>
        …

    </PropertyGroup>
    …

</Project>
```

It helps if you are a bit familiar with MSBuild, but it's not really needed. Just now that an additional `RestorePackages` task, triggering the `RestoreCommand`, is going to be executed in a prebuild step, for each Visual Studio project that has the property `RestorePackages` set to `True`. You can easily access this file from with Visual Studio in the `.nuget` solution folder that got added to your solution, as shown in Figure 6-6.

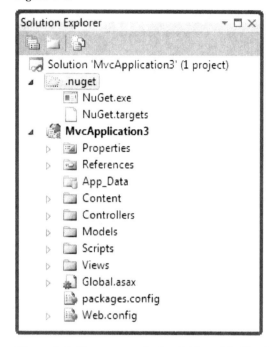

Figure 6-6. *The .nuget solution folder added by the Enable NuGet Package Restore feature*

You can adjust a couple of interesting settings in this file. The one that deserves some special attention is the `PackageSources` setting, allowing you to redirect your restore command to the NuGet package repository (or repositories) of your preference. If you want, for instance, to fetch NuGet packages from the ProNuGet feed on MyGet, you could use the following:

```
<PackageSources>"http://www.myget.org/F/pronuget"</PackageSources>
```

The default setting—empty quotes—indicates that the package sources defined in the `NuGet.config` file will be used. However, we prefer explicitly indicating the package source in this file, even when you are using only the official NuGet.org gallery feed, so you can track changes to it. It is also the only way to ensure that no external changes can break your build and to ensure that you always get the same output for a given changeset. If any external influence changes the `NuGet.config` file on the machine that compiles your project, NuGet might be redirected to a different package source than the one you intended.

It is important to point out that the NuGet package restore feature will install the exact same package version as defined in the project's `packages.config` file: it will *not* perform any upgrades for the exact same reasons.

Promoting Packages

NuGet packages, just like any other release vehicle (binaries, installers, etc.), need to undergo rigorous testing and quality assurance before being released to the masses. One cannot just build a complex NuGet package, complete with custom PowerShell hookpoints, push it to the repository and assume everything will work as expected, every single time, over and over again. If you're that good, you should be able to convince your managers to code directly onto the production servers.

We like Eric S. Raymond's approach of *release early, release often*. This is exactly what you should do with your NuGet packages as well. You not only release the package contents, you also release the package itself. It is your *release vehicle*. That is why your continuous integration builds should be producing NuGet packages as well if you intend to ship your product as a NuGet package (or multiple NuGet packages).

■ **Note** The concept of *release early, release often* (or RERO in short) actually has another part of the sentence: *"and listen to your customers."*

Besides ensuring quality, anticipating your customers needs and gathering feedback are among the most important requirements for your product to become a success. Continuously delivering high-quality releases enables you to do so. In addition, it's also the fastest way of delivering value to your clients.

Phill Haack has a great blog post on this topic: `http://haacked.com/archive/2011/04/20/release-early-and-often.aspx`

As your package goes through various stages of testing, you want to ensure nothing gets changed in those packages. No one is permitted to modify the package file or its contents. To facilitate the different teams that are involved in this process, one could choose to set up various NuGet feeds. An example set up could be as follows:

- *CI feed*: Every CI build pushes its output onto this feed, ready for consumption by development teams who want to play around with it but more importantly for QA teams to test them.

- *QA feed*: All packages from the CI feed that have been validated and approved by QA could then be pushed onto the QA feed. Whenever a release needs to get out, you can pick a version and push it to the Release feed.

- *Release feed*: This feed will be used for general consumption of your officially released packages.

With this setup, you have a very short track of releasing a package, while ensuring optimal quality and respecting the normal release processes. We like to call this flow *NuGet package promotion*. How you should move these packages from repository to repository is explained in the topic "Phasing Out Packages" later in this chapter.

Prereleasing Packages

NuGet v1.6 introduces the concept of prerelease packages. A prerelease NuGet package is considered *unstable*, and thus not ready yet for general consumption. A prerelease package is often indicated by the commonly used terms *alpha, beta, RC,* and so on. The concept of prereleases does not fit well with the concept of *release fast, release often* that we discussed in the previous section of this chapter. If we cannot modify the package contents (for example, the version number), and we don't know upfront whether our package will make it through the QA gate, how do we know when to tag our package with a certain release number? This is contradictory and counterintuitive. Then why does NuGet support prerelease tags at all?

Let's look at things from another perspective. We all know requirements change. Quite often, this happens very fast, and it occasionally impacts planning as well. Well, it nearly always impacts planning. It could be in the time dimension, resulting in shifting release dates. It could be in the scope dimension, resulting in adjusted functionality for a milestone. It could also have another impact on planning in the broader meaning of the word, any type of planning, including capacity or resource planning.

If planning is affected in the time dimension, you can choose to pick the latest QA-approved package and give it a prerelease tag before pushing it onto the Release feed. Probably more commonly, the opposite can happen as well, usually when changes have been made in scope: pick a prerelease package from QA, drop all version information after the dash (thus removing prerelease information), and push it out as an official release.

As explained in Chapter 3 of this book, NuGet also respects the `semver.org` notation and meaning of a prerelease package. Prerelease information is appended to the patch number, prefixed with a dash, as shown here:

```
major.minor.patch-prereleasetag (e.g. 1.0.0-RC1)
```

In our opinion, even prereleases are official releases. They only indicate a notion of potential instability or potential feature incompleteness. Prereleases should be considered milestones and be planned accordingly. A prerelease has a specific purpose—you want to get early feedback from your customers. This means that, ideally, your prerelease tags in the version information of your package should already be present in the CI build output.

Phasing Out Packages

In an enterprise environment, it is quite common to stop supporting an older, or maybe obsolete, framework. The same thing can happen to one or more of your NuGet package dependencies. If you want to discontinue a NuGet package, you either want to make sure that no one is still depending on it or that at least you can provide them with a working upgrade path.

On the official NuGet gallery feed, package owners can delete a package from the gallery. However, they don't have any idea who depends on that package and have no way of learning that either. A package owner could guess purely on the download count and, if by keeping track of this number over time, spot a trend in the usage of the package. However, a declining trend still does not justify the rude deletion of the package from a publicly available package source. If you ever contribute a package to the NuGet.org gallery, please keep this in mind.

So what should enterprises do with their desire to block certain packages from being installed by their development teams? Deleting any already listed packages from your package source can have a significant impact. As with anything, communication is key. Communicating that support for a certain package (version) will be discontinued is a *better practice*. At least, your developers are aware that they should mitigate the risk associated with this pending change.

If you are using multiple package sources, you could add an additional one for archiving those old or obsolete packages. If you delete a package without keeping a copy just in case, you're in for trouble. Archiving a package, after communicating its retirement, doesn't sound like a bad thing to us.

You could easily perform these actions by just moving the .nupkg file from one location to another, assuming you have enough permissions on both package sources. Moving those packages from filesystem path to filesystem path is straightforward. Moving a package from a feed to a filesystem path implies that you can download the package, store it on the archiving location, and delete it from the originating feed. This requires many more security permissions to be set properly. No matter how you move a package from one feed to another, you'll need all these permissions. This is a clear indication of how big an impact this action can have on your package consumers. Be cautious.

You could reuse Rob Reynold's command line extension for NuGet, the NuGet.copy.extension package. You can install it by executing the following commands in the NuGet Package Manager Console:

```
Install-Package NuGet.InstallCommandLineExtension
Install-CommandLineExtension NuGet.copy.extension
```

After installing this extension, your NuGet command line instances should have a new command available: the copy command. This command allows you to copy a package from one feed to another, by specifying the package ID (with optional version number), a source, a destination and optionally an API key for the destination.

An example usage of the copy command follows:

```
nuget copy WebActivator -Version 1.4 -Source http://www.myget.org/F/pronuget -Destination↵
http://www.myget.org/F/pronugetarchive
```

When you are using MyGet feeds, you might as well benefit from the built-in package retirement feature. MyGet gives you the option to set, on a per-package basis, whether the package is *listed* or not, without actually deleting it from the feed. By unlisting a package, you are preventing it from being consumed. Any newer versions of the package that are listed will still be available. Older ones as well, but you should probably ask yourself the why you didn't unlist those as well. This effectively means you are no longer supporting a specific package (version) while maintaining an upgrade path to a newer version for those that still rely on it. Remember, you should communicate a package retirement so people can take appropriate actions, such as mirroring the package you are about to retire or even check it into source control as a temporary measure. This is a nice, soft phase-out of a package. In fact, you give your consumers a polite and gentle push toward upgrading this dependency.

■ **Caution** Continue respecting core principles of software craftsmanship: package owners can decide when to stop support for a certain package, but it is still the consumer's decision when and if to upgrade to a newer version!

Listing or unlisting a package on a MyGet feed is the same as toggling support on or off for that package. When navigating to the package details page on MyGet.org, you'll see a link next to each package version in the Package History listing, as shown in Figure 6-7.

Package history

	Version	Size	Last updated	Downloads	Listed?	
	roundhouse 0.8.0.292	3.63 MB	Tuesday, May 17, 2011	28	yes	🗑 Delete
	roundhouse 0.8.0.291	3.63 MB	Tuesday, May 17, 2011	4	yes	🗑 Delete
	roundhouse 0.7.0.290	3.63 MB	Monday, May 16, 2011	6	yes	🗑 Delete
	roundhouse 0.7.0.281	2.99 MB	Monday, April 04, 2011	37	no	🗑 Delete

Figure 6-7. Listing and unlisting NuGet packages on a MyGet feed

If you toggle the state of a package version from listed to unlisted, you'll be prompted by a dialog warning you about the impact of your action, which you'll have to confirm, as shown in Figure 6-8.

> **The page at www.myget.org says:**
>
> Are you sure you want to unlist roundhouse 0.7.0.281 on the current private feed?
>
> This will prevent the package from being consumed while maintaining a package update scenario.
>
> [OK]   [Cancel]

Figure 6-8. A dialog will warn you and ask for confirmation when unlisting a package on MyGet.

In addition, because of the soft implementation of this functionality, the operation of unlisting a package *can* be undone, as opposed to deleting the package from the feed.

Summary

In this chapter, we focused on supporting the development environment and processes, as well as the application and package life cycle. We've explained how NuGet can live in perfect symbiosis with established techniques such as continuous integration.

We have provided you with guidance on how you can set up a no-commit strategy using various version control systems and considered a different approach of dealing with software dependencies outside of your VCS. We discussed both benefits and drawbacks of the no-commit strategy and highlighted some of the trade-offs being made.

Using a NuGet package as release vehicle of our product, we discussed how packages should respect a correct flow and how versioning and package promotion can help you in doing so. We've touched on the enterprise scenario of gently phasing out old or obsolete packages as well.

The next chapter will change perspectives from continuously integrating to continuously delivering and discuss optimizations in the field of automated delivery, using NuGet.

CHAPTER 7

Automated Delivery

Did you know NuGet is more than just a tool to manage dependencies in your software projects? Since NuGet is both a tool and a means of publishing and consuming packages, those packages may be used for scenarios other than the ones we've already covered. Agreed, packages contain assemblies by default, but they can also contain PowerShell scripts and other files. What if there were tools out there leveraging this idea?

Meet Octopus and Chocolatey. Both are projects that started early in the NuGet release wave and immediately saw advantage in using NuGet for more than it was originally intended. We'll cover both tools in this chapter, because they are great for optimizing your deployments. Octopus can be used to deploy *your* application packages to a variety of test, staging, and production environments and automates deploying to web and database servers. Chocolatey, on the other hand, is a NuGet extension that enables you to distribute and install software packages on a system, distributed through a NuGet feed. It uses NuGet as a system-level package manager, as opposed to NuGet's default solution-level purpose.

Both tools distribute software, but each does so in its own way and with its own goals. This chapter will explain how you can use Octopus to deploy your .NET solutions, packaged as a NuGet package, to your test, staging, and production servers. We'll also cover Chocolatey and how you can use it to install software prerequisites on either your machine or your servers.

Note If you are interested in how you can use NuGet in other scenarios make sure to read Chapter 9 of this book, where we explain how to use NuGet as a protocol and how you can use the NuGet.Core assembly to create similar experiences to the ones provided by Octopus and Chocolatey.

Deploying Artifacts with Octopus

Let's start this section with some background. Imagine you have a web application, and you need to deploy it to test, staging, and production environments. How do you deploy your application today? Most people are using one or more of the following solutions:

- The application is copied to a USB drive or DVD and given to a system administrator, who copies all files to the target machine.

- The web application is built on one of the developer's machines. That developer connects to the target server using FTP, Remote Desktop, or a file share and copies over all files, either manually or using a batch file.

- A batch script runs on the build server and copies all files to the target machine.

- Microsoft's WebDeploy is used to deploy the web application to the target servers.

All the methods we've just mentioned (and probably a lot more) are valid ways of deploying an application. Unfortunately, most of them are not standardized through the use of either a process or a tool supporting that process.

We've seen this all before. If you look a few years back, the same story could be told about builds. Some shops let one lead developer create the final build. Others had a script in place that could be run either locally or on a server. Build processes are becoming more and more standardized. Most software developers have some sort of build server in place—think TeamCity, Team Foundation Server build, CruiseControl.NET. These build servers are all focusing on one thing: making it easy to create builds in a standardized manner.

Today, deployments are in the situation builds were a few years ago. Some teams do it manually; some have a script; some have a code monkey to deploy their product. Why not make deployments easy as well? Why not standardize them so that every deployment is exactly the same? Microsoft is trying to do this using WebDeploy; others are creating different solutions, including Octopus, the deployment solution based on NuGet that we'll describe in this section.

What Is Octopus?

Octopus is a tool supporting a conventions-based process of automating deployments. It can be downloaded from `www.octopusdeploy.com`. The general idea is to create your source code and check it into source control, making use of standard conventions like `Web.config` transforms and using `appSettings`. Your build server such as TeamCity or Team Foundation Server (TFS) compiles this source code and packages this project into a NuGet package. This package is then published on a NuGet feed.

This is the moment where Octopus comes in play: you define a project and its target machines and environments. Octopus will then download the latest release of your software from a NuGet feed. It uploads each package to the target machines, which run a small agent called a Tentacle.

On each machine you plan to deploy to, the Tentacle agent accepts the NuGet package from Octopus and installs it using a set of conventions, such as configuration file transforms and calling PowerShell scripts. A schematic overview of Octopus' deployment flow is shown in Figure 7-1.

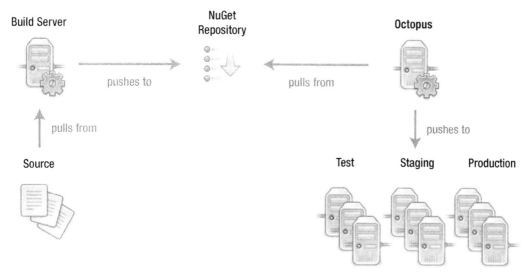

Figure 7-1. *High-level overview of Octopus deployment process (image taken from* `http://www.octopusdeploy.com/Features`)

In this chapter, we will not cover all options and conventions available in Octopus. We will only explain the basics of getting a deployment server up and running and how to deploy a simple application. All details—conventions, ways to configure your build server, and more—can be found on the Octopus web site at `http://help.octopusdeploy.com/kb`.

Installing Octopus

This section will guide you through installing Octopus. Since Octopus consists of the web portal for configuring and creating new deployments as well as Octopus Tentacle, we'll split this section into two parts.

■ **Note** To make things easy, we'll install both Octopus and Octopus Tentacle on the same machine. In production environments, you would ideally deploy Octopus to one server where you can manage deployments and releases and install Octopus Tentacle to every machine on which software will be deployed.

Installing Octopus

Octopus comes with an installer that can be downloaded from the official web site at `www.octopusdeploy.com/Download`. This page lists two different downloads: Octopus and Octopus Tentacle. We'll download the `Octopus.<some version>.msi` file. Save this file to disk, and double-click the installer.

You'll be greeted by a friendly Octopus, a favor you can return by just clicking Next until you have to click Install. After clicking the Install button, Octopus will be installed into C:\Octopus. At the end of the installation, you'll be prompted to launch the configuration wizard. Make sure this option is checked, and click Finish. This is where the real work comes in.

The Octopus Configuration dialog, shown in Figure 7-2, requires some additional information:

- *Database connection string*: Can be a local SQL Server or SQL Server Express database in which all Octopus application data will be stored.

- *X.509 certificates*: Used to encrypt communications between Octopus and Octopus Tentacle.

- *Octopus Windows Service*: Has to be installed to push out deployments

- *Octopus Portal*: Has to be installed to use the web portal to configure deployments and releases

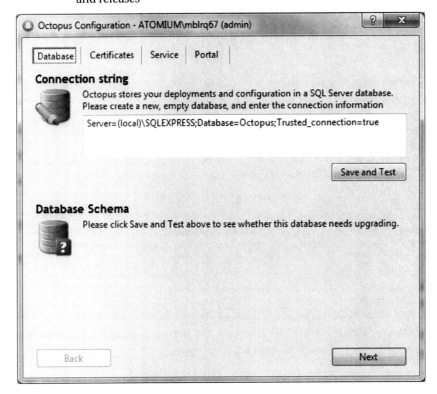

Figure 7-2. Octopus Configuration screen

Make sure you create a database and fill out your database connection string in the Octopus Configuration dialog. Afterward, click the "Save and Test" button. If Octopus can make a connection to your database, a new button titled Deploy will appear. Click it to install the Octopus database schema on your database server.

After configuring the database for Octopus, click the Certificates tab. This tab can create a certificate to encrypt all communications between Octopus and Octopus Tentacles. Click the New button to generate a new certificate. As Figure 7-3 shows, a certificate is generated, and certificate text is displayed. Make sure to copy this text somewhere, because it will have to be entered when installing an Octopus Tentacle.

Figure 7-3. Octopus certificate generation

The next tab in the Octopus Configuration is Service. Simply click the Install button to install a Windows service, which will be the hearth of Octopus and will take care of deploying applications to Octopus Tentacles.

As a final step, in the Portal tab, pick a port number on which the Octopus portal should be installed, and click Install. If that succeeds, you are good to go, and Octopus will be available on the URL you've just created. We've changed our port number to 8085, hence http://localhost:8085 displays the Octopus Portal shown in Figure 7-4. Since we have not configured any environments or projects yet, it looks a bit empty. But don't worry: after installing Tentacle, we'll configure Octopus further.

Figure 7-4. Octopus portal right after installation

■ **Tip** The Octopus portal is configured to run under the NT AUTHORITY\NETWORK SERVICE user. This user will typically not have access to your database. Make sure to either change the user under which the Octopus portal is running or allow access to the Octopus database for the NT AUTHORITY\NETWORK SERVICE user.

Installing Octopus Tentacle

Octopus Tentacle comes with an installer, which can also be downloaded from the official web site at www.octopusdeploy.com/Download. Recall that this page lists two different downloads: Octopus and Octopus Tentacle. This time, we'll download the Octopus.Tentacle.<some version>.msi file. Save this file to disk, and double-click the installer.

Again, a friendly Octopus welcomes you to the installation. After clicking the Install button, the Tentacle Configuration screen shown in Figure 7-5 is shown. In the Certificates tab, paste the certificate that was generated by the Octopus configuration earlier. If you are installing Octopus and Octopus Tentacle on the same machine, this field will be prepopulated for you.

In the Service tab, click the Install button to install the Octopus Tentacle Windows service to your machine. This service will accept deployments from Octopus and deploy them on the machine on which Octopus Tentacle is installed.

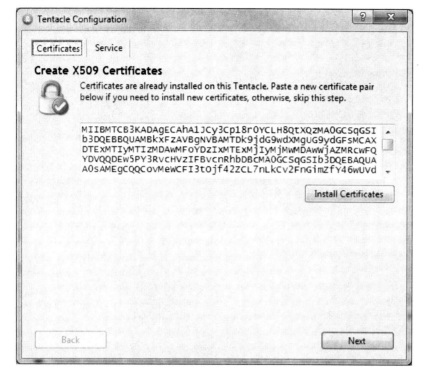

Figure 7-5. *The Tentacle Configuration screen*

You are now ready to start using Octopus.

Deploying a Project Using Octopus

This section will walk you through your first Octopus deployment. We'll start by setting up our Internet Information Services (IIS) environment to make sure Octopus knows where to deploy our web application. Next, we'll create a simple HelloWorld web application that we'll package using NuGet. Finally, we'll use Octopus to deploy this application to a webserver.

Let's start off with listing all Octopus conventions to give you some background on why we are doing certain things.

Convention-Based Deployments

Octopus relies heavily on conventions, a set of rules to which your environment and packages must adhere in order to make it easier for Octopus to discover all tasks it should execute when deploying an application. The following are the mayor conventions when working with Octopus:

- The XML configuration convention assumes your configuration files all have a filename ending with `.config` and that they are XML files. Octopus will update these files when deploying and updates connection strings and application settings. More details about this convention can be found at `http://help.octopusdeploy.com/kb/conventions/xml-configuration-convention`.

- The PowerShell convention defines that the Octopus Tentacle will look for `PreDeploy.ps1`, `Deploy.ps1`, and `PostDeploy.ps1` PowerShell scripts in the root folder of your NuGet package. If found, they will be executed. This can be useful to add configuration scripts into a NuGet package. More details about this convention can be found at `http://help.octopusdeploy.com/kb/conventions/powershell-deployps1-convention`.

- The IIS WebSite convention defines that the Octopus Tentacle will install the NuGet package containing your application to the Web Site with a name matching the name of your package. More about this convention at `http://help.octopusdeploy.com/kb/conventions/iis-web-site-convention`.

The IIS WebSite convention is the most important to take into account in this chapter. It states that if we create a NuGet package named HelloWorld, we should also make sure that the IIS web site to which we'll deploy must be named HelloWorld, as shown in Figure 7-6. Note that the web root of your web site does not matter; Octopus will update this for every deployment.

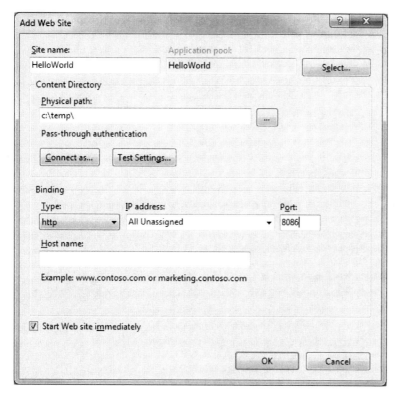

Figure 7-6. An IIS web site must be named identical to the NuGet package identifier.

Shipping an Application in a NuGet Package

To deploy a web application using Octopus, your application should be shipped as a NuGet package. This means creating a NuGet package containing your project's assemblies and artifacts. According to the author of Octopus, Paul Stovell, the best solution to do this is to publish your application to a local folder and package the application from there, either manually or using a build server.

There is another method that we slightly prefer because it is easier to set up. But before we go there, let's set up a quick sample. Create a new ASP.NET MVC application in Visual Studio, and make sure it is named HelloWorld. This application will be the one we'll ship using NuGet, a task that can be done using the excellent OctoPack package. In the Package Manager Console, issue the following command:

```
Install-Package OctoPack
```

This will instruct Visual Studio to create an Octopus-compatible NuGet package from your project on every compilation. The OctoPack package adds a new build target to your project that is typically located under your solution root, \packages\OctoPack.<version>\targets\OctoPack.targets.

NuGet always automatically adds your project's dependencies to the NuGet package as well. This is good in most situations but bad in combination with Octopus, because it does not support packages containing dependencies.

Fortunately, we can work around this: if you rename the packages.config file right before packaging and restore it after packaging, NuGet will ignore the dependencies listed in there. To do so, edit the \packages\OctoPack.<version>\targets\OctoPack.targets file, and add the lines of code highlighted in bold in Listing 7-1.:

Listing 7-1. Update NuGet.targets to Skip Listing Package Dependencies in the NuGet Package

```xml
<Project xmlns="http://schemas.microsoft.com/developer/msbuild/2003">
  <!-- Shortened for brevity  -->

  <!--
  Packaging Web Applications
  -->
  <Target Name="OctopusPackageWeb"
          DependsOnTargets="$(OnBefore_CopyWebApplicationDefault);OctopusFindNuGetSettings">
    <Message Text="Project was published to: $(OutDir)" />
    <Copy SourceFiles="$(OctopusNuSpecFileName)"
          DestinationFolder="$(WebProjectOutputDir)" />

    <Move SourceFiles="$(ProjectDir)\packages.config"
          DestinationFiles="$(ProjectDir)\octopackages.config"
          ContinueOnError="true" />

    <Exec Command='"$(NuGetExe)" pack
        "$(WebProjectOutputDir.TrimEnd(&quot;\&quot;))\$(OctopusNuSpecFileName)"
        -OutputDirectory "$(OutputPath.TrimEnd(&quot;\&quot;))"
        -basePath "$(WebProjectOutputDir.TrimEnd(&quot;\&quot;))"
        -Version "$(OctopusPackageVersion)" -NoPackageAnalysis' />

    <Move SourceFiles="$(ProjectDir)\octopackages.config"
          DestinationFiles="$(ProjectDir)\packages.config"
          ContinueOnError="true" />
  </Target>

  <!-- Shortened for brevity  -->
</Project>
```

We're not quite finished yet. OctoPack will look for a HelloWorld.nuspec file in your project, a package manifest like the ones we have created several times before over the course of this book. Add the HelloWorld.nuspec file to your project, and copy the code from Listing 7-2. Make sure to not use replacement tokens like id or $version$ when working with OctoPack.

Listing 7-2. NuGet Package Manifest for the HelloWorld application.

```xml
<?xml version="1.0"?>
<package >
  <metadata>
    <id>HelloWorld</id>
    <version>1.1.0.0</version>
    <title>HelloWorld</title>
    <authors>Maarten Balliauw &amp; Xavier Decoster</authors>
    <owners>Maarten Balliauw &amp; Xavier Decoster</owners>
```

```
    <description>HelloWorld sample application</description>
    <requireLicenseAcceptance>false</requireLicenseAcceptance>
    <releaseNotes>Summary of changes made in this release of the package.</releaseNotes>
    <copyright>Copyright 2011</copyright>
  </metadata>
</package>
```

Now, compile your application in the Release configuration. You should see a
HelloWorld.1.0.0.nupkg file in your application's bin folder. Note that you can change the configuration
in which OctoPack produces the package by adjusting the OctopusPackageConfiguration element in the
OctoPack.targets file. Ensure that all assemblies and content are copied into the NuGet package. Figure
7-7 shows our package's contents in NuGet Package Explorer.

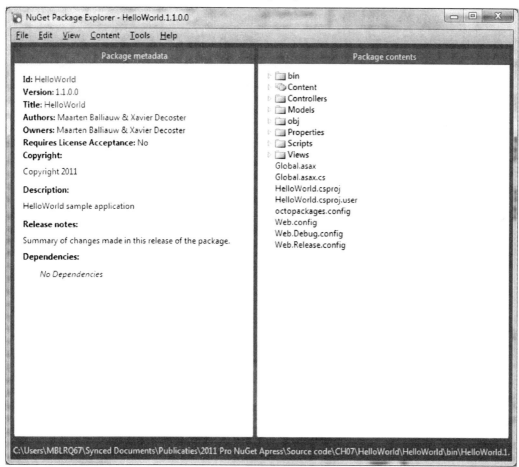

Figure 7-7. Using NuGet Package Explorer to verify package contents

The final step in shipping an application through NuGet is of course to push it to a NuGet feed. We've pushed the HelloWorld package to our ProNuGet feed on MyGet, www.myget.org/F/pronuget/. Feel free to use that one when configuring Octopus if you don't want to create a package yourself.

Configuring the Octopus Environment

Before we are able to deploy an application to a web server using Octopus, we'll have to define five things in Octopus. Don't worry; this is just some initial configuration, so there's no need to run through these steps on every deployment you want to create.

- Which environments do we have?
- Which servers are in those environments?
- Which NuGet feed has to be used to pull shipped applications from?
- Which projects do we have?
- Which packages have to be deployed for such project?

After making sure these items are configured, Octopus can be used to easily deploy an application across multiple environments.

Log in to the Octopus web portal (which we've deployed to http://localhost:8085). As a first step, we're going to configure a deployment environment. This is a logical unit of servers, typically named test, staging, and production. Of course, more than one environment can be created, and if you have a chucknorris environment as well, feel free to configure it. Click the Add Environment button, and provide a name and description for it.

After creating an environment, one or more servers should be added to it. Click the Add Machine button to configure a server on which Octopus Tentacle is installed. By default, tentacles are listening on port 10399, which means we can simply add our localhost Octopus Tentacle by entering http://localhost:10399. Figure 7-8 shows you an example of a machine being added to the Production environment.

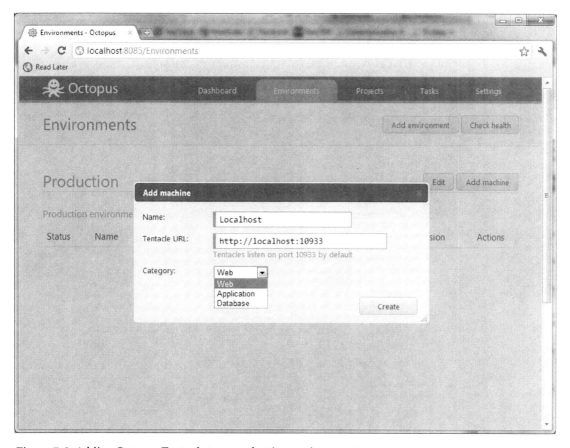

Figure 7-8. *Adding Octopus Tentacle to a production environment*

So far, we have configured an environment and added a machine to it. Since Octopus uses NuGet to distribute application packages to its tentacles, we'll have to configure the NuGet feed to use. In the Settings menu, click the Add Feed button, and enter the URL serving your application packages. Feel free to use our www.myget.org/F/pronuget feed on which we've published the HelloWorld application created earlier. Figure 7-9 shows you an example.

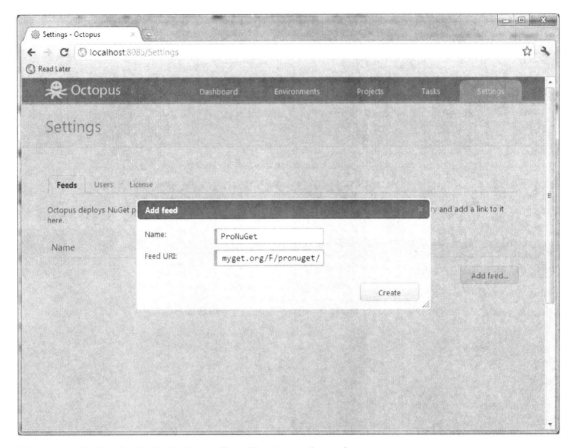

Figure 7-9. Define the NuGet feed to pull application packages from

We're almost good to go now. The only thing missing is a project and a deployment. A project in Octopus is a logical unit of packages. For example, if you are building a three-tier application, the project will group all three tiers. There is no need to create one project per tier! Also, there's no need to create a project for each environment either: Octopus can deploy a project to an environment of choice in a later step.

On the Projects page, click the "Create project" button. Enter a project name and description, and click the Create button. You will notice the project page is rather empty. The reason for that is the project does not know which application packages should be deployed. Click the "Add step" button to add a deployment step to your project. A *deployment step* indicates that a certain package from a certain feed should be deployed to a web, application, or database server. Figure 7-10 shows what you'll see after selecting the ProNuGet feed and entering the HelloWorld package identifier. Make sure to deploy it to Web.

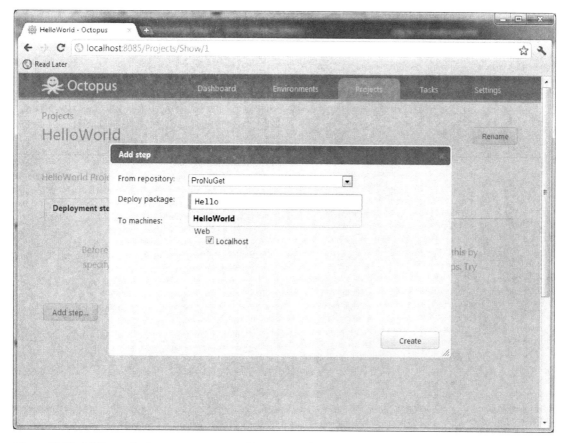

Figure 7-10. Adding a deployment step to an Octopus project

After clicking the Create button, we're ready to deploy the HelloWorld application to our servers.

Creating and Deploying a Release

Octopus defines a *release* simply as a version of a deployment of several packages to the target environment. Figure 7-11 shows the screen that is presented when you click the "Create release" button under the HelloWorld project we've just created. It requires you to enter a release version (think about semantic versioning for your releases as well!) and select the versions of application packages that should be released. This is the place where NuGet comes in: all available package versions are retrieved from the configured NuGet feed.

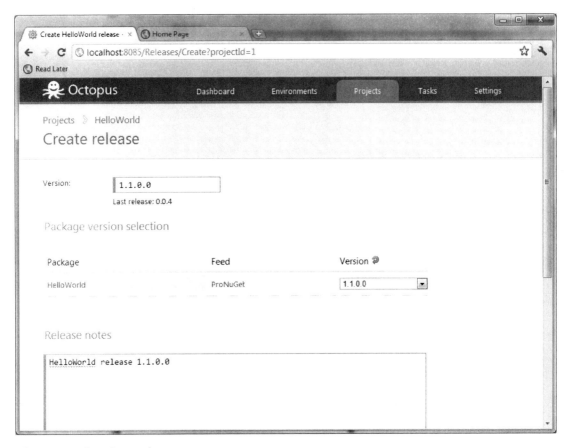

Figure 7-11. Creating a release

When you click the "Add to queue" button, the actual deployment is not executed yet. Your release comes in a *queue*, which a release manager in your team can inspect. Once a release is approved, that team member can click Deploy to trigger the actual deployment of your web application to an environment of choice.

Just like with a build server, you can see what Octopus is doing: a release log is created where you can see all steps of a deployment as well as eventual warnings or errors. Note that release logs are kept in Octopus' database: just as with builds, it's important to be able to roll back a release and/or to inspect what happened during a certain release. Part of this release log is shown in Figure 7-12. Note the fact that the HelloWorld 1.1.0.0 package is downloaded from a NuGet feed and then sent off to an Octopus tentacle.

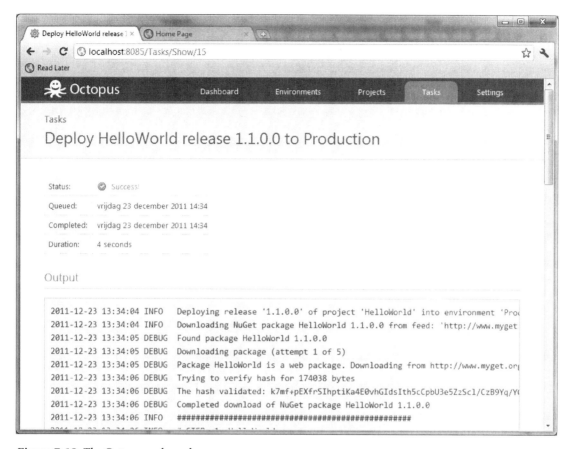

Figure 7-12. *The Octopus release log*

If the release yields "Success!", your application will be deployed to the IIS web site configured earlier. Note that Octopus automatically applied any configuration transforms to the web site, starting from `Web.config` (or `App.Config`). Octopus always applies the `Web.Release.config` first, and if the package is being deployed to an environment different than your release environment, it will also apply any available `Web.(Environment).config` transformations. For example, when you deploy to an environment with the name "QA", Octopus will transform the `Web.config` by first applying the transformations of `Web.Release.config`, followed by `Web.QA.config`.

The big benefit of Octopus is that you can simply *release* a single package and deploy it to multiple different environments without having to create a new *release version* in Octopus.. This also means that no modifications to the package can be done between various stages of the deployment pipeline, ensuring that what you deploy to the acceptance environment is exactly what will get deployed onto production as well.

Deploying Software with Chocolatey

The first part of this chapter focused on deploying a NuGet package remotely, but we'll now do the opposite and look at a very interesting way of installing a NuGet package locally—no, not within your code base, but on your system. Obviously, these NuGet packages will contain something of interest for the entire system. How about an application? That's right, an application! You can wrap an application installer into a NuGet package and have a common means of distributing those applications to various systems.

What Is Chocolatey?

Very early in the life of NuGet, Rob Reynolds and others in the community played with the idea of a systemwide package manager, much like apt-get, which is a very popular command-line advanced packaging tool (APT) use on (mainly Debian-based) Linux systems. Rob created one for Windows based on the NuGet command line and infrastructure, and called it Chocolatey (after "chocolatey nougat"). Who doesn't like chocolate after all (did we tell you we are from Belgium)?

If you're like us, you probably have quite a few tools installed on your workstation—tools that are nowhere to be found on your corporate standard workstation image, tools that actually make your device a *work*station. Quite often, we find ourselves installing new tools as well. We don't realize the amount of tools we use until we don't have them. Try working for a day on someone else's workstation to find out. If you have to switch workstations or repave your device, you better have a list of the tools you need.

Even if you have such list, you have to keep track of the location where you can find the latest version and manually go over the list to download, unblock, extract, and install the application yourself. This is a very time-consuming process during which you cannot do anything productive. What if you could feed this list to a tool that does it for you and grab a cup of coffee while your coworkers are struggling to keep up? What if this tool automatically fetches the latest versions available for every application in your list, so you no longer have to track the version or the download location of each application? What if, when returning from a well-deserved holiday, you could use that same tool to automatically update all your applications on the list to the latest version? Meet Chocolatey.

Chocolatey can be seen as a tool enabler or as a silent application installer. You can develop tools and applications and release them as NuGet packages with Chocolatey. And you can release *any* windows application or tool, not just .NET applications. That also means that Chocolatey is not necessarily developer focused, unlike NuGet.

■ **Tip** To get an instant Chocolatey experience, you can watch a video on YouTube showing you Chocolatey in action: http://bit.ly/chocolateyVideo.

Installing Chocolatey

Chocolatey has very few requirements. You have to have the .NET 4 Framework and PowerShell 2 installed. Installing Chocolatey really takes only a matter of seconds. You have multiple installation options, so just pick the one you prefer. Chocolatey itself exists as a NuGet package, so if you get a hold on the package, you get an opportunity to install it.

As of v1.0, Chocolatey installs by default into the %SystemDrive%\Chocolatey folder. Older versions target %SystemDrive%\NuGet instead. If you are not OK with that, you can define the desired installation directory before running the installation. To do so, adjust the user environment variable named ChocolateyInstall, and set it to the folder you want Chocolatey to install to.

Using PowerShell

Using PowerShell is the easiest installation method. Because of PowerShell's security strategy, make sure you have set your execution policy to unrestricted before installing Chocolatey. You can check your current execution policy by running the Get-ExecutionPolicy command in any PowerShell console. If it returns anything else than Unrestricted, you should run the Set-ExecutionPolicy Unrestricted command. To change the PowerShell execution policy, you should open a PowerShell console with elevated privileges, so run it as Administrator. On Windows 7, you simply right-click the PowerShell icon in the Start menu, and select "Run as administrator". Figure 7-13 illustrates how to change the PowerShell execution policy.

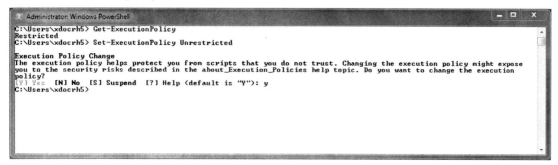

Figure 7-13. Ensuring the PowerShell ExecutionPolicy is set to Unrestricted

If your PowerShell execution policy is set to Unrestricted, you can run the following one-liner to install the latest version of Chocolatey on your system; Figure 7-14 shows you the Chocolatey installation process in a PowerShell console:

```
iex ((New-Object Net.WebClient).DownloadString("http://bit.ly/psChocInstall"))
```

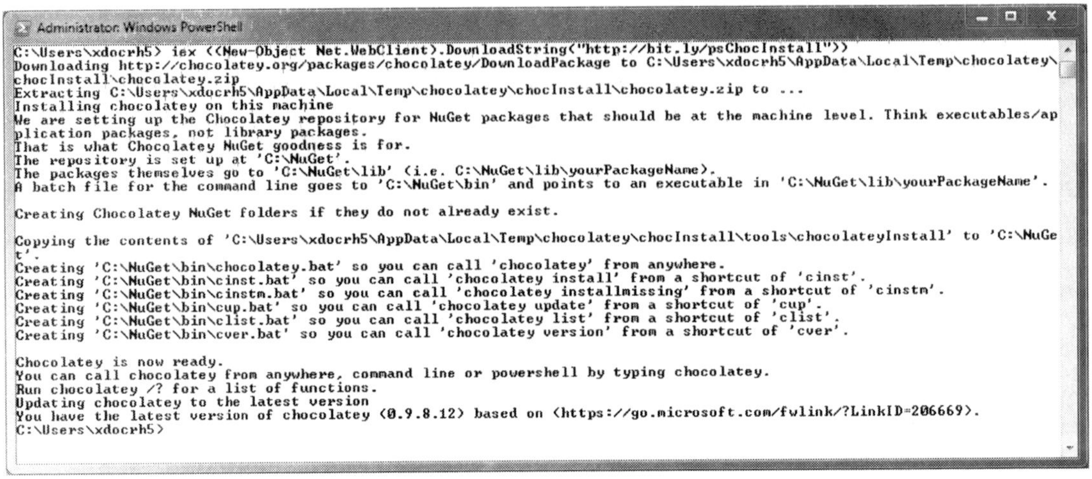

Figure 7-14. Installing Chocolatey from within PowerShell

If you have PowerShell ninja skills and want to find out what happens behind the scenes, you can take a look at the install script on GitHub (yes, Chocolatey is open source as well!). The install script can be found on the following location:

`https://raw.github.com/chocolatey/chocolatey/master/chocolateyInstall/InstallChocolatey.ps1`

Another way to install Chocolatey is by downloading the two files from the GitHub repository on the following location: `https://github.com/ferventcoder/chocolatey/tree/master/chocolateyInstall`. Simply run the `installChocolatey.cmd` batch file to finish the installation.

Using NuGet Package Manager Console

By now, you are familiar with the NuGet Package Manager Console, so you can install Chocolatey from within Visual Studio as well. This installation method is no one-liner and requires you to have a solution open in Visual Studio. Don't forget to select the official NuGet gallery feed as package source.

Whereas the PowerShell installation method executed the remote unsigned `install.ps1` script directly from the GitHub repository, the NuGet Package Manager Console installation method will make use of the Chocolatey NuGet package, available from the official NuGet.org gallery feed.

To install Chocolatey using the Package Manager Console, simply run the following commands:

```
Install-Package Chocolatey
Initialize-Chocolatey
Uninstall-Package Chocolatey
```

Figure 7-15 shows you the output of running the `Install-Package Chocolatey` command. If you read the instructions, you see you have to run `Initialize-Chocolatey` once, and after that, you can safely uninstall the package using the `Uninstall-Package Chocolatey` command. If you read the output a bit more carefully, you'll notice there is another, alternative method of installing Chocolatey—using NuGet outside of Visual Studio.

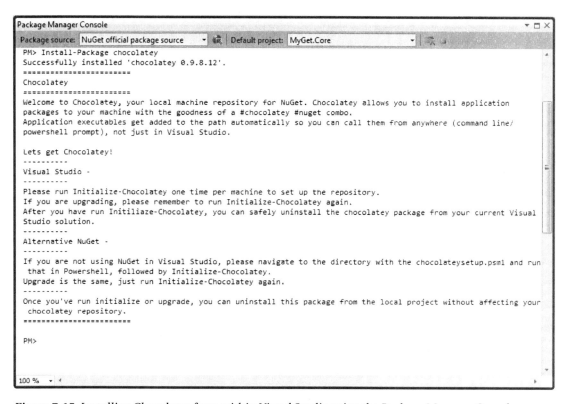

Figure 7-15. Installing Chocolatey from within Visual Studio using the Package Manager Console

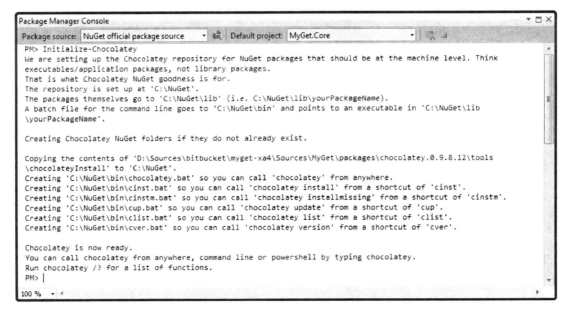

Figure 7-16. Initializing Chocolatey from within Visual Studio

If you installed the Chocolatey package using the NuGet.exe command line for instance, you can run the ChocolateySetup.psm1 file in a PowerShell console, followed by the Initialize-Chocolatey command.

The initialization of Chocolatey also mentioned another interesting thing: every tool or application you install using Chocolatey will be automatically available from within every command prompt on that system, because the install path is in the system environment path. You also get a glimpse at the various commands that Chocolatey exposes. Let's see what tasty ingredients Chocolatey has to offer.

Using Chocolatey

Chocolatey is a command-line tool that exposes quite a few options for you to manage applications. You install a single application or batch the installation of an application list. You can update a single application or update all applications that have been installed using Chocolatey at once. Let's take a look at the various commands.

▪ **Tip** For the latest up-to-date Chocolatey Commands reference, you can visit the following URL: https://github.com/chocolatey/chocolatey/wiki/CommandsReference.

Installing Tools and Applications

We are going to install Notepad++, our favorite replacement for the Windows built-in Notepad text editor, using Chocolatey. We can do this because Notepad++ is also available as a NuGet package on the Chocolatey Gallery feed on `http://chocolatey.org` (see Figure 7-17).

Figure 7-17. Searching for Notepad++ on the Chocolatey.org Gallery

Another way to find out if your favorite tool or application has been packaged and made available on Chocolatey is by using the Chocolatey command line. Chocolatey has a `chocolatey list` command (or `clist` for short) that you could use for that. To list all available packages on the Chocolatey gallery, you can run the following command (this might take a while to finish):

```
chocolatey list
```

or

```
clist
```

If you want to filter the list, simply add the beginning of the application name to the command, as shown here:

```
chocolatey list notepad
```

or

```
clist notepad
```

The preceding command will yield results for both Notepad2 and Notepad++ (or NotepadPlusPlus), so you can pick the one you prefer. We will go for Notepad++.

To actually install the application, you need to use the `install` command (or the `cinst` alias). For Notepad++, this looks as follows:

```
chocolatey install notepadplusplus
```

or

```
cinst notepadplusplus
```

Figure 5-18 illustrates the installation process for Notepad++, and Figure 5-18 shows the complete output logged by Chocolatey after successfully installing Notepad++ on your system.

Figure 7-18. Progress indication of the installation process of the Notepad++ Chocolatey package

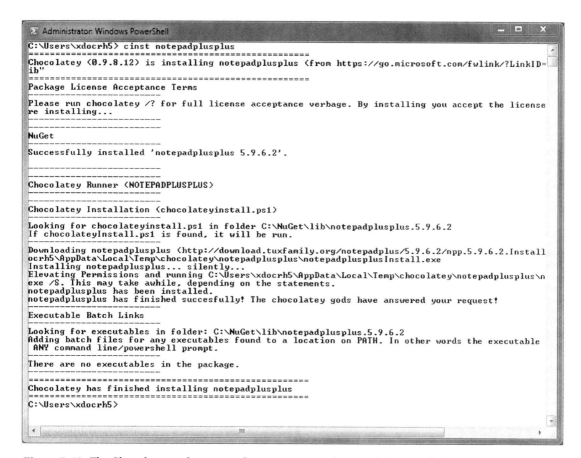

Figure 7-19. The Chocolatey gods answered your request and successfully installed Notepad++.

As easy as it is to install a single application using Chocolatey, you could actually batch the installation of multiple tools and applications at once. Because Chocolatey comes as a command-line tool and registers itself in the PATH environment variable, it is very convenient to call Chocolatey commands from any location on your system. Listing 7-3 shows you how you can install a sequence of tools in one go using Chocolatey. Save this listing into a script file (e.g., installMyTools.ps1 or installMyTools.bat) to distribute it to your colleagues, who can then simply double-click the file to execute this script on their machines as well.

Listing 7-3. An Example Batch File to Sequentially Install Various Tools Using Chocolatey

```
cinst sysinternals
cinst notepadplusplus
cinst adobereader
cinst msysgit
cinst fiddler
cinst filezilla
cinst putty -version 0.62
cinst tortoisesvn
cinst tortoisehg
cinst tortoisegit
cinst iisexpress -source webpi
```

Note that the install command will install the package unless the package is already installed on the system. If you want to reinstall the package, you should use the -force option. A few more options are available to pass on to the install command, and these are discussed in the "Distributing Chocolatey Goodness" section, when we will talk about configuring the native installer that is triggered by the Chocolatey package.

This is a very useful way of making sure your system is configured with the tools desired in one go. We've given the example of easily repaving your computer or quickly configuring a new system, but you could also use it to make sure all developers have the same (version of) specific tooling installed on their systems when working on your code base. By checking this script file into source control, everyone on the team can run it locally with ease.

In addition to manually creating batch files and duplicating a bunch of Chocolatey commands (cinst for instance) on every line, you could also just describe the packages you want and perform a single Chocolatey operation to process the file. Installing a list of packages would then result in a single install command, passing in a file containing your packages list to install. This also allows for internal optimization by Chocolatey to perform this operation.

What would be the best way to describe the packages you want to install onto your system? If you think about the parallelism with NuGet: how does NuGet describe which packages should be installed into a project? Does the packages.config file ring a bell to you?

The Chocolatey install command supports targeting a packages.config file. Simply list the package IDs and versions for the Chocolatey packages you want to have installed on your system in the exact same XML format as NuGet does to denote project package dependencies. Chocolatey supports a tiny deviation from the default *vanilla* packages.config file that NuGet uses. You can add a very convenient source attribute to each of the package elements in the packages.config file, to indicate what source should be used to fetch the package. Listing 7-4 defines the packages listed in Listing 7-3. Save this file, and give it a name, for instance, MyFavoriteChocolateyPackages.config. Note that you can add the version attribute within each package element to denote the desired package version.

Use cinst MyFavoriteChocolateyPackages.config to perform the batch installation of these packages onto your system. The packages are installed in the order defined in the file.

Listing 7-4. An Example packages.config File to Sequentially Install Various Tools Using Chocolatey

```xml
<?xml version="1.0" encoding="utf-8"?>
<packages>
  <package id="sysinternals" />
  <package id="notepadplusplus" />
  <package id="adobereader" />
  <package id="msysgit" />
  <package id="fiddler" />
  <package id="filezilla" />
  <package id="putty" version="0.62" />
  <package id="tortoisesvn" />
  <package id="tortoisehg" />
  <package id="tortoisegit" />
  <package id="iisexpress" source="webpi" />
</packages>
```

Last, but definitely not least, there is a third option to easily tell Chocolatey which packages you want to get installed on your system. What if you're like us and don't like messing around with script files, distributed over various systems, trying to remember which one was the latest one? If you need to repave your system, or want to tell someone how to install a bunch of tools, you want to give simple instructions—a simple command, preferably a single line, with no files involved.

You might have guessed it, but we will be using a feed for this. Chocolatey supports installing all listed packages directly from a custom feed. To do so, you need to create your own custom Chocolatey repository—you could use a MyGet.org feed for this—and target it in your commands. As such, you now have a central place to maintain your list of favorite tools and keep them up to date. Simply invite people to target your feed URL, and you can easily share this list with your colleagues and friends. Upload or mirror the packages you need on your feed and off you go. The Chocolatey command involved is the following one:

```
cinst all -source [feedURL]
```

This is a great way of installing many tools at once, but what if one of those tools is not available as a package on the Chocolatey Gallery? What if you want to install a tool, for instance IISExpress, using the Microsoft Web Platform Installer? You could use WebPI, the Web Platform Installer command line tool, but you might not have this additional tool yet on the system. No problem for the Chocolatey gods: Chocolatey has built-in support for WebPI. In fact, webpi is a command available in Chocolatey:

```
chocolatey webpi IISExpress
```

or

```
cwebpi IISExpress
```

Another way to install applications using WebPI as a source instead of the Chocolatey NuGet Gallery is by using the –Source switch of the Chocolatey install command.

```
cinst IISExpress -source webpi
```

■ **Tip** Once you have installed the WebPI command-line tool, using `cinst webpicommandline` for instance, you could use Chocolatey to list the available applications for the Web Platform Installer, using the `clist -source webpi` command.

It goes without saying that Chocolatey has been influenced and inspired by tooling outside of the .NET community, such as `apt-get` or Ruby Gems. If you want to benefit from Chocolatey goodness while working with Ruby, you'll be happy to learn that Chocolatey also has built-in support for Ruby Gems. According to Wikipedia, "RubyGems is a package manager for the Ruby programming language that provides a standard format for distributing Ruby programs and libraries (in a self-contained format called a 'gem'), a tool designed to easily manage the installation of gems, and a server for distributing them" (http://en.wikipedia.org/wiki/RubyGems).

To install Ruby Gems using Chocolatey, use the `chocolatey gem` or `cgem` command, followed by the package name. This command defaults to the latest version of the package available, so if you want to get a specific version of the package, you should use the `-version` option. The command to install the latest version of a Ruby Gem, for instance GemCutter, using Chocolatey would look as follows:

```
chocolatey gem gemcutter
```

or

```
cgem gemcutter
```

Much like you could for the built-in WebPI support, you could also install Ruby Gems using the install command and specify Ruby as the source to be used, as follows:

```
cinst gemcutter -source ruby
```

This command will result in the exact same operation being performed as when using the `cgem` command.

Keeping Your Toolbelt Up to Date

Of course, you don't want to simply install a bunch of tools and applications and then work with those happily ever after. Those applications evolve, and your tools have updates. A good reason to keep those installed applications up to date as well.

There's a very handy way of updating an application installed through Chocolatey. Simply use the update command, and target an installed package name to update that application to the latest version available. In addition, there is a very convenient short notation for the `chocolatey update` command: `cup` (as in "cup of Chocolatey").

```
chocolatey update notepadplusplus
```

or

```
cup notepadplusplus
```

Just as easily as you can batch the installation of multiple packages on your system, you can keep all these tools up to date with one simple command:

```
chocolatey update all
```

or

```
cup all
```

Much like you can on the NuGet command line, you can also perform an in-place update of Chocolatey itself. Simply run the following command to update Chocolatey to the latest version:

```
chocolatey update
```

or

```
cup
```

If you want to determine whether an update is available for any of your installed Chocolatey packages without immediately triggering the actual update operation, you could use the version command. This command will output the found version and the latest version of those packages:

```
chocolatey version all
```

or

```
cver all
```

Again, this command can be used similar to the update command. If you do not specify all or a package name, it will perform the action against the Chocolatey command-line tool itself. To check whether Chocolatey itself is up-to-date, run cver or chocolatey version.

Distributing Chocolatey Goodness

No, not distributing chocolates! At this point, we want you to contribute useful Chocolatey packages to the Chocolatey Gallery on http://chocolatey.org. That's right; you can produce packages yourself and make them available to the broader community as well.

Although you'll find quite a few useful packages already hosted on the Chocolatey Gallery, you might occasionally look for a missing one. If you ever find one of your favorite must-have tools or applications missing on the Chocolatey Gallery, you might consider creating and publishing a package for it yourself.

You know by now how to create various types of *vanilla* NuGet packages (Chapter 3 of this book explained this in detail). There are a few things you should know about creating and publishing Chocolatey packages however.

■ **Note** When we refer to "vanilla" NuGet packages, we are referring to the original NuGet packages to make a clear distinction with Chocolatey NuGet packages.

As with NuGet vanilla, you'll need to start from a .nuspec file. Let's take a look at the Notepad++ Chocolatey package we just installed onto our system.

■ **Tip** To browse the Chocolatey packages installed on your system through Windows Explorer, simply navigate to the `%SystemDrive%\Chocolatey\lib` folder. You should notice a folder structure very similar to the `$(SolutionDir)\packages` folder that NuGet vanilla installs solution-level packages into.

If you open `notepadplusplus.5.9.6.2.nupkg` (if you find a different version, note that version 5.9.6.2 was the latest version available at the time of this writing) using NuGet Package Explorer. You should see something unusual: where's the Notepad++ installer? The package almost has no contents at all, as shown in Figure 7-20.

Package contents

▲ 🗀 tools
       chocolateyInstall.ps1
   nppLogo.png

Figure 7-20. The Chocolatey package for Notepad++ has almost no contents at all.

You should notice, however, a single script file called `chocolateyInstall.ps1` in the `tools` folder. Using this filename by convention allows Chocolatey to recognize a Chocolatey package and makes sure NuGet vanilla is not doing anything with this package inside Visual Studio. This file will contain the script that will install this package onto your system. So to create Chocolatey package, you should start with having a `chocolateyInstall.ps1` script file into the package's `tools` folder. Don't worry about the image file for now, because it is just the logo for the package to be displayed on the Chocolatey Gallery web site.

Taking a closer look at the contents of the `chocolateyInstall.ps1` file, you might be surprised again: it contains only a single line of PowerShell! If you aren't surprised, probably things just got clearer to you. The reason why a Chocolatey package is so small in size and has almost no contents at all is because the contents are usually hosted elsewhere. Most of these tools already have a download URL on their originating web sites. This allows the `installChocolatey.ps1` script in your package to simply point to that URL and avoids copying the installers of the tool into your package. That's why Chocolatey packages are small in size, fast to download, and allow Chocolatey to provide immediate feedback during the installation process.

If we take a closer look at the one-liner in the `installChocolatey.ps1` file, you'll see the following piece of code:

```
Install-ChocolateyPackage 'notepadplusplus' 'exe' '/S'
'http://download.tuxfamily.org/notepadplus/5.9.6.2/npp.5.9.6.2.Installer.exe'
```

It is calling the `Install-ChocolateyPackage` cmdlet and passing in some values to the following arguments:

- PackageName: notepadplusplus
- PackageType: exe
- SilentArgs: /S

- Url: http://download.tuxfamily.org/notepadplus/5.9.6.2
  /npp.5.9.6.2.Installer.exe

In short, the `Install-ChocolateyPackage` cmdlet will download a file from a URL and install it on your system. The `PackageName` argument is arbitrary. You can name it whatever you want, but it would make sense to use the NuGet package ID of the package you are currently creating. The `PackageType` should either be exe or `msi`, depending on the installer that will be downloaded, which is referenced in the `Url` parameter.

If you want to provide a silent installation experience, without any wizards popping up asking for user input (mostly true for automated installations), you should pass in some value for the `SilentArgs` parameter. If you don't pass any value for this argument, you'll experience the default installation of the target installer. Please use the `notSilent` tag in your package's NuGet metadata if you choose a non-silent installation experience.

The `SilentArgs` arguments are being passed on to the exe or `msi` installer. For a `PackageType` of `msi`, this is easy: use `/quiet`. For an exe package, things are a bit different, because there is no standard format. Try any of these values to provide a silent installation experience: /s, /S, /q, /Q, /quiet, /silent, /SILENT, /VERYSILENT.

In addition to the arguments used by the `notepadplusplus` package, you could use a few other arguments in your own packages. One of them is the `Url64bit` argument, which could point to an alternative URL for the installer of the x64 version of the tool or application.

The `chocolatey install` or `cinst` command also has a few additional options available for use when installing a Chocolatey package. You can, for instance, pass on a set of arguments to the native installer being triggered by the package installation. This could be useful if you know some of the arguments being used or have some custom ones defined for your own installer. You can pass on these arguments to the `InstallArguments` parameter. By default, this parameter is empty and will be appended to any arguments already passed in by the package installation script. If you do not want to append these arguments and want to override all arguments the package already passes in, you could use the `OverrideArguments` switch. There's one last, additional shortcut to make the package install in a non-silent model: the `NotSilent` option. This will make the installer use the default interactive behavior, if any, disregarding any `SilentArgs` being passed on to it by the Chocolatey package installation script. You'll find a summary of these commands in Table 7-1.

Table 7-1. *Passing Arguments to a Native Installer Via Chocolatey*

Option	Description	Alternative Notation
InstallArguments	Specifies the installation arguments to be passed on to the native installer. Default behavior is to append these arguments to any arguments being passed on in the installChocolatey.ps1 script.	-ia -installArgs
OverrideArguments	Specifies whether the InstallArguments should be appended or overrides any arguments being passed internally in the package.	-o -overrideArgs
NotSilent	Specifies that the native installer should be run in non-silent mode, whatever the value of the SilentArgs parameter inside of the installChocolatey.ps1 script.	

■ **Caution** You can actually include executables in your Chocolatey packages if you have the right to distribute. If you feel uncertain about this, make sure you check out `https://github.com/chocolatey/chocolatey /wiki/Legal` for more information on legalities and distributions.

So, to create a Chocolatey package, you only have to create a `.nuspec` manifest, reference the `installChocolatey.ps1` file in its tools folder, and call the `Install-ChocolateyPackage` cmdlet within the script to point to the URL of your favorite tool's installer. Listing 7-5 shows how the `.nuspec` manifest could look like (metadata shortened for clarity):

Listing 7-5. An Example NuGet Manifest for Creating a Chocolatey Package

```xml
<?xml version="1.0"?>
<package xmlns="http://schemas.microsoft.com/packaging/2010/07/nuspec.xsd">
  <metadata>
    <id>notepadplusplus</id>
    <version>5.9.6.2</version>
    ...
    <description>Notepad++ is a free ...</description>
    <summary>Notepad++ is a free ...</summary>
    <tags>notepad notepadplusplus notepad-plus-plus chocolatey</tags>
  </metadata>
  <files>
    <file src="tools\chocolateyInstall.ps1" target="tools\chocolateyInstall.ps1" />
  </files>
</package>
```

In addition to the `Install-ChocolateyPackage` cmdlet, you might find the following helpers useful:

- `Install-ChocolateyPowerShellCommand`

- `Install-ChocolateyZipPackage`

All of these helper methods have built-in error handling, so there's no need to check for errors yourself when calling them from within `installChocolatey.ps1`. For more information on these helpers, check `https://github.com/chocolatey/chocolatey/wiki/CreatePackages`. This web page also provides information regarding some other helper methods you could use supporting some more advanced scenarios.

To create the Chocolatey package itself, the `.nupkg` file, Chocolatey exposes a `chocolatey pack` command, or `cpack` in short. Similar to the NuGet pack command, simply call `cpack myPackage.nuspec` (or `chocolatey pack myPackage.nuspec` if you like typing a lot) and out comes a Chocolatey package.

All that is left now is to make it available to the public for consumption. To do so, use the `chocolatey push` command, or `cpush` for short. Note that you must be a registered user on `http://chocolatey.org` and have a valid API key to be able to push your package to the Chocolatey Gallery. The package will be pushed, not published. Publishing will happen shortly, after the package has been reviewed by the Chocolatey gods.

Summary

We've looked at two projects in the NuGet ecosystem that focus on distributing applications using NuGet rather than distributing dependencies.

Octopus can be used to deploy *your* application packages to a variety of test, staging, and production environments and automates deploying to web and database servers. You learned that Octopus is the next step in formalizing the development process: build servers were introduced to automate and manage builds, and now, software like Octopus tries to provide a solution for the next step in the process: deployments.

We switched sides from remote deployments using NuGet packages to installing applications and tools, shipped in NuGet packages, using the Chocolatey command line. We touched briefly on how Chocolatey builds a bridge between NuGet and the Microsoft Web Platform Installer and Ruby Gems. You also learned how you can automate software installations, even in batches, and how you can keep those packages up to date with minimal effort. We also shed light on how easy it is to create and distribute tools and applications yourself using Chocolatey.

In the next chapter, we'll look at extending NuGet, a logical next step in creating software using NuGet in a tailor-made process.

CHAPTER 8

Extending NuGet

In the previous chapters, we've shown you how you can leverage NuGet in more advanced scenarios and how NuGet can be the tool of preference for managing external dependencies in your software projects. We've even touched some alternative scenarios where NuGet can be used to distribute releases and deploy them onto your server infrastructure.

While all of this is great, there are some use cases we haven't covered yet. The power of NuGet is its simplicity: it enables you to publish and consume packages. There are three mayor clients to work with NuGet. And all three of them can be extended to give you more power. For example, wouldn't you like to know how you can make yourself or your development team more productive? Or how you can get a grasp on what external dependencies are being used in your projects?

This chapter will focus on these questions and will provide you the required starting points to extend NuGet on your machine, or the machines of your team, to make software development more fun. We'll start with a quick "why?" before we dive in to the more technical part, where we'll be creating plug-ins and extensions for all three clients. Simple, basic things that you can extend or build upon to achieve super powers.

Why Extend NuGet?

The enthusiast software developer in you may answer the question of why one should extend NuGet with an energetic "because I can!" While that is a valid reason (and also the reason why Xavier and Maarten started looking into extending NuGet), there are some better reasons to do so as well.

If you've heard about git, a distributed version control system (DVCS) that gained enormous popularity in the open-source world thanks to GitHub.com, you may be aware that git offers various extensions. In fact, the git source control system is fairly easy and does not contain a lot of commands at its core. The real value of git as a source control system comes from its easy-to-create extensions, of which a lot are available.

A parallel can be drawn to NuGet. Out of the box, the NuGet command line knows the commands list, pack, push, setApiKey, install, upgrade, and uninstall. Those commands give you a great base set of functionality; you can do everything you probably want to do with them. But what about copying a package from one feed to another? A nuget copy command would come in handy there. What about knowing about all packages and their dependencies without having to open every single project in Visual Studio? Wouldn't nuget analyze be useful?

Similarly, for the NuGet Package Manager Console, it's great to have some functionality out of the box. Knowing the Package Manager Console is just a PowerShell console with some added variables (like $dte, an object representing Visual Studio) makes it an incredibly powerful tool to extend your development process. What about creating Team Foundation Server (TFS) work items from the package Manager Console? What about writing packages that add some to-do tasks to your list of work items? What about adding code generation or even a Bing search in there?

NuGet Package Explorer (NPE) is a great tool to work with NuGet packages and inspect what is going on in there. The lib folder in NuGet packages typically contains only an assembly and not source code. How about creating a NPE plug-in that allows you to decompile assemblies in a NuGet package and browse through the source code of the packages you download?

We've just scratched the surface in this section: all tools are there for you to use; all extension points are available. This chapter will give you some starters on how to extend the various tools, but we'll leave the implementation of the cool stuff to you. And when you're finished, why not publish your extensions on NuGet so everyone can use them?

Extending the NuGet Command Line

The NuGet command line tool is built in a very extensible fashion. For starters, every command that the command line tool exposes implements the same `ICommand` interface. In addition, the tool is using the Managed Extensibility Framework (MEF) to import (actually `ImportMany`) these commands within the scope of the application's lifetime. It does this by scanning its own assemblies and a special extensions folder defined by the command line tool. This special extensions folder can be found in the following location on your system:

`%LocalAppData%\NuGet\Commands`

Note The NuGet command line tool is a very nice example of how one could design an application open for extensibility, by making good use of the Managed Extensibility Framework (MEF). MEF is an interesting topic on its own and ships as part of the .NET Framework 4.0. If you haven't heard about it before, we highly recommend you read up on MSDN (`http://msdn.microsoft.com/en-us/library/dd460648.aspx`). Did you know you can actually dive into the sources on Codeplex (`http://mef.codeplex.com`)?

Because the NuGet command line is scanning this extension folder upon startup, it will automatically detect any assembly within that directory, or any of its subdirectories, that contains an *export* of a well-known type, such as an implementation of NuGet's `ICommand` interface. The `ICommand` interface is decorated with MEF's `InheritedExport` attribute, as shown in Listing 8-1, declaring that any implementing type will be exported as an implementation of type `ICommand`.

Listing 8-1. The NuGet Command Line ICommand Interface

```
[InheritedExport]
public interface ICommand
{
    CommandAttribute CommandAttribute { get; }
    IList<string> Arguments { get; }
    void Execute();
}
```

To be able to create your own custom `ICommand` implementation, you'll have to add a reference in your project to the `nuget.exe` file—that's right, to the NuGet command line tool itself! All you need to do is implement the interface, compile your assembly that exports your custom commands, and deploy it into the NuGet extensions directory. The concept is very simple yet so powerful.

■ **Tip** The commands available in NuGet are implemented in the same way as a command line extension is created for NuGet. This means that, if you want to create a command similar to the existing NuGet commands, you can easily peek at the NuGet source code. Also, if you want to borrow code that accesses an external package source, many good examples can be found in the NuGet source code.

One such example is the NuGet install command of which you can find the sources at https://hg01.codeplex.com/nuget/file/01f7db273fbd/src/CommandLine/Commands/InstallCommand.cs. Note these are not the latest sources but instead the latest version we found when writing this book. The ideal way to look at the NuGet source code would be by accessing https://hg01.codeplex.com/nuget/.

Creating a custom NuGet command

Creating a custom NuGet command is as easy as implementing the ICommand interface or its easy-to-use companion, the Command class. This interface (and companion class) can be found in the NuGet.exe assembly. Here are the steps required to get started in Visual Studio:

1. Create a new Visual Studio Solution, and add a class library (full .NET 4.0 framework).

2. Add a NuGet reference to Nuget.CommandLine (Install-Package Nuget.CommandLine)

3. Manually add a reference to NuGet.exe. You'll find it in your solution's packages folder where you installed Nuget.CommandLine in the previous step.

4. Adding a reference to NuGet.exe gives you access to the ICommand interface, the Command class, and the CommandAttribute class.

5. Add a reference to System.ComponentModel.Composition (the managed extensibility framework).

The ICommand interface is very straightforward to implement as it only contains one method Execute() and a read-only property IList<string> Arguments. Obviously, the Execute method executes the command, the Arguments property gives you access to any command line arguments received by the console.

To make things even easier for you, you can also inherit from a base class implementing this ICommand interface and providing you with some common NuGet command behavior, such as integrated help from the command line. This integrated help gives your custom command support for the help (or ?) option, so you can output some help information to the user instead. This way, you can provide guidance to users requesting help by executing the command nuget help or nuget help myCustomCommand. The base class we refer to is called Command and can be found in the NuGet.Commands namespace of the nuget.exe assembly.

> ▪ **Tip** We really encourage you to reuse this base class and benefit from its integrated help functionality to provide your users with a consistent nuget command line experience.

To get started, take a look at the NuGet.Analyze package, which provides some analysis functionality on top of source code repositories consuming NuGet packages. The package is a first attempt to automate the creation of a dependency grid for a given project, which is currently a manual and time-consuming task, often forgotten or allowed to become out of date. However, NuGet stores all your dependencies in a nice XML file (the packages.config file) relative to each Visual Studio project, as well as storing a reference to all these XML files in a central repositories.config file in the solution's packages folder. This is very useful information stored in a well-known format, so analysis of these files should be pretty straightforward.

For any solution that is consuming NuGet packages, you can find out which module of the product (or project of the solution) has which dependencies, even without parsing the information inside the source code itself. Therefore, one should be able to point NuGet to a solution file and get a real-time view on its dependencies. The output could be used as a generated dependency matrix for the given target solution.

The NuGet.Analyze package has support for both Team Foundation Server source control and local (or remote) file system folders. This should cover most source control systems in a first attempt. Of course, as the entire thing is open source as well, feel free to contribute your own ideas and send a pull request. The source code can be found at https://github.com/xavierdecoster/NuGet.Analyze.

Let's take a closer look at the AnalyzeCommand, which you can find in the source code. You'll notice the usage of a few attributes in that class, as shown in Listing 8-2.

Listing 8-2. Implementing a Custom NuGet Command Line Command

```
[Command(typeof(AnalyzeCommandResources), "analyze", "AnalyzeCommandDescription",
UsageSummaryResourceName = "AnalyzeCommandUsageSummary",
MinArgs = 0, MaxArgs = 1,AltName = "analyse")]
public class AnalyzeCommand : Command
{
    public override void ExecuteCommand()
    {
        ...
    }
}
```

To create a basic command, you simply inherit from Command and implement the abstract ExecuteCommand method. However, you still need to expose a little metadata for the NuGet command line to know how to deal with this command. That's where the CommandAttribute comes in, which you can see decorated on top of the class declaration. NuGet.exe will process this information and learn that the analyze command corresponds to the AnalyzeCommand type. An alternative name for the command has been provided as well: analyse.

Helpful information, such as a usage summary, can be found in the AnalyzeCommandResources file using the key AnalyzeCommandUsageSummary. Figure 8-1 shows you what the AnalyzeCommandResources file looks like.

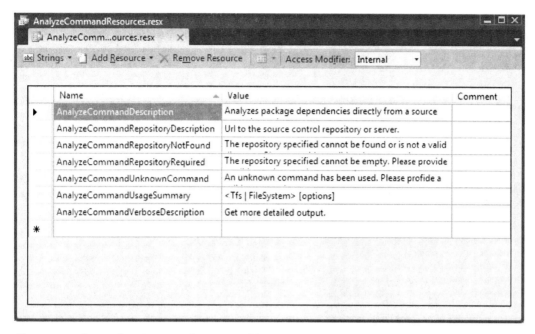

Figure 8-1. *The AnalyzeCommandResources file containing all messages related to the Analyze command we are creating*

Using the `CommandAttribute`, the NuGet command line also knows that zero or one argument can be passed to this command. That's a lot of information in a single attribute, but it gives you a lot of flexibility to implement your command as you want, without needing to take care of plumbing your command into the command line tool to make it integrate nicely.

We already mentioned that you *inherit* support for the help option when deriving from `Command`, but you can create additional options or flags that can give an extra meaning or different behavior to your custom command. For example, Listing 8-3 implements an argument as a simple property, decorated with the `OptionAttribute`. Figure 8-1 contains the messages referred to by The `OptionAttribute` as well.

Listing 8-3. *Implementing an Optional Flag for a Custom Command*

```
[Option(typeof(AnalyzeCommandResources), "AnalyzeCommandVerboseDescription")]
public bool Verbose { get; set; }
```

Installing a Custom NuGet Command

You now have learned all there is to it to extend the NuGet command line with your own custom commands: inherit `Command` and distribute the compiled assembly to the NuGet extensions directory.

The *classical* way of installing a command line extension is shown in Listing 8-4.

Listing 8-4. *Installing a NuGet Command Line Extension the Classical Way*

```
nuget.exe install /excludeversion /outputdir "%LocalAppData%\NuGet\Commands" MyCustomExtension
```

How do you feel about distributing those assemblies? What if we could make NuGet extend itself and distribute NuGet command line extensions using NuGet packages?

Luckily for you, there is a package for that! It's called NuGet.InstallCommandLineExtension and is available with the official NuGet package source. Figure 8-2 shows NuGet.InstallCommandLineExtension in action.

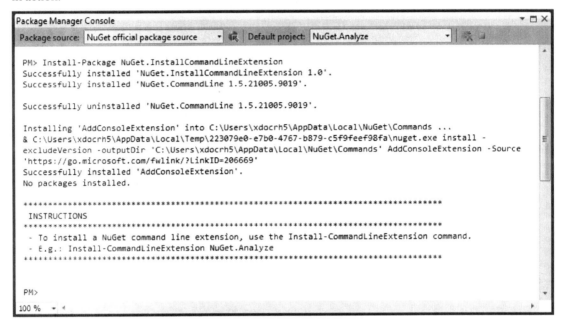

Figure 8-2. Installing the NuGet.InstallCommandLineExtension package using the NuGet Package Manager Console

Installing the NuGet.InstallCommandLineExtension package performs two actions: it will install a first NuGet command line extension, called AddConsoleExtension, and it will install a custom PowerShell cmdlet into the Package Manager Console, called Install-CommandLineExtension. This gives you two different ways of extending the NuGet command line in a way you already know and love—by using NuGet itself.

The AddConsoleExtension was installed into the NuGet command line extension directory and added the addExtension command to nuget.exe. Basically, if you would want to install the NuGet.Analyze command line extension, containing the nuget analyze command, you can now simply execute the following command from within the NuGet command line tool, as shown in Listing 8-5.

Listing 8-5. Extending the NuGet Command Line Tool from within the NuGet Command Line

```
nuget addExtension NuGet.Analyze
```

The addExtension command in itself is a NuGet command line extension. As with the NuGet.Analyze command we created in the previous section of this chapter, it inherited all the functionality for supporting the help command. Figure 8-3 shows you the addExtension command help after invoking nuget help addExtension from the command line.

Note The addExtension command line extension can be found separately in the official NuGet package source at http://nuget.org/List/Packages/AddConsoleExtension.

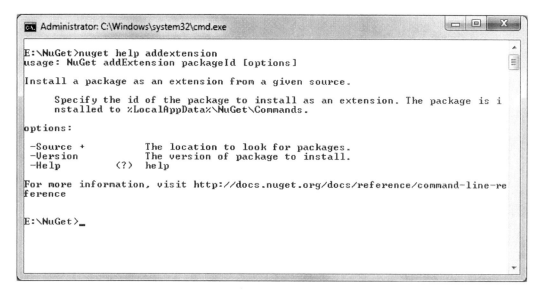

Figure 8-3. Displaying help for the NuGet addextension command

A great example of a NuGet extension is the copy command created by Rob Reynolds. You can use it to copy a NuGet package from one feed to another. Figure 8-4 shows you how you can install it on your system, simply by invoking the nuget addextension nuget.copy.extension command.

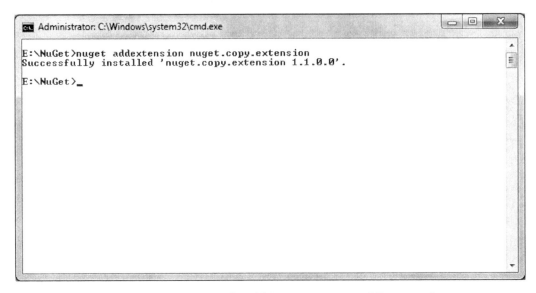

Figure 8-4. Installing an extension using the addExtension command line extension

When you installed the NuGet.InstallCommandLineExtension package, another item was installed on your system: a utility that can be used from within the Package Manager Console in Visual Studio. To extend the NuGet command line tool on your development machine with a given command, such as NuGet.Analyze, you can now simply run the script in Listing 8-6 from within the Package Manager Console, by making use of the newly installed Install-CommandLineExtension cmdlet:

Listing 8-6. Extending the NuGet Command Line Tool from within the Package Manager Console

```
Install-CommandLineExtension NuGet.Analyze
```

This section showed you two clean ways of installing a NuGet command line extension using the NuGet client tools, while distributing these extensions as NuGet packages: inception!

Extending the Package Manager Console

So far, you've seen how you can extend the NuGet command line. While handy, NuGet extensions of this type only worked from the command prompt. What about extending Visual Studio? The Package Manager Console is just a PowerShell console with additional variables like $dte, an object representing Visual Studio itself.

NuGet already speeds up your development in terms of dependency management, but having the Package Manager Console at hand inside Visual Studio makes NuGet incredibly powerful for extending your Visual Studio environment as well.

This section will guide you through the creation of PowerShell cmdlets that can be run in the Package Manager Console. It starts with some simple cmdlets that (of course) will be distributed through NuGet. After that, we'll create a more advanced cmdlet that also includes tab completion to make using the cmdlet even easier.

■ **Tip** An interesting Package Manager Console extension we've found is Steve Sanderson's MvcScaffolding package. It adds additional PowerShell cmdlets to the NuGet Package Manager Console and enables you to generate code in ASP.NET MVC.

Creating and Distributing a Package Manager Console Extension

Let's start the creation of a NuGet Package Manager Console extension by defining what we want to achieve. Visual Studio exposes a lot of functionality hidden in menus and keyboard shortcuts. Some developers are very keyboard-oriented in their day-to-day jobs, and to support them, we want to provide two PowerShell cmdlets for use in the Package Manager Console.

The first cmdlet, Remove-Usings, will enable any developers who have installed the extension we're creating to sort and remove using directives in their source code for the entire project. The second cmdlet, Find-Symbol, will enable those developers to find symbols, such as a class or interface, using the Package Manager Console.

Figure 8-5 shows you the NuGet Package Manager Console where the cmdlet Find-Symbol DeckController has been invoked. This cmdlet is not available out of the box but has been defined in a PowerShell module added to the Package Manager Console

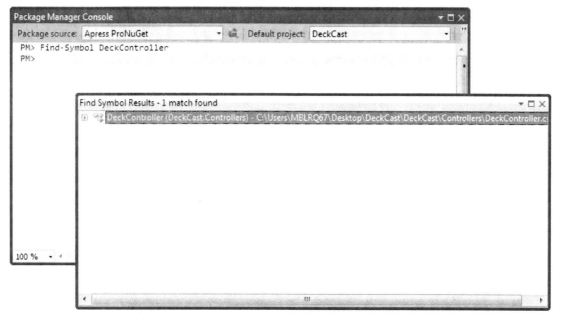

Figure 8-5. *The Package Manager Console executing a custom cmdlet named Find-Symbol*

Creating a NuGet Package Folder Structure

The Package Manager Console extension we are creating will be distributed through NuGet, so we'll have to create a NuGet package for that. In this section, we'll be using a simple approach to create a NuGet package: create a folder, create a NuGet package manifest, and invoke the nuget pack command.

Let's do that step by step. First of all, create a folder on your hard drive that will mimic the NuGet package contents. Maarten has created C:\Users\MBLRQ67\Desktop\Samples\VsCommands for that, but the exact location does not really matter. Next, open a command prompt, and run the nuget spec VsCommands command. This will create a NuGet Package Manifest (the .nuspec file) named VsCommands.nuspec. Open the file in Notepad (or any other text editor), and update the XML to something along the lines of Listing 8-7.

Listing 8-7. The NuGet Package Manifest for Our Package Manager Console Extension

```
<?xml version="1.0"?>
<package>
  <metadata>
    <id>VsCommands</id>
    <version>1.0.0</version>
    <authors>Maarten Balliauw</authors>
    <owners>Maarten Balliauw</owners>
    <requireLicenseAcceptance>false</requireLicenseAcceptance>
    <description>Adds cmd-lets NuGet PowerShell Console.</description>
    <releaseNotes>Adds cmd-lets to the NuGet PowerShell Console.</releaseNotes>
    <copyright>Copyright Maarten Balliauw 2011</copyright>
    <tags>nuget powershell pronuget apress</tags>
  </metadata>
</package>
```

■ Tip Did you know that Windows (since Windows 95, according to http://support.microsoft.com /kb/126449) has a hidden context menu item to open a console window at the current location? In your Windows Explorer, hold the Shift key and right-click the folder. This will show a context menu containing the "Open command window here" item.

The next step is to create a folder called tools under your VsCommands folder structure. As you saw in Chapter 3, the tools folder can contain scripts like install.ps1 (runs when the package is installed into a project), uninstall.ps1 (runs when the package is uninstalled from a project), and init.ps1 (runs every time you open the project into which the package is installed).

As you may have already guessed, we're going to take advantage of one of these scripts to dynamically load our Remove-Usings and Find-Symbol cmdlets into the Package Manager Console. Create a file called init.ps1 under the tools folder, and add the code you see in Listing 8-8. This code is a (short) PowerShell script that will be executed every time Visual Studio loads a project containing the VsCommands NuGet package we are creating.

Listing 8-8. *The init.ps1 PowerShell script for our Package Manager Console extension.*

```
param($installPath, $toolsPath, $package)
Import-Module (Join-Path $toolsPath VsCommands.psm1)
```

There are two important things to note in the init.ps1 script. The first line of code accepts some parameters the Package Manager Console hands to our PowerShell script. These contain the install path to your package, the tools path and the package itself. You are not obliged to use them, but there are scenarios where you may want to use this data to take action. For example, you can use the $installPath parameter to write additional files into the project.

The second line of code imports a PowerShell module into the Package Manager Console. As you can see, we're loading the module named VsCommands.psm1. Aha! This is where the actual Package Manager Console extension is defined. The VsCommands.psm1 file is a regular PowerShell module, which is simply being imported into the Package Manager Console PowerShell host. Create a new file named VsCommands.psm1 in the tools folder.

▨ **Note** Advice on writing PowerShell script modules, like we will be doing in the VsCommands.psm1 file, is worth a book in itself. If you want to know everything about it, or just want to dive into specifics like providing output when the Get-Help cmdlet is invoked on your extensions, refer to the MSDN pages at http://msdn.microsoft.com/en-us/library/dd878340(v=VS.85).aspx. Also, the Apress book *Pro Windows PowerShell* by Hristo Deshev (ISBN: 978-1-59059-940-2) may come in handy.

Creating the Package Manager Console Extension

In the previous section, we created the required NuGet package folder structure. The VsCommands.psm1 in the tools folder is still empty. In this section, we'll add the required PowerShell code that implements our Remove-Usings and Find-Symbol cmdlets.

The VsCommands.psm1 script will have access to the NuGet Package Manager Console and therefore to global variables like $dte, an object representing Visual Studio. Cmdlets you already know (and love?) such as Get-Project and Install-Package are available as well; the complete list of available NuGet PowerShell cmdlets can be found in Appendix C of this book.

Given the fact that we have access to the $dte object, the Package Manager Console has access to the Visual Studio environment. This opens the possibility we are looking for: to interact with Visual Studio.

▨ **Tip** A list of properties and methods available on the $dte object can be found on the MSDN page at http://msdn.microsoft.com/en-us/library/envdte.dte.aspx. James Chambers also did a great job collecting some PowerShell snippets in various NuGet packages and posted a list of $dte interactions and other samples at http://jameschambers.com/blog/powershell-script-examples-for-nuget-packages.

Let's start with implementing the `Remove-Usings` cmdlet. Since it will accept no parameters, it's just a PowerShell function that executes a method on the $dte object. Here's the definition of the Remove-Usings cmdlet:

```
function Remove-Usings {
    $dte.ExecuteCommand("ProjectandSolutionContextMenus.Project.RemoveandSortUsings")
}
```

When the `Remove-Usings` command is executed, the $dte object's `ExecuteCommand` method is called, passing the Visual Studio command name we expect to be executed. A list of possible Visual Studio commands is hidden inside Visual Studio: open the Tools ➤ Options menu and find the Environment ➤ Keyboard tab. This will give you a searchable list of all commands available in Visual Studio.

The `Find-Symbol` cmdlet for our VsCommands Package Manager Console extension will accept a parameter: if we want to find a class or interface, it'll be crucial to know what to search for. Here's the code for the `Find-Symbol` cmdlet:

```
function Find-Symbol {
    param(
        [parameter(ValueFromPipelineByPropertyName = $true)]
        [string]$Name
    )

    $dte.ExecuteCommand("Edit.FindSymbol", $Name)
}
```

Again, we're simply delegating the actual work to Visual Studio. The `Edit.FindSymbol` cmdlet exposed by the $dte object's `ExecuteCommand` method will search for the symbol.

There is one missing part in our `VsCommands.psm1` file: we need to tell PowerShell to expose all cmdlets to the outside world. In their current state, the only place where `Remove-Usings` and `Find-Symbol` can be executed is inside the `VsCommands.psm1` file itself. Solving that is easy: PowerShell's `Export-ModuleMember` cmdlet will allow you to expose all (or some specific) functions to the Package Manager Console PowerShell host.

The complete source code for `VsCommands.psm1`, including the call to `Export-ModuleMember` at the bottom, can be seen in Listing 8-9.

Listing 8-9. *The VsCommands.psm1 File Containing the Actual Implementation of the Package Manager Console Extension*

```
function Remove-Usings {
    $dte.ExecuteCommand("ProjectandSolutionContextMenus.Project.RemoveandSortUsings")
}

function Find-Symbol {
    param(
        [parameter(ValueFromPipelineByPropertyName = $true)]
        [string]$Name
    )

    $dte.ExecuteCommand("Edit.FindSymbol", $Name)
}

Export-ModuleMember -Function *
```

Distributing the Package Manager Console Extension

Now that the PowerShell scripts for our Package Manager Console extension are ready, it's time to gather everything as a NuGet package and get the extension out there. Packaging the extension is easy: by now, you should know the nuget pack command. Distributing the package is easy as well: nuget push should do the trick.

In the folder containing the VsCommands.nuspec file, open a command prompt, and run the nuget pack command. After you've run this command, a NuGet package for your Package Manager Console extension has been created.

The VsCommands.1.0.0.nupkg file can be pushed to the official NuGet package source or to your private NuGet feed. For this book, Maarten has pushed the package to a feed on MyGet that we've created for this book, http://www.myget.org/F/pronuget—feel free to add this package source in Visual Studio and install the VsCommands package. Figure 8-6 shows the output for both the nuget pack and nuget push commands.

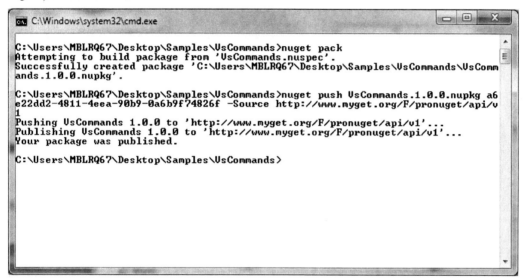

Figure 8-6. Results of packaging and publishing the VsCommands.1.0.0.nupkg package

Adding Tab Expansions to Package Manager Console Extensions

The VsCommand commands we created in the previous section were simple to create and use. There was no need for a lot of documentation or samples because both cmdlets were straightforward. Things are different if you create more complex cmdlets.

One of the things you may have noticed when using the NuGet Package Manager Console is the support for tab expansions, an idea similar to the IntelliSense you know and love when editing code in Visual Studio. Figure 8-7 shows you an example of tab expansion. When working with the Get-Package cmdlet, every option available features a menu of possible values when pressing the Tab key.

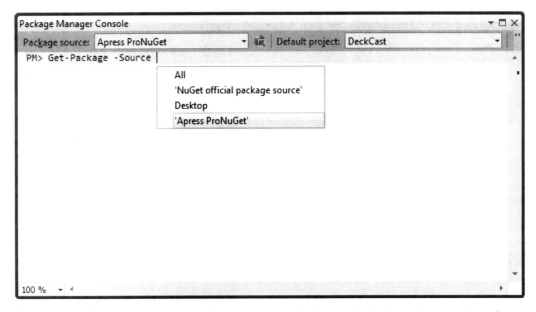

Figure 8-7. Tab expansion in action after pressing the Tab key in the Package Manager Console

For this section, find the source code related to this book on the Apress web site. We'll not dive into creating a Package Manager Console extension from scratch again; instead, we'll have a quick look at the `TfsCommands.psm1` PowerShell module, which you can download from the Apress web site. If you just want to test the TfsCommands commands, find them on the `http://www.myget.org/F/pronuget` NuGet feed for this book.

The TfsCommands extension features several PowerShell cmdlets that can be used when your project is added to a Team Foundation (TFS) server and a connection to that server has been established in Visual Studio. It features the following cmdlets:

- `Get-CurrentTfsCollectionUri`: Returns the URL for the TFS server to which you are currently connected

- `Get-CurrentTfsProjectName`: Returns the TFS project name to which you are currently connected

- `Get-TfsProjectNames`: Returns all projects for the TFS server to which you are currently connected

- `Get-WorkItemTypes`: Returns the work item types available in the TFS project to which you are currently connected

- `Add-WorkItem`: Creates a TFS work item in a specified project

The `Add-WorkItem` cmdlet is a hard to use in the Package Manager Console. It requires you to specify a number of parameters (`-Title`, `-Description`, `-WorkItemType`, `-TfsCollectionUri` and `-Project`). Wouldn't it be great to have tab expansions for these cmdlets? Figure 8-8 shows you what we are aiming for.

Figure 8-8. Our Add-WorkItem cmdlet featuring tab expansions (Project names have been blurred for confidentiality.)

The Add-WorkItem cmdlet has been implemented just as we've implemented the cmdlets in the previous section of this book. To achieve tab expansions, we've added some code at the bottom of the TfsCommands.psm1 file. Using the Register-TabExpansion PowerShell cmdlet, we can instruct the Package Manager Console to enable tab expansions for a given cmdlet. Listing 8-10 shows you how to do this.

Tab expansions can be static or dynamic. In Listing 8-10, note the Title and Description tab expansions will simply return a list of strings containing some sample data of what the user may pass into these cmdlet parameters. The WorkItemType, TfsCollectionUri, and Project tab expansions are slightly more complicated: these call into another PowerShell cmdlet to retrieve their data.

Listing 8-10. The Tab Expansion Registration

```
Register-TabExpansion 'Add-WorkItem' @{
    'Title' = {
        "Implement feature X",
        "Verify bug Y"
    }
    'Description' = {
        "Please implement feature X",
        "Bug Y has not been verified yet. Please take care of it."
    }
    'WorkItemType' = { Get-WorkItemTypes | Select -ExpandProperty Name }
    'TfsCollectionUri' = { Get-CurrentTfsCollectionUri }
    'Project' = { Get-TfsProjectNames | Select -ExpandProperty Name }
}
```

PUTTING TOGETHER THE MODULE'S CODE

In this section, you'll find the complete source code for this module.

```
function Get-CurrentTfsCollectionUri {
    [System.Reflection.Assembly]::LoadWithPartialName(
        "Microsoft.VisualStudio.TeamFoundation") | Out-Null

    if ($dte -ne $null) {
        $tfs = $dte.GetObject(
            "Microsoft.VisualStudio.TeamFoundation.TeamFoundationServerExt")
        $tfs.ActiveProjectContext.DomainUri
    }
}

function Get-CurrentTfsProjectName {
    [System.Reflection.Assembly]::LoadWithPartialName(
        "Microsoft.VisualStudio.TeamFoundation") | Out-Null

    if ($dte -ne $null) {
        $tfs = $dte.GetObject(
            "Microsoft.VisualStudio.TeamFoundation.TeamFoundationServerExt")
        $tfs.ActiveProjectContext.ProjectName
    }
}

function Get-TfsProjectNames {
    [System.Reflection.Assembly]::LoadWithPartialName(
        "Microsoft.VisualStudio.TeamFoundation") | Out-Null

    if ($dte -ne $null) {
        $tfs = $dte.GetObject(
            "Microsoft.VisualStudio.TeamFoundation.TeamFoundationServerExt")
        $TfsCollectionUri = $tfs.ActiveProjectContext.DomainUri

[psobject]$tfs =
[Microsoft.TeamFoundation.Client.TeamFoundationServerFactory]::GetServer($TfsCollectionU
ri)
    $wit = $tfs.GetService(
            [Microsoft.TeamFoundation.WorkItemTracking.Client.WorkItemStore])

return $wit.Projects
    }
}

function Get-WorkItemTypes {
    param(
        [parameter(Mandatory = $false)]
        [string]$TfsCollectionUri,
        [parameter(Mandatory = $false)]
        [string]$Project
```

```
    )

    [System.Reflection.Assembly]::LoadWithPartialName(
        "Microsoft.VisualStudio.TeamFoundation") | Out-Null
    [System.Reflection.Assembly]::LoadWithPartialName(
        "Microsoft.TeamFoundation.Client") | Out-Null
    [System.Reflection.Assembly]::LoadWithPartialName(
        "Microsoft.TeamFoundation.WorkItemTracking.Client") | Out-Null
    [System.Reflection.Assembly]::LoadWithPartialName(
        "Microsoft.TeamFoundation.WorkItemTracking.Client.WorkItemStore") | Out-Null

    if ($TfsCollectionUri -ne $null -and $dte -ne $null) {
        $tfs = $dte.GetObject(
            "Microsoft.VisualStudio.TeamFoundation.TeamFoundationServerExt")
        $TfsCollectionUri = $tfs.ActiveProjectContext.DomainUri
    }

    if ($Project -eq $null -ne $null -and $dte -ne $null) {
        $tfs = $dte.GetObject(
            "Microsoft.VisualStudio.TeamFoundation.TeamFoundationServerExt")
        $Project = $tfs.ActiveProjectContext.ProjectName
    }

    [psobject]$tfs =[Microsoft.TeamFoundation.Client.TeamFoundationServerFactory]
        ::GetServer($TfsCollectionUri)
    $wit = $tfs.GetService(
        [Microsoft.TeamFoundation.WorkItemTracking.Client.WorkItemStore])
    return $wit.Projects[$Project].WorkItemTypes
}

function Add-WorkItem {
    param(
        [parameter(ValueFromPipelineByPropertyName = $true)]
        [string]$Title,
        [parameter(Mandatory = $false)]
        [string]$Description,
        [parameter(Mandatory = $false)]
        [string]$WorkItemType = "Task",
        [parameter(Mandatory = $false)]
        [string]$TfsCollectionUri,
        [parameter(Mandatory = $false)]
        [string]$Project
    )

    [System.Reflection.Assembly]::LoadWithPartialName(
        "Microsoft.VisualStudio.TeamFoundation") | Out-Null
    [System.Reflection.Assembly]::LoadWithPartialName(
        "Microsoft.TeamFoundation.Client") | Out-Null
    [System.Reflection.Assembly]::LoadWithPartialName(
        "Microsoft.TeamFoundation.WorkItemTracking.Client") | Out-Null
    [System.Reflection.Assembly]::LoadWithPartialName(
        "Microsoft.TeamFoundation.WorkItemTracking.Client.WorkItemStore") | Out-Null
```

223

```
    if ($TfsCollectionUri -ne $null -and $dte -ne $null) {
        $tfs = $dte.GetObject(
            "Microsoft.VisualStudio.TeamFoundation.TeamFoundationServerExt")
        $TfsCollectionUri = $tfs.ActiveProjectContext.DomainUri
    }

    if ($Project -eq $null -ne $null -and $dte -ne $null) {
        $tfs = $dte.GetObject(
            "Microsoft.VisualStudio.TeamFoundation.TeamFoundationServerExt")
        $Project = $tfs.ActiveProjectContext.ProjectName
    }

    [psobject]$tfs = [Microsoft.TeamFoundation.Client.TeamFoundationServerFactory]
        ::GetServer($TfsCollectionUri)
    $wit = $tfs.GetService(
        [Microsoft.TeamFoundation.WorkItemTracking.Client.WorkItemStore])
    $workItem = new-object Microsoft.TeamFoundation.WorkItemTracking.Client.WorkItem(
        $wit.Projects[$Project].WorkItemTypes[$WorkItemType])
    $workItem.Title = $Title
    if ($Description -ne $null) {
        $workItem.Item("System.Description") = $Description
    }
    $workItem.Save()
}

Register-TabExpansion 'Add-WorkItem' @{
    'Title' = {
        "Implement feature X",
        "Verify bug Y"
    }
    'Description' = {
        "Please implement feature X",
        "Bug Y has not been verified yet. Please take care of it."
    }
    'WorkItemType' = { Get-WorkItemTypes | Select -ExpandProperty Name }
    'TfsCollectionUri' = { Get-CurrentTfsCollectionUri }
    'Project' = { Get-TfsProjectNames | Select -ExpandProperty Name }
}

Export-ModuleMember -Function *
```

Extending NuGet Package Explorer

If you often use NuGet Package Explorer, you're probably doing some repetitive work without even paying too much attention to it. For example, you might need to take a look at the sources of a given assembly inside a NuGet package. We personally like to use ILSpy, a free and open source .NET assembly browser and decompiler, to disassemble binaries and investigate their inner workings. If you want to do this for an assembly inside a NuGet package you opened in NuGet Package Explorer, you would first need to extract it, save it to disk (and remember its location), open ILSpy, and open the assembly you just saved. This is too much manual effort, and if you do this a lot, you can easily consume too much valuable time.

When dealing with scenarios as these, it's worth considering if a plug-in could help you with this task. That's exactly what Xavier Decoster's ILSpy plug-in for NuGet Package Explorer does! We will use this plug-in as an example of how to create plug-ins, and we'd like to invite you to create your own and share them with the world. The ILSpy plug-in is open source and can be found at http://npeilspy.codeplex.com.

NuGet Package Explorer has been designed to support plug-ins by making good use of the Managed Extensibility Framework. It has a full-blown plug-in manager built in, allowing you to add plug-ins from within the application itself. Starting from version 2.5, it has pushed the limit even further by supporting plug-ins to be delivered through NuGet packages, hosted on a dedicated NuGet feed on MyGet.org, available at www.myget.org/F/npe. As such, NuGet Package Explorer supports both local and feed plug-ins. You can see dialog for adding a plug-in in Figure 8-9.

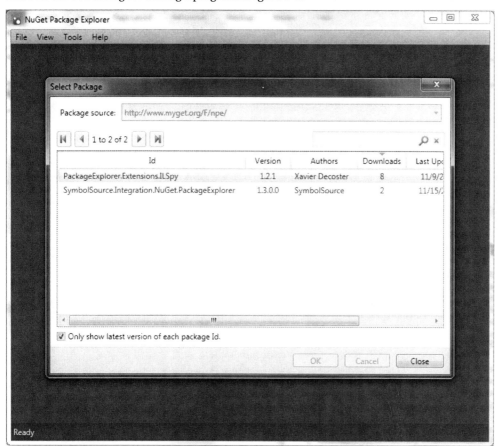

Figure 8-9. Adding a feed plug-in in NuGet Package Explorer's built-in plug-in manager

NuGet Package Explorer features three different types of extensions:

- *Content viewer extensions* provide support for visualizing files in NuGet packages. For example, if you open a package containing an image, the standard NPE image visualizer will show you a preview of the selected image.

- *Package validation rules* provide the ability to analyze packages you create using NPE. When a user clicks the Analyze Package command, your custom package validation rules will be activated to check the package you are creating conforms the rules you define for creating packages.

- *Package commands* provide support to add menu items and actions to the NPE application. For example, if you always publish a package to a specific feed using the exact same API key, why not create a `PublishToMyFeed` command to do exactly that without interrupting you with other dialog windows?

Creating any of these three types of extensions is done using the same pattern:

- Create a new Visual Studio Solution, and add a class library (make sure you target the full .NET 4.0 Framework, and not the .NET 4.0 Framework Client Profile).

- Add a NuGet Reference to `NuGetPackageExplorer.Types` (`Install-Package NuGetPackageExplorer.Types`).

This will make sure your project has the required references and will install some sample code files into your project, ready for modification to suit your needs.

Creating a Custom Content Viewer

The main purpose of NuGet Package Explorer Content Viewer plug-ins is to attach custom visualizers to certain file types. By default, NuGet Package Explorer does not handle every possible file extension, except for the most common NuGet package contents. Whenever a user triggers the View Content command on a certain file, by double clicking it for instance, NuGet Package Explorer scans the application for a command that can handle the requested file extension.

After installing the `NuGetPackageExplorer.Types` package, described in the previous section, the installer has injected your project with a class named `MyCustomContentViewer`, shown in Listing 8-11. This class is a sample content viewer that you can adjust to suit your needs. For starters, you might want to pick a proper file extension to tell the tool what kind of files your plug-in will target. Notice that your plug-in can register itself for more than one extension at the same time. The integer parameter of the `PackageContentViewerMetadata` attribute sets your plug-in's priority. The lower the value, the higher its priority.

Listing 8-11. Default Sample of a Custom Content Viewer for NuGet Package Explorer

```
// TODO: replace '.extension' with your custom extension
[PackageContentViewerMetadata(0, ".extension", ".anotherextension")]
internal class MyCustomContentViewer : IPackageContentViewer
{
    public object GetView(string extension, Stream stream)
    {
        throw new NotImplementedException();
    }
}
```

The content viewer has only one significant method—GetView. It returns an object, but please bear in mind that NuGet Package Explorer is a WPF application and will put the result of this method into a ContentPresenter control's Content property. Therefore, you can return either a simple string or any deriving object of the Visual class. The GetView method has access to information regarding the file it will need to handle: its file extension and its content stream.

A simple sample is shown in Listing 8-12. This is an NPE content viewer plug-in that handles .txt files and simply returns their content stream as a string.

Listing 8-12. A Simple .txt file Content Viewer Example

```
[PackageContentViewerMetadata(0, ".txt")]
internal class TextFileContentViewer : IPackageContentViewer
{
    public object GetView(string extension, Stream stream)
    {
        StreamReader reader = new StreamReader(stream);
        return reader.ReadToEnd();
    }
}
```

The ILSpy plug-in for NuGet Package Explorer goes a little further and works with a modal WPF dialog showing a custom ConfigurationControl, as shown in Listing 8-13. Because it targets files with a .dll or .exe extension and has a priority of 0, it will be used as the default content viewer for assembly files inside a NuGet package.

Listing 8-13. A Content Viewer Using a Custom WPF Control in a Modal Dialog

```
[PackageContentViewerMetadata(0, ".dll", ".exe")]
internal class ILSpyPackageContentViewer : IPackageContentViewer
{
    private ConfigurationControl configControl;
    private Window dialog;

    public object GetView(string extension, Stream stream)
    {
        try
        {
            configControl = new ConfigurationControl(extension, stream);
            dialog = new Window();
            dialog.Content = configControl;
            dialog.Topmost = true;
            dialog.Width = 300;
            dialog.Height = 120;
            dialog.ResizeMode = ResizeMode.NoResize;
            dialog.WindowStartupLocation = WindowStartupLocation.CenterOwner;
            dialog.ShowInTaskbar = false;
            dialog.ShowDialog();

            return configControl.Assembly.FullName;
        }
        catch (Exception exception)
        {
```

```
            return exception.ToString();
        }
    }
}
```

A user who double-clicks an assembly contained in a NuGet package open in NuGet Package Explorer and has the ILSpy plug-in installed will see the configuration control in a dialog, as shown in Figure 8-10.

Figure 8-10. The configuration control of NuGet Package Explorer's ILSpy plug-in

After choosing the correct path to your ILSpy executable and clicking the OK button, you'll see ILSpy opening up the requested file, as shown in Figure 8-11.

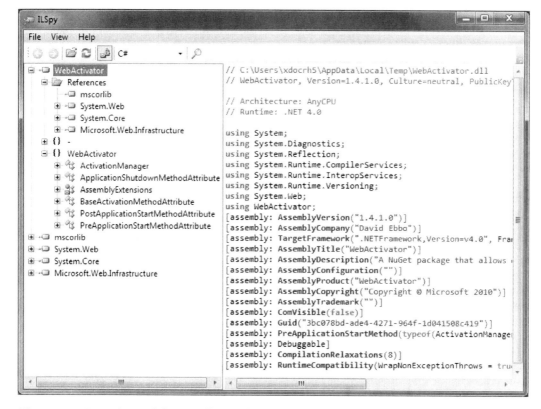

Figure 8-11. Browsing and decompilling a .dll assembly with ILSpy

Creating a Custom Package Validation Rule

In addition to a custom content viewer, you'll notice that after installing the
NuGetPackageExplorer.Types package, two more classes were injected into your project. One of them,
the MyCustomPackageRule class, is implementing IPackageRule, which allows you to add your own
validation logic for NuGet packages, for example, to enforce all packages produced in your company
have correct copyright information and a proper logo in its manifest. Do not forget to *export* these
package rules by marking them with the Export attribute, as shown in Listing 8-14.

Listing 8-14. Default Sample of a Custom Package Rule for NuGet Package Explorer

```
[Export(typeof(IPackageRule))]
internal class MyCustomPackageRule : IPackageRule
{
    public IEnumerable<PackageIssue> Validate(IPackage package)
    {
        throw new NotImplementedException();
    }
}
```

Whenever a user triggers the Analyze Package command in NuGet Package Explorer for the first time, the application will import all available IPackageRule implementations and call their `Validate` method for the currently opened package.

A sample of a package validation rule can be found in Listing 8-15. The `SamplePackageRule` yields one `PackageIssue` of the `PackageIssueLevel.Error`. A title, description, and a possible solution are added to the `PackageIssue` object to provide the user running this validation rule with enough information to comply with the rule defined.

Listing 8-15. A Sample Package Validation Rule

```
[Export(typeof(IPackageRule))]
internal class SamplePackageRule : IPackageRule
{
    public IEnumerable<PackageIssue> Validate(IPackage package, string packageFileName)
    {
        yield return new PackageIssue(
            PackageIssueLevel.Error, "Sample error",
            "The sample error is just being used for sample purposes.",
            "There's no solution to this.");
    }
}
```

The `PackageIssue`(s) being returned will be shown in the package analysis pane of NPE, as shown in Figure 8-12.

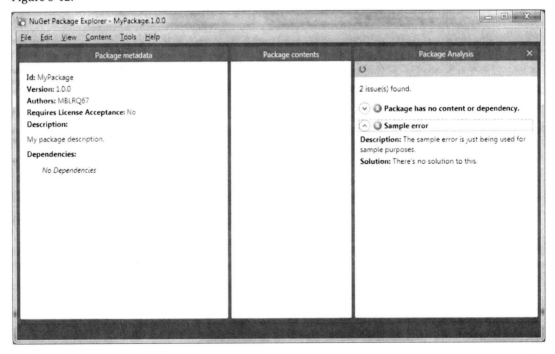

Figure 8-12. NuGet Package Explorer displaying an error message created by a package validation rule

---

■ **Warning** Do not store any *state* into your custom rule classes, because all package rules will be instantiated only *once per session* of the NuGet Package Explorer application. As such, all package rule instances are likely to be shared among multiple invocations of the Analyze Package command.

Creating a Custom Package Command

The third piece of code that has been added to your project after installing the NuGetPackageExplorer.Types package is a sample custom package command. A custom package command has access to the opened package and appears as a menu item in the Tools menu. A custom package command implements the IPackageCommand interface and exposes some metadata through the PackageCommandMetadata attribute, as shown in Listing 8-16.

Listing 8-16. Default sample of a custom package command for NuGet Package Explorer

```
[PackageCommandMetadata("My custom command")]
internal class MyCustomPackageCommand : IPackageCommand
{
    public void Execute(IPackage package)
    {
        throw new NotImplementedException();
    }
}
```

By implementing your own custom package commands, you can plug in your own useful commands into NuGet Package Explorer and reuse them for any NuGet package, for instance, a command that easily clones a package and saves a copy on disk.

NuGet Package Explorer offers you a lot of extensibility in three different domains: file content viewers, package validation rules, and custom package commands. Each of them are useful on their own, and combined, they can possibly be a huge asset in your NuGet tool belt.

Summary

In this chapter, we covered the power of NuGet: its simplicity (it enables you to publish and consume packages) and its extensibility (the three mayor clients to work with NuGet can be extended with more power).

We've created extensions for all three clients: we've extended the NuGet command line with an analyze command and have demonstrated an easy way to install these additional commands.

The Package Manager Console was extended with several cmdlets; some simple commands that instruct Visual Studio to search for symbols or remove and sort using directives. We've covered how to create more complex commands with tab expansions support for creating an experience similar to IntelliSense for the users of your extensions.

NuGet Package Explorer can also be extended. We've demonstrated this with a plug-in providing you with ILSpy integration, allowing you to disassemble binary package content right from within NuGet Package Explorer. No need to extract the desired assembly from the package, open Windows Explorer windows to find ILSpy.exe and then manually dragging the assembly onto the ILSpy window. It is a much better experience to automate such things.

If you find yourself executing repetitive tasks when working with any of these NuGet client tools, consider if writing a simple extension or plug-in could help you out and save you, and others, lots of time in the future.

In the next chapter, we'll go one step further. NuGet is great for managing packages but if we change perspective you'll see NuGet can be considered a protocol too—a protocol that enables you to automatically update your applications or to extend your own applications with plug-ins that are distributed through NuGet. And that's exactly what we'll do in the next chapter.

NuGet as a Protocol

So far, you've seen how to consume and create NuGet packages and how to host your own feed containing packages. Using NuGet, we've managed to set up a means of continuous package delivery and extended the NuGet command line and Package Manager Console.

The concepts and techniques demonstrated in the previous chapters of this book focused on using NuGet as a means of managing dependencies when developing software using Visual Studio. We've looked at NuGet as a package manager. How about we change our perspective and look at NuGet as a protocol for distributing packages?

You've already seen that complete deployments can be shipped as NuGet packages and that complete software installations can be distributed through NuGet (see Chapter 7). Why not leverage these techniques ourselves? All NuGet components have been built around one central assembly, `NuGet.Core`, which provides the base functionalities used in NuGet: working with feeds (or repositories) and installing and uninstalling packages based on such feeds.

This chapter will demonstrate how you can use `NuGet.Core` in your applications. If you are working with any form of plug-ins that users can install into your application or want to work with a self-updating executable (much like `nuget.exe update -self`), the techniques described in this chapter will be of use to you. In this chapter, we'll create a simple ASP.NET Model View Controller MVC application that supports loading plug-ins from external assemblies and we'll distribute these plug-ins through NuGet.

Understanding Protocols

Let's have a look at Wikipedia's definition for a protocol:

> *A communications protocol is a system of digital message formats and rules for exchanging those messages in or between computing systems and in telecommunications. A protocol may have a formal description.*
>
> *Protocols may include signaling, authentication and error detection and correction capabilities.*

> Wikipedia, `http://en.wikipedia.org/wiki/Communications_protocol`

If we break down the definition for a protocol, there are two important concepts to note: *exchanging messages* and *formal description*. When you think of NuGet, it supports exactly that: NuGet provides a means of *exchanging messages* through the use of a feed containing packages. These feeds conform to the OData feed format, a *formal description* of what a feed should look like. Packages are also created according to a *format description*: the Open Packaging Conventions are used to create a compressed archive containing multiple files and the relations between them. The NuGet package manifest adds an additional layer of information to these packages containing data like package authors, versioning information, and tags.

That leaves one conclusion to make: NuGet is a protocol—not a low-level protocol like TCP but a high-level protocol for exchanging packages between a server and a client. If you take into account that packages can be pushed onto a feed, that also means an exchange between client and server is possible. Where TCP packages transport only a few bytes, NuGet packages can potentially transport gigabytes of data. NuGet provides a protocol for distributing those packages through a feed.

To make this explanation more clear, let's look at an example. Paint.NET, a well-known image editor written in .NET and available freely at www.getpaint.net has plug-ins. If you want to create an image effect filter that performs some specific actions on the input image, you can do so. It's a pity, though, that community contributed plug-ins are only available on a bulletin board, from which you have to manually download the plug-in and copy it into Paint.NET's installation directory.

Of course, this could be done using a web site where a ZIP file containing a plug-in is available for download. Using some C# or VB.NET code, it would be easy to download these files and copy them to a specific folder. But why go through all the hassle of supporting proxies and authentication and creating conventions on how a plug-in should be compressed?

It would make sense to use NuGet as a protocol in this situation: if the members of the team behind Paint.NET chose NuGet as a protocol, they could provide a user interface where users can pick the plug-ins to install from a feed (a NuGet feed, but that fact would be invisible to the user). Using NuGet under the cover, Paint.NET would be able to download the plug-in packages and copy the contents to the Paint.NET plug-ins folder. Authors of plug-ins could publish their plug-ins to the same NuGet feed to share their work with the world. All the infrastructure to establish this scenario is available in NuGet.Core!

Similarly, in the next section, we'll create an ASP.NET MVC application supporting plug-ins and distribute these plug-ins through a NuGet feed.

Creating a Pluggable Application Using NuGet

This chapter will make use of a sample application called SearchPortal, for which you can find the source code in the downloads for this book. SearchPortal is a web application written in ASP.NET MVC, which can be installed in any company and serves as a portal to one or more search engines. As Figure 9-1 demonstrates, anyone navigating to the SearchPortal homepage can enter a string to search for, select a search engine, and perform a web search based on that information.

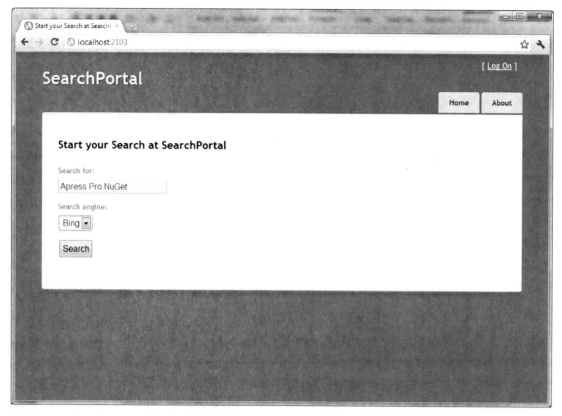

Figure 9-1. SearchPortal home page allowing a user to specify a search string and select a search engine which should be used to perform the search

The list of search engines that can be used is specific to the IT department installing SearchPortal on its servers: some companies may choose to allow searches using only Bing, while others may allow Bing, Google, and maybe even their own internal search engine. Figure 9-2 shows you a search for "Pro NuGet" after selecting Bing from the list of search engines.

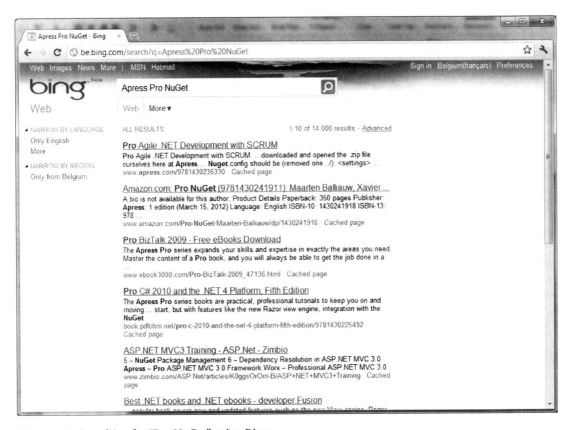

Figure 9-2. Searching for "Pro NuGet" using Bing

An administrator can log in to the administration area of the application (conveniently located at /administration). As Figure 9-3 shows, the administration area features a list of available search engines that can be installed or uninstalled. Using this page, the administrator picks the search engines to be shown in the drop-down list on the SearchPortal home page.

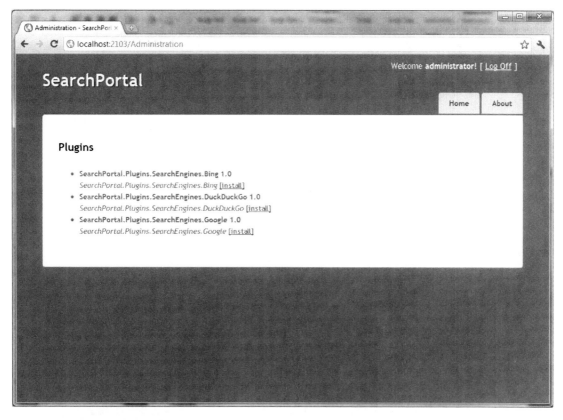

Figure 9-3. The SearchPortal administration area

The Plugins list shown in the administrative area is based on a NuGet feed located at www.myget.org/F/pronuget, the same feed that we've used as a sample in previous chapters of this book. All plug-ins for SearchPortal are, in fact, NuGet packages containing a search engine that can be plugged into SearchPortal. This enables any user of SearchPortal to create a search engine plug-in that can be installed in any SearchPortal deployment by administrators of SearchPortal. The list of packages on the MyGet feed can be seen in Figure 9-4.

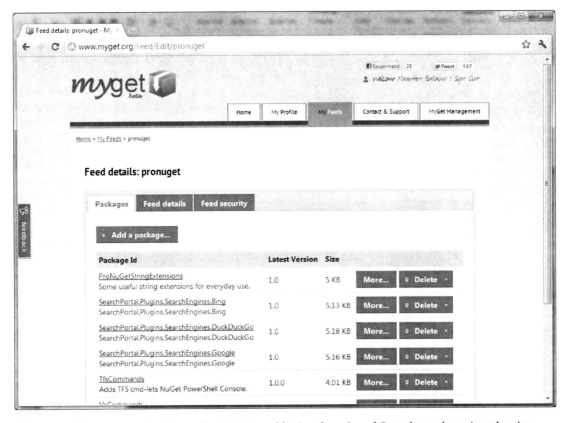

Figure 9-4. The pronuget feed hosted on MyGet and listing three SearchPortal search engine plug-ins

Defining Architecture and Technologies

Before we dive into how SearchPortal is developed, it is important to identify a suitable architecture and pick suitable technologies to support that architecture. SearchPortal uses two concepts that require a well-thought-out architecture:

- SearchPortal has to be extensible. The application architecture should support loading plug-ins from assemblies that were not originally shipped with the SearchPortal installation files. Extensions should be discovered and loaded by the application and integrated at runtime.

- Plug-ins should be easily discoverable. Distributing plug-ins to SearchPortal administrators should be simple and easy to do.

To build SearchPortal, we will make use of the following technologies:

- ASP.NET MVC will be used to develop the web interface for SearchPortal.

- Microsoft's Managed Extensibility Framework (MEF) will be used to make the application extensible. Living in the System.ComponentModel.Composition namespace, MEF is a framework that enables your application to load external assemblies at runtime and integrate them into your application.

- NuGet will be used for plug-in distribution. Plug-ins containing additional search engines will be compiled into an assembly and packaged into a NuGet package.

Tip If you are not familiar with the Managed Extensibility Framework (MEF), refer Maarten's "MEF is cool as ICE" blog post at http://blog.maartenballiauw.be/post/2010/03/04/MEF-will-not-get-easier-its-cool-as-ICE.aspx. Using MEF, classes can import dependencies by adding the [Import] attribute to a property. These imports are satisfied by composing the application and looking for matching exports, which have an [Export] attribute. Have a look at this blog post to quickly grasp the ideas and principles behind MEF.

Figure 9-5 shows a schematic view of the SearchPortal architecture. The SearchPortal.Web application will be created as an ASP.NET MVC application using Visual Studio. It will make use of MEF to load search engine plug-ins such as Bing or Google. These plug-ins will be distributed using NuGet and can be installed through an administration area, which makes use of the NuGet.Core assembly.

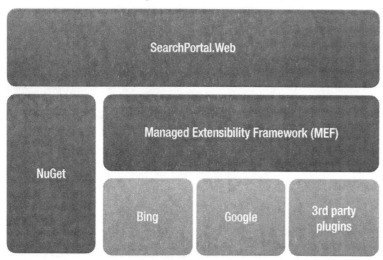

Figure 9-5. Schematic view of the SearchPortal architecture

Defining the ISearchEngine Interface

As discussed in the previous section of this chapter, SearchPortal will make use of MEF to load and integrate plug-ins at runtime. Since MEF is part of the .NET Framework, it is easy to make an application support a form of plug-ins:

- Add an assembly reference to System.ComponentModel.Composition.

- Create an interface for the search engines plug-ins.

The first part, adding a reference to a .NET Framework assembly to a Visual Studio project, should be easy. Let's do something more interesting; let's define an interface for search engine plug-ins.

The ISearchEngine interface in Listing 9-1 shows you an interface that exposes a property and a method. The Name property should return the name for the search engine plug-in, for example "Bing". The GenerateSearchUri method should return a Uri object based on a given searchTerm. For example, when searching for "Pro NuGet", the GenerateSearchUri should return a URL in the form of http://www.bing.com/search?q=Pro%20Nuget. This URI can then be used by SearchPortal to initiate the actual search on the selected search engine.

Listing 9-1. The ISearchEngine Interface That Has to Be Implemented by Search Engine Plug-ins to be Discoverable by the SearchPortal Application

```
[InheritedExport]
public interface ISearchEngine
{
    string Name { get; }

    Uri GenerateSearchUri(string searchTerm);
}
```

Note that the ISearchEngine interface has the [InheritedExport] attribute, which will tell MEF that any class implementing the ISearchEngine interface will be exposed as a plug-in and can be loaded at runtime. This is the basis for the plug-in architecture in SearchPortal.

An example of such ISearchEngine implementation is shown in Listing 9-2. The Bing class implements the ISearchEngine interface and because that interface was attributed with the [InheritedExport] attribute, SearchPortal will know about the Bing class being a search engine implementation.

Listing 9-2. The Bing Class Exposing Search Functionalities Through the Bing Search Engine

```
public class Bing
    : ISearchEngine
{
    public string Name
    {
        get { return "Bing"; }
    }

    public Uri GenerateSearchUri(string searchTerm)
    {
        return new Uri(string.Format("http://www.bing.com/search?q={0}", searchTerm));
    }
}
```

Importing Search Engines

In the previous section of this chapter, we've defined the ISearchEngine interface. This interface defined what a search engine plug-in should look like and how MEF can discover implementations of this interface.

MEF will look for implementations of the ISearchEngine interface in a so-called catalog of components. This catalog is created once when the application starts and is exposed through a CompositionContainer. Although it's feasible to create this catalog yourself and integrate MEF's CompositionContainer in your ASP.NET MVC application, that task takes some time and effort on your part. Since you are reading a book about NuGet and we want to encourage you to use NuGet as much as possible, the following commands can be run from the Package Manager Console in Visual Studio:

```
Install-Package MefContrib -Version 1.2.0.0
Install-Package MefContrib.MVC3 -Version 1.2.0.0
```

Note You might be wondering why we explicitly specify the version in the preceding commands. The explanation is very straightforward: we want our samples to give you an "it just works" experience. At the time of this writing, version 1.2.0.0 of these packages was the latest available, and we know this version works with our sample. If we didn't specify a version, you might risk installing a newer version that potentially breaks our sample. However, don't hesitate to try it out another version by omitting the version specification.

The MefContrib and MefContrib.MVC3 packages contain everything you need to work with MEF in an ASP.NET MVC application without having to worry about implementing interfaces such as ASP.NET MVC's IControllerFactory. Instead, the MefContrib.MVC3 package contains these implementations and registers them with ASP.NET MVC for you by adding a file called /App_Start/AppStart_MefContribMVC3.cs to your Visual Studio project.

The AppStart_MefContribMVC3 class contains the Start() method, which does all the wiring of MEF for you, including the creation of a catalog containing possible plug-ins. Since we'll have to add the plug-ins installed through NuGet to this catalog later on, let's quickly go though the AppStart_MefContribMVC3 class's source code. A trimmed-down version of it is shown in Listing 9-3. If you want the full source code for this class, see the related source code download for this book.

Listing 9-3. MefContrib's AppStart_MefContribMVC3 Class, Which Does All the MEF Wiring in the
SearchPortal Application

```
[assembly: WebActivator.PreApplicationStartMethod(
    typeof(SearchPortal.Web.App_Start.AppStart_MefContribMVC3), "Start")]

namespace SearchPortal.Web.App_Start
{
    public static class AppStart_MefContribMVC3
    {
        public static void Start()
        {
            // Register the CompositionContainerLifetimeHttpModule HttpModule.
            // This makes sure everything is cleaned up correctly after each request.
            CompositionContainerLifetimeHttpModule.Register();

            // Create MEF catalog based on the contents of ~/bin.
            //
            // Note that any class in the referenced assemblies implementing in
            // "IController" is automatically exported to MEF. There is no need for
            // explicit [Export] attributes on ASP.NET MVC controllers.

            var catalog = new AggregateCatalog(
                new DirectoryCatalog("bin"),
                new ConventionCatalog(new MvcApplicationRegistry()));
                // Note: add your own (convention)catalogs here if needed.

            // Tell MVC3 to use MEF as its dependency resolver.
            var dependencyResolver = new CompositionDependencyResolver(catalog);
            DependencyResolver.SetResolver(dependencyResolver);

            // Tell MVC3 to resolve dependencies in controllers
            ControllerBuilder.Current.SetControllerFactory(
                new CompositionControllerFactory(
                    new CompositionControllerActivator(dependencyResolver)));

            // ... trimmed ...
        }
    }
}
```

The MefContrib.MVC3 package has a dependency on a NuGet package called WebActivator. The first line of code in Listing 9-3 registers the AppStart_MefContribMVC3 class' Start() method with WebActivator to register all MEF components whenever the SearchPortal application is started.

In the Start() method, an AggregateCatalog is created in which MEF will look for plug-ins. This AggregateCatalog is an aggregate of two other catalogs, a DirectoryCatalog that scans for plug-ins in the /bin folder of the SearchPortal application and a ConventionCatalog that is an internal implementation of the MefContrib.MVC3 package to automatically register all ASP.NET MVC controller classes with MEF. Remember that the definition of this catalog is where we will have to add the plug-ins distributed through NuGet later in this chapter.

From now on, we can easily retrieve a list of all ISearchEngine implementations that are found by MEF. For example, the HomeController for SearchPortal can import an IEnumerable of ISearchEngine in its constructor, which is illustrated in Listing 9-4. This IEnumerable will contain all ISearchEngine implementations discovered by MEF, if there are any, and can be used by the HomeController to decide which search engines should be shown in the drop-down list on the home page. The bold sections in Listing 9-4 illustrate using this IEnumerable.

Listing 9-4. The HomeContoller Importing an IEnumerable of ISearchEngine

```
public class HomeController : Controller
{
    private readonly IEnumerable<ISearchEngine> _searchEngines;

    [ImportingConstructor]
    public HomeController(IEnumerable<ISearchEngine> searchEngines)
    {
        _searchEngines = searchEngines;
    }

    public ActionResult Index()
    {
        var viewModel = new SearchFormViewModel();
        viewModel.SearchTerm = "";
        viewModel.SearchEngine = _searchEngines.Select(e => e.Name).FirstOrDefault();
        viewModel.AvailableSearchEngines = _searchEngines.Select(
            e => new SelectListItem()
                    {
                        Text = e.Name,
                        Value = e.Name
                    }).ToList();

        return View(viewModel);
    }

    [HttpPost, ActionName("Index")]
    public ActionResult Index_Post(SearchFormViewModel model)
    {
        if (ModelState.IsValid)
        {
            var searchEngine = _searchEngines.FirstOrDefault(
                e => e.Name == model.SearchEngine);
            if (searchEngine != null)
            {
                return Redirect(
                    searchEngine.GenerateSearchUri(model.SearchTerm).ToString());
            }
        }

        return View(model);
    }
}
```

Installing Plug-ins into SearchPortal

SearchPortal features an administration area that enables administrators to install a search engine plug-in from a list of available search engines that can be installed or uninstalled. Using this page, the administrator picks the search engines to show in the drop-down list on the SearchPortal home page.

The administration area of the application is located at /administration. If you are running the sample code, administrator is both the username and password. This administrative interface has been developed as a dedicated ASP.NET MVC controller, the AdministrationController.

Listing 9-5 lists the source code for the AdministrationController class. As you can see, it is only available for uses in the Administrator role (hence the [Authorize(Roles = "Administrator")] attribute). The AdministrationController class consists of three action methods:

- Index: This method queries an IPluginManager interface for a list of available and installed plug-ins. The IPluginManager interface and its implementation will be covered later in this section.

- Install: This action method instructs the IPluginManager implementation to install a specific plug-in into the SearchPortal application.

- Uninstall: This action method instructs the IPluginManager implementation to uninstall a specific plug-in from the SearchPortal application.

Listing 9-5. The AdministrationController Enabling the Administrator of SearchPortal to List, Install, and Uninstall Search Engine Plug-ins

```
[Authorize(Roles = "Administrator")]
public class AdministrationController : Controller
{
    private readonly IPluginManager _pluginManager;

    public AdministrationController(IPluginManager pluginManager)
    {
        _pluginManager = pluginManager;
    }

    public ActionResult Index()
    {
        var plugins = _pluginManager.ListPlugins();

        var viewModel = new AdministrationViewModel();
        viewModel.Plugins = plugins
            .Select(p => new PluginViewModel()
            {
                PackageId = p.PackageId,
                PackageVersion = p.PackageVersion,
                PackageDescription = p.PackageDescription,
                IsInstalled = p.IsInstalled
            })
            .ToList();

        return View(viewModel);
    }
```

```
    public ActionResult Install(string packageId, string packageVersion)
    {
        _pluginManager.Install(packageId, packageVersion);

        return RedirectToAction("Index");
    }

    public ActionResult Uninstall(string packageId, string packageVersion)
    {
        _pluginManager.Uninstall(packageId, packageVersion);

        return RedirectToAction("Index");
    }
}
```

The IPluginManager interface is a simple interface that enables its consumers to ListPlugins and to Install or Uninstall a plug-in. Listing 9-6 is the source code for this interface, which serves as an abstraction used by the AdministrationController.

***Listing 9-6.** The IPluginManager Interface Used by the AdministrationController*

```
[InheritedExport]
public interface IPluginManager
{
    IEnumerable<PluginModel> ListPlugins();
    void Install(string packageId, string packageVersion);
    void Uninstall(string packageId, string packageVersion);
}
```

Of course, no NuGet magic will happen if we don't implement the IPluginManager interface. This implementation will do the actual integration with the NuGet.Core namespace. The NuGet.Core assembly can be installed through NuGet itself. Simply use Install-Package NuGet.Core.

Among other classes, NuGet.Core features two interesting symbols:

- The IPackageRepository interface is used to query a NuGet feed for information.

- The PackageManager class manages installing, updating, and uninstalling packages to a local folder based on an IPackageRepository instance to retrieve a list of packages.

We'll use both of these symbols in the constructor for our PluginManager class:

```
public class PluginManager
    : IPluginManager
{
    private readonly string _pluginFolder;
    private readonly IPackageRepository _packageRepository;
    private readonly PackageManager _packageManager;

    public PluginManager()
    {
        _pluginFolder = HostingEnvironment.MapPath("~/App_Data/Plugins");
        _packageRepository = PackageRepositoryFactory.Default
```

```
        .CreateRepository("http://www.myget.org/F/pronuget/");
    _packageManager = new PackageManager(_packageRepository, _pluginFolder);
    }
}
```

First of all, a plug-in folder is determined. This folder will hold all installed search engine plug-ins. We've chosen the /App_Data/Plugins folder for this. We're using the HostingEnvironment class's MapPath() method to determine the absolute path to this folder.

Next, a package repository reference is created. NuGet.Core features a default PackageRepositoryFactory, which can create a repository by simply passing the URL of the feed to consume. We're passing in http://www.myget.org/F/pronuget, because this is the URL to the NuGet feed that holds search engine plug-ins.

Finally, a PackageManager instance is created linking the package repository to a local folder where installed packages will be stored. In essence, this is the inner working of all NuGet components such as the NuGet command line and the Package Manager Console.

We still have some methods to implement. Let's start with the ListPlugins() method:

```
public IEnumerable<PluginModel> ListPlugins()
{
    IPackage dummy = null;

    return _packageManager.SourceRepository.GetPackages()
        .Where(p => p.Tags.Contains("chapter9plugin"))
        .OrderBy(p => p.Id)
        .ToList()
        .Select(p => new PluginModel()
            {
                PackageId = p.Id,
                PackageVersion = p.Version.ToString(),
                PackageDescription = p.Description,
                IsInstalled = _packageManager.LocalRepository
                    .TryFindPackage(p.Id, p.Version, out dummy)
            })
        .ToList();
}
```

Using the PackageManager created in the constructor of our PluginManager class, we query the source repository for all packages having the tag "chapter9plugins". Of course, other queries are possible here as well. You can search any property a NuGet package has in this query: you can look for packages having a specific ID, containing a search string in their title or summary, a specific package version, and so on. Be as creative as you want here.

The ListPlugins() method returns an IEnumerable of PluginModel instances. The PluginModel class is a simplified representation of a NuGet package that will be used by the AdministrationController mentioned earlier in this section. The PluginModel class only contains the package ID, the package version, the description, and a Boolean that tells SearchPortal whether or not the package is installed.

To check if a package is installed, call PackageManager's local repository method TryFindPackage.

Finally, the PluginManager should be able to install and uninstall NuGet packages. The Install method consists of only two lines of code:

```
public void Install(string packageId, string packageVersion)
{
    _packageManager.InstallPackage(packageId, new Version(packageVersion));

    HostingEnvironment.InitiateShutdown();
}
```

As you can see, the Install method calls into the PackageManager's Install method with the package ID and package version to install. From then on, the PackageManager will take care of downloading the package from the NuGet feed at www.myget.org/F/pronuget and extracting the package to the /App_Data/Plugins folder.

The second line of code in the Install method is interesting and is only required when working with web applications. The HostingEnvironment.InitiateShutdown() method requests the web server, for example, Internet Information Server (IIS) to shut down the running instance of SearchPortal and to restart the application pool in which SearchPortal is running. We have a two good reason for doing this:

- The MEF catalog containing all available plug-ins is only created once at startup of the SearchPortal application. This catalog is rebuilt when the application is restarted and only then is our newly installed search engine plug-in discovered.

- The Common Language Runtime (CLR), .NET's runtime, locks the assemblies loaded at runtime. This means that if we install a search engine plug-in, the CLR will lock the assembly containing the search engine plug-in. We will never be able to remove the assembly again because the file will be in use by the CLR. In addition to restarting the application pool, we'll be using a technique named shadow copying which will be explained in the next section.

The complete source code for the PluginManager class is listed in Listing 9-7.

Listing 9-7. The PluginManager Class Can List, Install, and Uninstall pacKages from a Specific NuGet Feed

```
public class PluginManager
    : IPluginManager
{
    private readonly string _pluginFolder;
    private readonly IPackageRepository _packageRepository;
    private readonly PackageManager _packageManager;

    public PluginManager()
    {
        _pluginFolder = HostingEnvironment.MapPath("~/App_Data/Plugins");
        _packageRepository = PackageRepositoryFactory.Default
            .CreateRepository("http://www.myget.org/F/pronuget/");
        _packageManager = new PackageManager(_packageRepository, _pluginFolder);
    }

    public IEnumerable<PluginModel> ListPlugins()
    {
        IPackage dummy = null;

        return _packageManager.SourceRepository.GetPackages()
```

```
                .Where(p => p.Tags.Contains("chapter9plugin"))
                .OrderBy(p => p.Id)
                .ToList()
                .Select(p => new PluginModel()
                    {
                        PackageId = p.Id,
                        PackageVersion = p.Version.ToString(),
                        PackageDescription = p.Description,
                        IsInstalled = _packageManager.LocalRepository
                            .TryFindPackage(p.Id, p.Version, out dummy)
                    })
                .ToList();
    }

    public void Install(string packageId, string packageVersion)
    {
        _packageManager.InstallPackage(packageId, new Version(packageVersion));

        HostingEnvironment.InitiateShutdown();
    }

    public void Uninstall(string packageId, string packageVersion)
    {
        _packageManager.UninstallPackage(packageId, new Version(packageVersion));

        HostingEnvironment.InitiateShutdown();
    }
}
```

Loading Installed Plug-ins into MEF's Catalog

So far, you've seen how to integrate MEF into an ASP.NET MVC application using the MefContrib and MefContrib.MVC3 packages. We've also downloaded search engine plug-ins from a NuGet feed and installed them into the /App_Data/Plugins folder. Now, its time to link both by adding the installed plug-ins to the MEF catalog.

As mentioned earlier, the AppStart_MefContribMVC3 class contains a Start() method that does all the wiring of MEF for you, including the creation of a catalog containing possible plug-ins. Adding the installed plug-ins to the catalog used by MEF to discover search engine plug-ins is easy as adding the correct folder as an additional catalog to the AggregateCatalog already defined in there. Listing 9-8 shows you the code to add the /App_Start/ShadowedPlugins folder to MEF's global catalog.

Listing 9-8. Adding the Installed Search Engine Plug-ins to MEF's Catalog

```
var catalog = new AggregateCatalog(
    new DirectoryCatalog("bin"),
    new RecursiveDirectoryCatalog(HostingEnvironment.MapPath("~/App_Data/ShadowedPlugins")),
    new ConventionCatalog(new MvcApplicationRegistry()));
```

There is a good reason for adding the /App_Start/ShadowedPlugins folder to the catalog instead of the /App_Start/Plugins folder, where the PluginManager installs its packages. The CLR locks the assemblies loaded at runtime. This means that all assemblies in the /App_Start/Plugins folder would be locked, and we would be unable to uninstall packages once installed.

To overcome this problem, we'll use a technique called *shadow copying*, which is also used by Microsoft to make it possible to compile ASP.NET web pages at runtime without being affected by CLR locks. Shadow copying may sound difficult, but it isn't. It consists of creating a copy of the original assemblies and using that copy instead of the original assemblies. Doing this allows us to modify the original set of assemblies by, for example, installing or uninstalling a search engine plug-in. The shadow copy is then updated whenever the application pool is restarted.

Listing 9-9 shows a simple technique to create a shadow copy of the /App_Data_Plugins folder to a folder called /App_Data/ShadowedPlugins.

Listing 9-9. *Creating a Shadow Copy of the /App_Data/Plugins Folder to Overcome CLR Locks*

```
private static void ShadowCopyPlugins()
{
    var shadowedPlugins = new DirectoryInfo(
        HostingEnvironment.MapPath("~/App_Data/ShadowedPlugins"));

    // Remove old shadow copies
    if (shadowedPlugins.Exists)
    {
        shadowedPlugins.Delete(true);
    }
    shadowedPlugins.Create();

    // Shadow copy plugins (avoid the CLR locking DLLs)
    var plugins = new DirectoryInfo(HostingEnvironment.MapPath("~/App_Data/Plugins"));
    if (plugins.Exists)
    {
        plugins.Copy(shadowedPlugins);
    }
}
```

Creating and Publishing Plug-ins

Until now, we've only discussed making the SearchPortal application pluggable. To make use of it, we'll have to create some search engine plug-ins. You can do this by creating a new class library project in Visual Studio. Name the project SearchPortal.Plugins.SearchEngines.Google.

To ensure that the ISearchEngine interface is known by our plug-in, add a reference to the SearchPortal.Web project, which you can find in the downloads for this book. This project contains the ISearchEngine interface that we'll use to implement a Google search engine plug-in for SearchPortal.

Add a class named Google to the project, and add the code in Listing 9-10 to it.

Listing 9-10. Source Code for the Google Search Engine Plug-in

```
using System;
using SearchPortal.Web.Code.Contracts;

namespace SearchPortal.Plugins.SearchEngines.Google
{
    public class Google
        : ISearchEngine
    {
        public string Name
        {
            get { return "Google"; }
        }

        public Uri GenerateSearchUri(string searchTerm)
        {
            return new Uri(string.Format("http://www.google.com/search?q={0}", searchTerm));
        }
    }
}
```

To publish this plug-in to a NuGet feed, we'll have to package it. Open a command prompt in the root folder of the newly created project SearchPortal.Plugins.SearchEngines.Google, and run the nuget spec command. This will create a file named SearchPortal.Plugins.SearchEngines.Google.nuspec that contains a package manifest for the Google search engine plug-in we are creating. Listing 9-11 lists the markup for the package manifest that will be used to create a NuGet package for this plug-in. Note that the tags element contains a tag named chapter9plugins; this is the tag we've specified in the PluginManager, because we want to show only packages having this tag in the SearchPortal application.

Listing 9-11. The Package Manifest Used to Package the Google Search Engine Plug-in

```
<?xml version="1.0"?>
<package >
  <metadata>
    <id>$id$</id>
    <version>$version$</version>
    <title>$title$</title>
    <authors>$author$</authors>
    <owners>$author$</owners>
    <requireLicenseAcceptance>false</requireLicenseAcceptance>
    <description>$description$</description>
    <copyright>Copyright Maarten Balliauw and Xavier Decoster 2011</copyright>
    <tags>pronuget apress plugin chapter9plugin</tags>
  </metadata>
</package>
```

From now on, you can use the knowledge you have gained from this book to package your project. Run the nuget pack command to create a package from the Google plug-in project, and publish this package to a NuGet feed of choice. If you have an account on MyGet.org, you can also push to the www.myget.org/F/pronuget feed using your MyGet API key.

■ **Tip** As an alternative to manually running the `nuget pack` command, you can also `Install-Package` `NuGetPowerTools` and invoke the `Enable-PackageBuild` cmdlet. This will change the project file for the `SearchPortal.Plugins.SearchEngines.Google` project and will trigger the `nuget pack` command automatically on every build.

Creating a Self-Updating Application Using NuGet

In addition to distributing plug-ins, why not distribute your application itself through NuGet? In fact, the NuGet command line is nothing more than a small bootstrapper downloading the `NuGet.CommandLine` package from the official NuGet package source on first run. The `nuget update -self` command does the exact same thing and updates the `NuGet.CommandLine` package to its latest version.

In this section, we'll use the NuGet source code that you can find at `https://hg01.codeplex.com/nuget`. You can clone this URL using Mercurial. To clone the NuGet repository, simply run the following command using the hg executable in a command prompt, while making sure you are in the directory into which you want to clone the remote repository.

```
hg clone https://hg01.codeplex.com/nuget
```

This command will work only if you have a Mercurial client installed. If not, use Chocolatey (described in Chapter 7), and invoke the `cinst hg` command. If you don't want to install a Mercurial client, you can also navigate to the `https://hg01.codeplex.com/nuget` URL in your browser and browse through the NuGet source code online.

Let's look at the `nuget update` command. The source code for this command is in the NuGet source code at `/src/CommandLine/Commands/UpdateCommand.cs` (for the browser minded: `https://hg01.codeplex.com/nuget/file/2588375a1dbb/src/CommandLine/Commands/UpdateCommand.cs`). This class contains a method named `SelfUpdate`, for which you can see the source code in Listing 9-12.

Listing 9-12. Source Code for NuGet's UpdateCommand SelfUpdate Method

```
private const string NuGetCommandLinePackageId = "NuGet.CommandLine";
private const string NuGetExe = "NuGet.exe";
private const string PackagesFolder = "packages";

internal void SelfUpdate(string exePath, SemanticVersion version)
{
    Console.WriteLine(NuGetResources.UpdateCommandCheckingForUpdates,
        NuGetConstants.DefaultFeedUrl);

    // Get the nuget command line package from the specified repository
    IPackageRepository packageRepository =
        RepositoryFactory.CreateRepository(NuGetConstants.DefaultFeedUrl);

    IPackage package = packageRepository.FindPackage(NuGetCommandLinePackageId);

    // We didn't find it so complain
    if (package == null)
    {
```

```
        throw new CommandLineException(NuGetResources.UpdateCommandUnableToFindPackage,
            NuGetCommandLinePackageId);
    }

    Console.WriteLine(NuGetResources.UpdateCommandCurrentlyRunningNuGetExe, version);

    // Check to see if an update is needed
    if (version >= package.Version)
    {
        Console.WriteLine(NuGetResources.UpdateCommandNuGetUpToDate);
    }
    else
    {
        Console.WriteLine(NuGetResources.UpdateCommandUpdatingNuGet, package.Version);

        // Get NuGet.exe file from the package
        IPackageFile file = package.GetFiles().FirstOrDefault(f =>
            Path.GetFileName(f.Path).Equals(NuGetExe, StringComparison.OrdinalIgnoreCase));

        // Get the exe path and move it to a temp file (NuGet.exe.old)
        // so we can replace the running exe with the bits we got
        // from the package repository
        string renamedPath = exePath + ".old";
        Move(exePath, renamedPath);

        // Update the file
        UpdateFile(exePath, file);

        Console.WriteLine(NuGetResources.UpdateCommandUpdateSuccessful);
    }
}
```

The `SelfUpdate` method contains a simple code flow that does the following:

1. Get the `NuGet.CommandLine` package from the official NuGet repository.

2. Compare the current version and the new version of this package to verify whether an update is required.

3. Rename the current `NuGet.exe` to `NuGet.exe.old`.

4. Extract the package (in memory), and extract the `NuGet.exe` file from it to the current path.

These four simple steps are all it takes to create a self-updating application using NuGet.

Summary

In this chapter, we've changed our perspective and looked at NuGet as being a protocol for distributing packages. We've leveraged techniques used by all NuGet components: using its central assembly, NuGet.Core, we have created a plug-in system for an ASP.NET MVC application which makes use of NuGet's features for working with feeds (or repositories) and installing and uninstalling packages based on such feed.

This technique is also used by NuGet Package Explorer, as you saw in Chapter 8. Plug-ins for NuGet Package Explorer are distributed through a NuGet feed to which you can contribute your NuGet plug-ins.

You've also seen how the NuGet command line tool is, in essence, also using this technique: when invoking the `nuget update -self` command from the command line, NuGet updates itself by querying the official NuGet package source for the `NuGet.CommandLine` package.

If you are working with any plug-ins that users can install into your application or want to work with a self-updating executable (much like `nuget.exe update -self`), the techniques described in this chapter will be of use to you. It's up to you to find a creative use case for these techniques.

Package Manifest (.nuspec) Reference

In previous chapters of this book, you've seen NuGet package manifests or .nuspec files being created a number of times. When creating packages, NuGet uses a *convention over configuration* approach. These conventions are rather simple by default but relying on them may not be enough to mold the package you wish to create. A NuGet package manifest, also known as a .nuspec file, describes the contents and metadata of your package. It is included in each NuGet package, or .nupkg, file, and it is the file you'll need to create the actual package. In short, before you can create a package, you'll need to describe it.

This appendix covers all details about available options in the XML of a package manifest. It is largely based on the information available on the official NuGet web site at http://docs.nuget.org/docs/reference/nuspec-reference. NuGet documentation (from the Outercurve Foundation) is licensed under Creative Commons license BY 3.0 (http://creativecommons.org/licenses/by/3.0/).

Note Editing .nuspec files in Visual Studio or any XML editor can be made easier using the XSD schema of the package manifest. This can be installed into a Visual Studio project using NuGet: Install-Package NuGet.Manifest.Schema.

Creating the Metadata Section

The package manifest metadata section is a mandatory section within the package manifest. The metadata section itself also has a set of mandatory elements. These required elements must be specified before you can create a package based on the .nuspec manifest. Here is the list of all required metadata fields:

- ID
- Version
- Description
- Authors

The first pieces of metadata your package exposes are the package ID and the package version. This pair of fields will uniquely identify your package on any NuGet feed. The package description and authors are used to search in the NuGet gallery.

Table A-1 lists the possible elements in the package manifest metadata section and their descriptions.

Table A-1. Elements in the Package Manifest Metadata Section

Element	Required?	Description
id	Yes	The unique identifier for the package. This is the package name that is shown when packages are listed using the Package Manager Console and used when installing a package using the Install-Package command within the Package Manager Console. Package IDs may not contain any spaces or characters that are invalid in an URL.
version	Yes	The version of the package in a format like 1.2.3.
title	No	The human-friendly title of the package displayed in the Manage NuGet Packages dialog. If none is specified, the ID is used instead.
authors	Yes	A comma-separated list of authors of the package code.
owners	No	A comma-separated list of the package creators. This is often the same list as in authors. This is ignored when uploading the package to the NuGet.org Gallery.
description	Yes	A long description of the package. This shows up in the right pane of the Add Package Dialog as well as in the Package Manager Console when listing packages using the Get-Package command.
releaseNotes	No	A description of the changes made in each release of the package. This field only shows up when the _Updates_ tab is selected and the package is an update to a previously installed package. It is displayed where the description would normally be displayed.
summary	No	A short description of the package. If specified, this shows up in the middle pane of the Add Package Dialog. If not specified, a truncated version of the description is used instead.
language	No	The locale ID for the package, such as en-us.
projectUrl	No	A URL for the home page of the package.

Element	Required?	Description
iconUrl	No	A URL for the image to use as the icon for the package in the Manage NuGet Packages dialog box. This should be a 32 × 32–pixel .png file that has a transparent background.
licenseUrl	No	A link to the license that the package is under.
copyright	No	Copyright details for the package.
requireLicenseAcceptance	No	A Boolean value that specifies whether the client needs to ensure that the package license (described by licenseUrl) is accepted before the package is installed.
dependencies	No	The list of dependencies for the package.
references	No	Names of assemblies under lib that are added as project references. If unspecified, all references in lib are added as project references. When specifying a reference, only specify the name, not the path inside the package.
frameworkAssemblies	No	The list of .NET Framework assembly references that this package requires. These are references to assemblies that exist in the .NET Framework and thus should already be in the GAC for any machine. Specifying framework assembly references ensures these references are added when installing the package.
tags	No	A space-delimited list of tags and keywords that describe the package. This information is used to help make sure users can find the package using searches in the Add Package Reference dialog box or filtering in the Package Manager Console window.

Populating Replacement Tokens

NuGet package manifests can be generated based on either a compiled assembly or a project file, for example MyProject.csproj. NuGet populates some replacement tokens within the metadata section of a package manifest with the data defined in the project's assembly name, AssemblyVersionAttribute, AssemblyCompanyAttribute, and AssemblyDescriptionAttribute. The MyProject.nuspec file adjacent to the MyProject.csproj file may contain the replacement tokens listed in Table A-2, which are populated by the values within the project.

Table A-2. Package Manifest Metadata Section Replacement Tokens

Token	Source
id	The assembly name
$version$	The assembly version as specified in the assembly's `AssemblyVersionAttribute`
$author$	The company as specified in the `AssemblyCompanyAttribute`
$description$	The description as specified in the `AssemblyDescriptionAttribute`

Referencing Dependencies

If your NuGet package depends on other NuGet packages, the listing of these dependencies will be generated based on the `packages.config` file found in your project, if any. External assemblies referenced in your project will also be added to the project manifest based on the files contained in the from the `lib` folder. These conventions are overridden by adding a `<dependencies>` element for NuGet package references or a `<references>` element to add external assembly references.

Specifying Dependencies

The dependencies element is a child element of the `metadata` element and contains a set of dependency elements. Each dependency element is a reference to another package that this package depends on. When installing a package that contains a list of package dependencies through NuGet, these package dependencies will be downloaded and installed as well. The following is an example list of dependencies:

```
<dependencies>
  <dependency id="RouteMagic" version="1.1.0" />
  <dependency id="RouteDebugger" version="1.0.0" />
</dependencies>
```

NuGet supports using interval notation for specifying version ranges. This way, you can create a package that references another NuGet package based on a specific version, a range of versions, or any latest version of the package. Limiting the version ranges may limit dependency hell in your projects. The NuGet specification was inspired by the Maven Version Range Specification but is not identical to it. The following summarizes how to specify version ranges:

```
1.0 = 1.0 • x
(,1.0] = x • 1.0
(,1.0) = x < 1.0
[1.0] = x == 1.0
(1.0) = invalid
(1.0,) = 1.0 < x
(1.0,2.0) = 1.0 < x < 2.0
[1.0,2.0] = 1.0 • x • 2.0
empty = latest version
```

Specifying Explicit Assembly References

Use the `<references />` element to explicitly specify assemblies that the target project should reference.

For example, if you add the following, only the `xunit.dll` and `xunit.extensions.dll` will be referenced from the appropriate framework or profile subdirectory of the `lib` folder even if there are other assemblies in the folder:

```
<references>
    <reference file="xunit.dll" />
    <reference file="xunit.extensions.dll" />
</references>
```

If this element is omitted, the usual behavior applies, which is to reference every assembly in the `lib` folder.

Specifying Framework Assembly References from the GAC

In some cases, a package may depend on an assembly that's in the .NET Framework. For example, your package may depend on the Managed Extensibility Framework (MEF), which is a .NET framework assembly that should be added as a reference to a project explicitly. When specifying Framework assembly references, NuGet will explicitly add a reference to a framework assembly when installing your NuGet package.

The `<frameworkAssemblies>` element, a child element of the metadata element, allows you to specify a set of `frameworkAssembly` elements pointing to a framework assembly in the Global Assembly Cache (GAC). Note the emphasis on "framework assembly." These assemblies are not included in your package, because they are assumed to be on every machine as part of the .NET Framework.

```
<frameworkAssemblies>
    <frameworkAssembly assemblyName="System.ServiceModel" targetFramework="net40" />
    <frameworkAssembly assemblyName="System.SomethingElse"  />
</frameworkAssemblies>
```

Table A-3 lists all attributes of the `frameworkAssembly` element.

Table A-3. Attributes for the framleworkAssembly Element

Attribute	Required?	Description
assemblyName	Yes	The fully qualified assembly name.
targetFramework	No	If specified, the specific target framework that this reference applies to. For example, if a reference only applies to .NET 4, the value should be "net40". If the reference applies to *all* frameworks, omit this attribute.

Specifying Files to Include in a Package

By convention, you do not have to explicitly specify a list of files in the `.nuspec` file. In some cases, however, it may be useful to explicitly list the files in your project that should be included in the NuGet package. Do note that if you specify any files, the conventions are ignored, and only the files listed in the package manifest are included in the package.

The files element is an optional child element of the package element and contains a set of file elements. Each file element specifies the source and destination of a file to include in the package via the src attribute and target attribute, respectively.

Table A-4 lists the possible attributes of the file element.

Table A-4. Attributes for the file Element

Attribute	Required?	Description
src	Yes	The location of the file or files to include. The path is relative to the .nuspec file unless an absolute path is specified. The wildcard character (*) is allowed. Using a double wildcard character (**) implies a recursive directory search.
target	Yes	This is a relative path to the directory within the package where the source files will be placed.
exclude	No	The file or files to exclude. This is usually combined with a wildcard value in the src attribute. The exclude attribute can contain a semicolon-delimited list of files or a file pattern. Using a double wildcard character (**) implies a recursive exclude pattern.

File Element Examples

This section describes some example usages of the file element to give you a better understanding of how it's used in NuGet. These use cases have been copied from the NuGet documentation at docs.nuget.org mostly, but we've added a few as well.

Single Assembly

Copy a single assembly in the same folder as the .nuspec file into the package's lib folder:

```
<file src="foo.dll" target="lib" />
```

The source contains foo.dll.
The packaged result is lib\foo.dll.

Single Assembly with a Deep Path

Copy a single assembly into the package's lib\net40 folder so that it only applies to projects targeting the .NET 4 framework:

```
<file src="assemblies\net40\foo.dll" target="lib\net40" />
```

The source contains foo.dll.
The packaged result is lib\net40\foo.dll.

Set of DLLs

Copy a set of assemblies within the bin\release folder into the package's lib folder:

```
<file src="bin\release\*.dll" target="lib" />
```

The source contains one of these:

- bin\releases\MyLib.dll
- bin\releases\CoolLib.dll

The packaged result is one of these:

- lib\MyLib.dll
- lib\CoolLib.dll

Set of DLLs, Excluding a Specific DLL

Copy a set of assemblies within the bin\release folder into the package's lib folder, omitting one assembly:

```
<file src="bin\release\*.dll" target="lib" exclude="bin\release\CoolLib.dll" />
```

The source contains one of these:

- bin\releases\MyLib.dll
- bin\releases\CoolLib.dll

The packaged result is lib\MyLib.dll.

DLLs for Different Frameworks

Copy a set of assemblies compiled for various versions of the .NET Framework:

```
<file src="lib\**" target="lib" />
```

Note that the double wildcard character implies a recursive search in the source for matching files. The source contains one of these:

- lib\net40\foo.dll
- lib\net20\foo.dll

The packaged result is one of these:

- lib\net40\foo.dll
- lib\net20\foo.dll

Content Files

Copy content files from a source folder into a specific folder in a NuGet package:

```
<file src="css\mobile\*.css" target="content\css\mobile" />
```

The source contains one of these:

- `css\mobile\style1.css`
- `css\mobile\style2.css`

The packaged result is one of these:

- `content\css\mobile\style1.css`
- `content\css\mobile\style2.css`

Content Files with a Directory Structure

Recursively copy content files from a source folder into a NuGet package:

```
<file src="css\**\*.css" target="content\css" />
```

The source contains one of these:

- `css\mobile\style.css`
- `css\mobile\wp7\style.css`
- `css\browser\style.css`

The packaged result is one of these:

- `content\css\mobile\style.css`
- `content\css\mobile\wp7\style.css`
- `content\css\browser\style.css`

Content Files with a Deep Path

Copy content files from a source folder into a folder in a NuGet package which has a different folder hierarchy than the source files:

```
<file src="css\cool\style.css" target="Content" />
```

The source contains `css\cool\style.css`.
The packaged result is `content\style.css`.

Content Files Copied to a Folder with "Dot" in Its Name

Copy content files from a source folder into a folder in a NuGet package which has a "dot" in its name:

```
<file src="images\Neatpic.png" target="Content\images\foo.bar" />
```

Note that, because the target extension doesn't match the src extension, NuGet treats it as a directory.

The source contains images\Neatpic.png.

The packaged result is content\images\foo.bar\Neatpick.png.

Content File with a Deep Path and a Deep Target

Copy a content file from a source folder into a NuGet package can be done using either of the following two lines:

```
<file src="css\cool\style.css" target="Content\css\cool" />
<file src="css\cool\style.css" target="Content\css\cool\style.css" />
```

Because the file extensions of the source and target match, the target is assumed to be the file name, not a directory name.

The source contains css\cool\style.css.

The packaged result is content\css\cool\style.css.

Content File Copy and Rename

Copy a content file from a source folder into a NuGet package to a different file name in the NuGet package:

```
<file src="ie\css\style.css" target="Content\css\ie.css" />
```

The source contains ie\css\style.css.

The packaged result is content\css\ie.css.

Excluding Files from the Package Manifest

The <file> element within a .nuspec file can be used to include a specific file or a set of files using a wildcard character. When doing so, there's no way to exclude a specific subset of the included files. For example, suppose you want all text files within a directory except a specific one:

```
<files>
    <file src="docs\*.txt" target="content\docs" exclude="docs\admin.txt" />
</files>
```

Use semicolons to specify multiple files:

```
<files>
    <file src="*.txt" target="content\docs" exclude="admin.txt;log.txt" />
</files>
```

Use a wildcard character to exclude a set of files, such as all backup files:

```
<files>
    <file src="tools\*.*" target="tools" exclude="tools\*.bak" />
</files>
```

Or use a double wildcard character to exclude a set of files recursively across directories:

```
<files>
    <file src="tools\**\*.*" target="tools" exclude="**\*.log" />
</files>
```

Note By convention, NuGet ignores a series of files automatically. Every file starting with a dot (.) is ignored by default. The reason for this is that NuGet packages should not contain files and folders created by some source control clients such as TortoiseSVN or Git. If these files are required to be shipped in a NuGet package, make sure to explicitly add them using the `file` element.

NuGet Command Line Reference

In previous chapters of this book, you've seen the NuGet command line being used. While we've covered most commands, this appendix lists all available commands from the NuGet command line. Parts of this appendix are based on the information available on the official NuGet web site at http://docs.nuget.org/docs/reference/command-line-reference. NuGet documentation (from the Outercurve Foundation) is licensed under Creative Commons license BY 3.0 (http://creativecommons.org/licenses/by/3.0/).

Deleting Packages

After publishing a package to a NuGet feed, the NuGet delete command enables a user to delete a package from the server. Note that some NuGet feeds, like the official NuGet gallery at NuGet.org, may not allow package deletion. The reason for this is threefold:

- Other packages may depend on that package. Those packages might not necessarily be on the same feed.

- It ensures that folks who are not committing packages (package restore) will not have broken builds.

- It helps ensure that important community owned packages are not mass deleted.

Here's an example:

```
nuget delete <package Id> <package version> [API Key] [options]
```

Available options are shown in Table B-1.

Table B-1. Available Options for the NuGet delete Command

Option	Description
Source	Specify the server URL.
NoPrompt	Do not prompt when deleting.
Help	Help information for the command.

Using the help Command

This command displays general help information and help information about other commands:

```
nuget help [command]
```

For example, retrieving help for the NuGet push command may be done by issuing the following command:

```
nuget help push
```

Available options are shown in Table B-2.

Table B-2. Available Options for the NuGet help Command

Option	Description
All	Print detailed information for all available commands.
Markdown	Print detailed help in markdown format.
Help	Help information for the command.

Installing Packages

The following command installs a package using the specified sources:

```
nuget install packageId|pathToPackagesConfig [options]
```

If no sources are specified, all sources defined in %AppData%\NuGet\NuGet.config are used. If NuGet.config specifies no sources, the default NuGet feed is used.

Note that when no package name is specified to the install command and instead packages.config is referenced, the install command will install all packages listed in packages.config. This may be very useful to restore a set of dependencies in a project without having to explicitly install all packages manually.

Available options are shown in Table B-3.

Table B-3. Available Options for the NuGet install Command

Option	Description
Source	Specify the server URL.
OutputDirectory	Specify the directory in which packages will be installed.
Version	The version of the package to install.
ExcludeVersion	If set, the destination folder will contain only the package name, not the version number.

Option	Description
PreRelease	Allow prerelease packages to be installed. This flag is not required when restoring packages from packages.config.
NoCache	If set, the NuGet package cache will not be used for installing the specified package.
Help	Help information for the command.

Listing Packages

The following command displays a list of packages from a given source:

```
nuget list [search terms] [options]
```

If no sources are specified, all sources defined in %AppData%\NuGet\NuGet.config are used. If NuGet.config specifies no sources, the default NuGet feed is used.

Available options are shown in Table B-4.

Table B-4. Available Options for the NuGet list Command

Option	Description
Source	A list of package sources in which to search.
Verbose	Display detailed information for each package.
AllVersions	List all versions of a package. By default, only the last version is displayed.
PreRelease	Allow prerelease packages to be listed.
Help	Help information for the command.

Using the pack Command to Create Packages

Create a NuGet package based on the specified .nuspec file, a project file, or an assembly name using the pack command:

```
nuget pack <nuspec | project | assembly> [options]
```

Available options are shown in Table B-5.

Table B-5. Available Options for the NuGet pack Command

Option	Description
OutputDirectory	Specify the directory for the created NuGet package file. If none is specified, use the current directory.
BasePath	The base path of the files defined in the .nuspec file.
Verbose	Show verbose output for package building.
Version	Override the version number from the .nuspec file.
Exclude	Specify one or more wildcard patterns to exclude when creating a package.
Symbols	Determine if a package containing sources and symbols should be created. When specified with a .nuspec file, create a regular NuGet package file and the corresponding symbols package.
Tool	Determine if the output files of the project should be in the tools folder.
Build	Determine if the project should be built before building the package.
NoDefaultExcludes	Prevent default exclusion of NuGet package files and files and folders starting with a dot (e.g., .svn).
NoPackageAnalysis	Specify if the command should not run package analysis after building the package.
Properties	Provide the ability to specify a semicolon-delimited list of properties when creating a package.
Help	Help information for the command.

Publishing Packages

The following command publishes a package that was uploaded to the server but not added to the feed:

```
nuget publish <package id> <package version> [API key] [options]
```

For example, some NuGet feeds like the official NuGet gallery at NuGet.org support listing and unlisting a package. The publish command can list a package that has previously been unlisted.

Available options are shown in Table B-6.

Table B-6. Available Options for the NuGet publish Command

Option	Description
Source	The package source to publish to. By default, NuGet assumes you are publishing to a v2 feed and appends /api/v2/package to the specified package source URL. To overcome this or to publish to a v1 feed, you have to explicitly specify the source URL
Help	Help information for the command.

Pushing a Package

The following command pushes a package to the server:

```
nuget push <package path> [API key] [options]
```

Depending on the NuGet feed you are pushing to, the package will immediately be published as well. Optionally, this behavior can be disabled by specifying the -CreateOnly option.

Available options are shown in Table B-7.

Table B-7. Available Options for the NuGet push Command

Option	Description
CreateOnly	Specify if the package should be created and uploaded to the server but not published to the server. False by default.
Source	The package source to publish to. By default, NuGet assumes you are pushing to a v2 feed and appends /api/v2/package to the specified package source URL. To overcome this or to push to a v1 feed, you have to explicitly specify the source URL
ApiKey	The API key for the server.
Help	Help information for the command.

Using the setApiKey Command

This command saves an API key for a given server URL:

```
nuget setapikey <API key> [options]
```

When no URL is provided, the API key for the official NuGet gallery is saved. API keys are stored in %AppData%\NuGet\NuGet.config.

Available options are shown in Table B-8.

Table B-8. Available Options for the NuGet setApiKey Command

Option	Description
Source	The package source to store the API key for.
Help	Help information for the command.

Using the sources Command

This command provides the ability to manage list of sources located in %AppData%\NuGet\NuGet.config:

```
nuget sources <List|Add|Remove|Enable|Disable> -Name [name] -Source [source]
```

Available options are shown in Table B-9.

Table B-9. Available Options for the NuGet sources Command

Option	Description
Name	Name of the source.
Source	Path to the package source.
Help	Help information for the command.

Using the spec Command

Generate a nuspec for a new package with the following command:

```
nuget spec [package id]
```

If this command is run in the same folder as a project file (.csproj, .vbproj, or .fsproj), it will create a package manifest that uses replacement tokens, such as id, $version$, $description$, and $authors$.

Available options are shown in Table B-10.

Table B-10. Available Options for the NuGet spec Command

Option	Description
AssemblyPath	Assembly to use for metadata.
Force	Overwrite a .nuspec file if it exists.
Help	Help information for the command.

Updating Packages

Update packages to latest available versions using the following command, which also updates NuGet.exe itself.

```
nuget update <packages.config|solution>
```

Available options are shown in Table B-11.

Table B-11. Available Options for the NuGet update Command

Option	Description
Source	A list of package sources to search for updates.
Id	Package IDs to update.
RepositoryPath	Path to the local packages folder (location where packages are installed).
Safe	Looks for updates with the highest version available within the same major and minor version as the installed package.
Self	Update the running NuGet.exe file to the newest version available from the server.
Verbose	Show verbose output while updating.
Prerelease	Allow updating to prerelease versions. This flag is not required when updating prerelease packages that are already installed.
Help	Help information for the command.

NuGet Package Manager Console PowerShell Reference

Throughout this book, you've seen the NuGet Package Manager Console making use of PowerShell. Although those chapters already covered the most important NuGet commands, this appendix lists all available NuGet commands exposed in the NuGet Package Manager Console.

This appendix builds on top of the contents of this book and will provide references to other parts of this book as well. However, this appendix is not meant to be a full PowerShell reference: there are plenty of good books on that topic.

Parts of this appendix are based on the information available on the official NuGet web site at http://docs.nuget.org/docs/reference/package-manager-console-powershell-reference. The NuGet documentation (from the Outercurve Foundation) is licensed under Creative Commons license BY 3.0 (http://creativecommons.org/licenses/by/3.0/).

Support for Common Parameters

Note that the PowerShell commands listed in this appendix all support the following set of common PowerShell cmdlet parameters, indicated by the [<CommonParameters>] option:

- Verbose
- Debug
- ErrorAction
- ErrorVariable
- WarningAction
- WarningVariable
- OutBuffer
- OutVariable

For more detailed information, you can simply type Get-Help About_CommonParameters in the NuGet Package Manager Console.

Adding Binding Redirects

This command adds binding redirects to the app.config or web.config file:

```
Add-BindingRedirect [-ProjectName] <string>
```

It has not been explicitly mentioned earlier in this book because, as of NuGet v1.2, this command is run automatically when needed during package installation. The available parameter for this command is shown in Table C-1.

Table C-1. *Available Option for the NuGet Add-BindingRedirect Command*

Option	Description	Required
ProjectName	Specify the project to analyze and add binding redirects to.	*True*

Getting a Set of Packages

This command gets the set of packages available from the package source:

```
Get-Package -Source <string> [-ListAvailable] [-Updates] [-ProjectName] [-Recent] [-Filter↵
  <string>] [-First <int>] [-Skip <int>] [-AllVersions] [-IncludePrerelease]
```

This command defaults to showing only the list of installed packages. Use the -ListAvailable flag to list packages available from the package source. Available options for this command are shown in Table C-2.

Table C-2. *Available Options for the NuGet Get-Package Command*

Option	Description	Required
Source	Specify the URL or directory path for the package source containing the package to install. When set to a local file system path, Source can be either absolute or relative to the current directory. If omitted, NuGet looks in the currently selected package source to find the corresponding package URL.	No
ListAvailable	Get packages available from the online package source.	*False*
ProjectName	Specify the project to get installed packages from. If omitted, the command will return installed projects for the entire solution.	*False*
Recent	Get the list of recently installed packages.	*False*
Updates	Get packages that have an update available from the package source.	*False*
Filter	Specify a filter string used to narrow down the list of packages returned. The filter is searched for in the package ID, the description, and tags.	*False*
First	Specifies the number of packages to return from the beginning of the list.	*False*

Option	Description	Required
Skip	Skip (do not return) the specified number of packages, counting from the beginning of the list.	*False*
AllVersions	Display all available versions of a package. The latest version of each package is listed by default.	*False*
IncludePrerelease	Indicate whether to include prerelease packages in the returned results.	*False*

Using this command, you can easily loop through all installed packages on the currently targeted project. The following command prints all installed package IDs for the current project into the Package Manager Console window:

```
Get-Package | % { Write-Host "$_.Id is installed" }
```

Getting Project Information

This command gets the specified project. If none is specified, it returns the default project.

```
Get-Project [[-Name] <string>] [-All] [<CommonParameters>]
```

Available parameters for this command are shown in Table C-3.

Table C-3. Available Options for the NuGet Get-Project Command

Option	Description	Required
Name	Specify the project to return. If omitted, the default project selected in the Package Manager Console is returned.	*False*
All	Return every project in the solution.	*False*

An example of calling Get-Project is shown in Figure C-1; it illustrates the output including the ProjectName, Type, and FullName properties of the object.

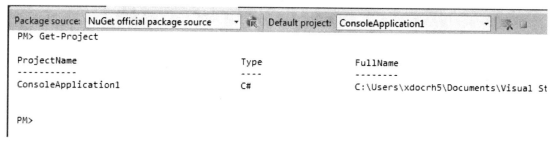

Figure C-1. Example output of the Get-Project cmdlet in NuGet Package Manager Console

This command opens up quite a few interesting opportunities to further automate the way we work with NuGet, and by extension, Visual Studio.

An example use case could be to install a package in multiple target projects at once, based on some selection criteria. For instance, let's say we want to install the NUnit package into all of our testing projects, which are named using the convention *Tests.csproj. This is not something you can easily achieve using the user interface dialogs of the NuGet Visual Studio Extension. Smart usage of the Get-Project command, however, allows you to achieve this very easily, as shown in Listing C-1.

Listing C-1. Installing a Package in Selected Target Projects Using the Get-Project Cmdlet

```
Get-Project -All | Where { $_.Name.EndsWith("Tests.csproj") } | Install-Package NUnit
```

When combining the Get-Project command with the Get-Package command, you could also list all installed packages for each project. Listing C-2 shows you how you can do this using a single line in PowerShell.

Listing C-2. Listing All Installed Packages for All Projects in the Current Visual Studio Solution

```
Get-Project -All | % { Write-Host $_.ProjectName; Get-Package -ProjectName ↵
$_.ProjectName | % { Write-Host "  $_.Id is installed" } }
```

Installing Packages

This command installs a NuGet package and, by default, also its dependencies into the target project:

```
Install-Package [-Id] <string> [-IgnoreDependencies] [-ProjectName <string>] [[-Version]↵
<string>] [[-Source] <string>] [-IncludePrerelease] [<CommonParameters>]
```

Available parameters for this command are shown in Table C-4.

Table C-4. Available Parameters for the NuGet Install-Package Command

Option	Description	Required
Id	Specify the package ID of the package to install.	*True*
IgnoreDependencies	Install only this package and not its dependencies.	*False*
ProjectName	Specify the project to install the package into. If omitted, the default project is chosen.	*False*
Version	Specify the version of the package to install. If omitted, defaults to the latest version.	*False*
Source	Specify the URL or directory path for the package source containing the package to install. When set to a local file system path, Source can be either absolute or relative to the current directory. If omitted, NuGet looks in the currently selected package source to find the corresponding package URL.	*False*
IncludePrerelease	Indicate whether this command will consider prerelease packages. If omitted, only stable packages are considered.	*False*

Creating Packages

This command creates a new package when supplied with a .nuspec package specification file:

```
New-Package [[-ProjectName] <string>] [-SpecFileName] <string> [-TargetFile] <string>
[-NoClobber] [<CommonParameters>]
```

Available parameters for this command are shown in Table C-5.

Table C-5. Available Parameters for the NuGet New-Package Command

Option	Description	Required
ProjectName	Specify the project containing the .nuspec file to use when creating the package. If omitted, the current project selected in the console is used.	*False*
SpecFileName	Specify the .nuspec file used to create the package. If omitted, the .nuspec file within the current project is used if there is only one such file.	*True*
TargetFile	Specify the full name of the output NuGet package file.	*True*
NoClobber	If specified, the target file is not overwritten.	*False*

To create a new NuGet package based on the currently selected project in the NuGet Package Manager Console, you simply call New-Package. This will work if you have a single .nuspec file—yes, only one!—within this project.

If you want to specify the NuGet manifest file and project to be used, you could provide those values as follows:

```
New-Package -Project MyProjectName -SpecFileName MyPackage.nuspec
```

Open Package Pages

This command will open the browser pointing to ProjectUrl, LicenseUrl, or ReportAbuseUrl of the specified package.

```
Open-PackagePage -Id <string> [-Version] [-Source] [-License] [-ReportAbuse] [-PassThru]↵
  [<CommonParameters>]
```

Available parameters for this command are shown in Table C-6.

Table C-6. Available Parameters for the NuGet Open-PackagePage Command

Option	Description	Required
Id	Specify the ID of the NuGet package to search for.	*False*
Version	Specify the version of the package to search for. If omitted, defaults to the latest version.	*False*
Source	Specify the source of the repository to search for package. If omitted, defaults to the selected source in the package source drop-down control.	*False*
License	Indicate that the cmdlet should open the LicenseUrl of the specified package. If neither LicenseUrl nor ReportAbuseUrl is set, the cmdlet will open the ProjectUrl by default.	*False*
ReportAbuse	Indicate that the cmdlet should open the ReportAbuseUrl of the specified package. If neither LicenseUrl nor ReportAbuseUrl is set, the cmdlet will open the ProjectUrl by default.	*False*
PassThru	If specified, the cmdlet will return the value of the requested URL.	*False*

Uninstalling Packages

This command uninstalls a NuGet package. If other packages depend on this package, the command will fail unless the –Force option is specified.

```
Uninstall-Package [-Id] <string> [-RemoveDependencies] [-Force] [-Version <string>]↵
  [-ProjectName <string>] [<CommonParameters>]
```

Available parameters for this command are shown in Table C-7.

Table C-7. Available Parameters for the NuGet Uninstall-Package Command

Option	Description	Required
Id	Specify the package ID of the package to uninstall.	*True*
RemoveDependencies	Uninstall the package and its *unused* dependencies.	*False*
Force	Force uninstalling this package and its dependencies, whether they are used by other packages or not.	*False*
Version	The version of the package to uninstall. If omitted, defaults to the latest version.	*False*
ProjectName	Indicate whether to include prereleases when searching for updates. If omitted, only stable packages are considered.	*False*

Updating Packages

This command updates a package and its dependencies to a newer version:

```
Update-Package [-Id] <string> [-IgnoreDependencies] [-ProjectName <string>] [-Version↵
  <string>] [-Safe] [-Source <string>] [-IncludePrerelease] [<CommonParameters>]
```

Available parameters for this command are shown in Table C-8.

Table C-8. Available Parameters for the NuGet Update-Package Command

Option	Description	Required
Id	Specify the package ID of the package to update. If omitted, every package is updated.	*True*
IgnoreDependencies	Update all of the package's dependencies to the latest version.	*False*
ProjectName	Specify the project containing the package to update. If omitted, the package is updated in every project with the package installed.	*False*
Version	Specify the version that the package will be upgraded to. If omitted, defaults to the latest version.	*False*
Safe	Constrain upgrades to newer versions with the same major and minor version components.	*False*
	For example, if version 1.0.0 of a package is installed, and versions 1.0.1, 1.0.2, and 1.1 are available in the feed, the -Safe flag updates the package to 1.0.2.	

Option	Description	Required
Source	Specify the URL or directory path for the package source containing the package to update. When set to a local file system path, Source can be either absolute or relative to the current directory. If omitted, NuGet looks in the currently selected package source to find the corresponding package URL.	*False*
IncludePrerelease	Indicate whether to include prereleases when searching for updates. If omitted, only stable packages are considered.	*False*

Index

CPSIA information can be obtained at www.ICGtesting.com
Printed in the USA
LVOW132152070312

272125LV00007B/7/P